Continuity and Disruption

PITT SERIES IN POLICY AND
INSTITUTIONAL STUDIES

Bert A. Rockman, Editor

Continuity

AND Disruption

ESSAYS IN
PUBLIC
ADMINISTRATION

Matthew Holden, Jr.

University of Pittsburgh Press

Published by the University of Pittsburgh Press, Pittsburgh, Pa., 15260

Library of Congress Cataloging-in-Publication Data
Holden, Matthew, 1931–
    Continuity and disruption : essays in public administration / Matthew Holden.
       p.   cm. — (Pitt series in policy and institutional studies)
    Includes bibliographical references and index.
    ISBN 0-8229-3885-5 (cl. : alk. paper)
    1. Public administration.   I. Title.   II. Series.
JF1351.H65   1995
350—dc20   95-16081

A CIP catalog record for this book is available from the British Library.
Eurospan, London

To
the love of my wife
and the continuity of our several families:
Holden   /   Welch
Garvin   /   Howard
Clark   /   Kennedy
Spinks

CONTENTS

ACKNOWLEDGMENTS

These essays result from the Ransone Lectures that I was invited to give at the University of Alabama in 1987. In the intervening years, my wife, Dorothy Holden, has been an ever present help and source of encouragement. Victor Gibean, who acted as my official host at the University of Alabama, was unusual in his intellectual interest in the subject, as well as in collegial courtesy, at the time of the visit. Harvey Kline, who was department chair at the time, was kind to show interest in this material well outside his field of comparative politics. Mylon Winn and Stephen Percy enhanced my understanding of what colleagues who have entered the discipline since 1980, more or less, perceive about the history and foundations of the discipline. Terrence Harwick helped with my understanding of Mary Parker Follett. Donald F. Kettl contributed greatly, as our discussions ranged over many issues of administration, and David O'Brien perceptively commented on the issues of law and administration. Martha Derthick was most helpful in her response to the chapter on public administration and the plural society.

James A. (Dolph) Norton, then director of the Center for Public Service, University of Virginia, gave me the equivalent of a subsidy by allowing me virtually unrestricted use of the offices and equipment of the Center. Frances H. Granger, executive assistant to the director of the Center, and Gail H. Moore, Faculty of Arts and Sciences Word Processing Center, along with their respective clerical staffs, were equally helpful. Sandra Wiley was a helpful adviser; and Lisa A. Miller, Kirsten Nakjavani, and Susan MacDonald read copy, looked up citations, and handled extensive word processing and other logistical tasks. Morgan Emily Adams worked without complaint through all the minutiae in finishing the job. I gladly accept the obligation to extend public thanks to them all.

Continuity and Disruption

INTRODUCTION

Walter de la Mare wrote a poem in which these lines appear:

Thou hast come, by some dark, dark catastrophe
Far, far from home.

These lines seemed remarkably appropriate to someone transformed in six months from being a political science graduate student in Evanston, Illinois, to being an army private in the replacement depot in Inchon, South Korea. These words, copied into a little notebook, soon settled into memory.

Similarly, public administration, as taught in American universities, also shows signs of having come far from home. There is much useful information conveyed in the hot topical issues discussed in journals, in academic courses oriented to practice, and in the more abstract exercises presented in other courses. But the field of public administration as a whole seems little guided by a sense of the fundamental problems from which its inquiries and teachings derive. Igor Diakanoff, an Assyriologist, is quoted as saying: "Man is always man in any age."[1] If one believes this to be true over the long periods that an Assyriologist studies, it is also true over the short period of recent decades.

Hence, the subject of the following chapters—the fundamental problem—is derived from a comment made by Albert B. Martin. Martin said that one of the central problems of the administrator is to reduce turbulence in the operating environment of administration.[2] Turbulence arises in the continual exchange between continuity and disruption. Understandably, continuity is the goal in administration, and sometimes it is achieved. Yet disruption is recurrent, whether in a repressive dictatorship experiencing popular unrest or in a social democracy of pacifist inclinations faced with a tough insurrection. The interplay between continuity and disruption—turbulence—is my subject.

The underlying thesis of this work is that administration is central to politics. There is a permanence to politics, even when people profess to dislike politics or to act without politics. Groups are necessarily diverse, and the needs or interests of a group's members will vary. This is true for families or clans, churches or clubs, corporations or universities, and so it is for governments. There must be some process for expressing differences, bringing differences into controlled conflict, and bringing conflicts to some resolution. *Politics* is the name of that process, whether formally recognized or furtively practiced, whether expressed in overt ideologies, doctrines, professions of religious faith, or even raw egoism. Politics involves, preeminently, making decisions where there is no necessary or overriding criterion that logically and psychologically causes the contending parties to reach agreement. Politics may thus amount to making decisions about incommensurate elements.

Politics, in brief, is the process of organizing power within human groups, large and small, public and private. To organize power means to control or to seek to control. By extension, it also includes those who seek to reject control, or even any association with existing powers and principalities. Thus engagement with politics is first a factual matter, not a question of values or states of mind and loyalty.

If one takes this view, then any attempt to maintain a false dichotomy between politics and administration, whether in old forms or new, impoverishes our understanding of public administration. Even more decisive from the viewpoint of political science is that such a dichotomy impoverishes our understanding of politics. It obscures the essential proposition that administration is the central process in politics.[3] Administration cannot be separated from politics, and no political system can be sustained when its administrative core collapses.

Administration is the imperative process of diffusing into the body politic whatever choices have been deemed compelling by those who purport to hold authority at the center. It entails discretion about the actual use (not the mere pronouncement of rules and norms) of information, money, and force—the basic resources of power. Diffusion does not, of course, stand alone, for its obverse is aggregation.

Public administration necessarily involves the public.[4] If a political system is to be viable, some process must aggregate and bring to the center the various bits of information (demands, protests, manifestations of loyalty) expressed by the body politic. In simple, face-to-face political units, there is little need for formality. Aggregation is exemplified in the New England town meeting, for example. Various East African peoples once had communal gatherings called *barazas*. In the Arab world, there was a gathering called a *majlis*. Parliaments of various kinds have arisen when delegates, deputies, or representatives assemble to aggregate the diversity of wills and interests found in a body politic. Aggregation is, however, rendered nugatory without some means of diffusion. Legislatures can order armies to disband, but armies do not obey unless soldiers have internalized the belief that they should obey or unless they are compelled by other force. On the other hand, armies can actually control or disband legislatures if they choose, as when Oliver Cromwell marched his troops into the House of Commons.

Administration is not the only diffusion process; adjudication is also diffusionary. The difference is that the judicial process lacks the means to carry out its choices. A judge may pronounce that someone is to be evicted or executed, but it is the sheriff, or the prison warden, who ensures that the act is performed. Adjudication is a form of diffusion in the trial courts of urban America, where many routine decisions are made repeatedly. They are settings of mass justice, to borrow a term from Judge Henry Friendly.[5] Judges dealing with "mass justice" pay some attention to rights, but they also pay substantial attention to policies and preferred outcomes, whether in the public interest or some highly particular private interest. Decisions are not tailor-made. The careful attention to facts and circumstances associated with the ideal court trial are given short shrift. The judge in a housing court, as reported by Jones, who deals constantly with inspection reports,[6] is engaged in adjudication; this is in a sense quite different from the judicial process at the appellate level. Similarly, the judge in a lower criminal court has decisions structured as much by the availability of clerks to process cases, or by space in the jails to receive potential prisoners, as by abstract justice. These judges act remarkably like routine field administrators in government agencies; and like those field administrators, they constitute the witness of authority to people who, in Austin Ranney's words, "almost never see anyone or have dealings with anyone other than 'administrators.' "[7]

Administrative government is normal in human society, although I do not use *normal* in the common usage that contrasts *normal* to *abnormal*. I use normal in the statistical sense. Among the variety of political units, other than very small face-to-face representative groups, administrative government is inevitably necessary. Conversely, one expects to find that the loss of control over actual use of force, money, and information is equivalent to the loss of power. A large-scale quantitative comparison of various types of governments would show this to be the case.

History also helps by multiplying the number of ways one can test these hypotheses. Dwight Waldo urges scholars to pay more attention to "the Roman experience of government and its consequences for the contemporary world." The methodological force of Waldo's admonition is powerful, though the Romans were latecomers on the scene. Records of government institutions go back to 3,000–4,000 B.C.[8] Mesopotamia, with its complex bureaucratic structure, existed 2,000 years before the Romans began to extend their power beyond the Italian peninsula.[9] The Hindu kingdom of Maurya predated Alexander's fourth-century B.C. march into Asia and long survived it. Certain features of Maurya's financial administration and management control seem familiar today. The king was advised to be "ever wakeful," to set aside regular times to hear his subordinates, to oversee funds received and spent, and to receive gold. The Mauryan kingdom attempted to forecast revenues, attempted to control expenditures, drafted formal budgets with fixed allocations of expenses for important purposes, rewarded subordinates who saved the king money, penalized those who lost him money, and had auditing and surveillance systems to detect error or fraud.[10]

During Maurya's time, the Romans still had not gained control over Egypt, something they achieved only in the first century B.C.[11] Rome learned bureaucracy from Egypt, which had the world's largest administrative structure for at least 1,400 years.[12] Initially, the Romans sought to control Egypt without annexing it; they could not hope to match the Egyptians' administrative skills: "The senatorial proconsuls of the [Roman] Republic lacked the expertise to manage a complex bureaucratic system, and without it the agricultural and commercial wealth of Egypt would never be drawn effectively into the public treasury." When, in due course, Augustus decided there was no choice but to annex Egypt, "he created cadres of Roman officials out of professional army officers, military tribunes and former leading centurions, trained in the practical operation of the Roman legionary establishment, who were capable of managing the departments of the Egyptian administration, manned by Greek personnel."[13]

The Roman administrative format was spread throughout Western Europe by the Roman Catholic church, which adapted the imperial structure for ecclesiastical government. Because that structure reveals itself in modern secular governments, Rome's experience is part of our own cultural tradition and continues to interest historians and researchers.[14]

We know much less about other past cultures, such as the African king-doms and empires that existed before colonization of the continent.[15] Max Weber knew enough about them to say, "The numerous great Negro empires, and similar formations, have had only an ephemeral existence primarily be-cause they lacked an apparatus of officials." Weber cites these units to make the point that not "every historically known and genuine formation of great states has brought about a bureaucratic administration."[16] The fact that they were not bureaucratic does not mean that they were not administered, however. Such entities could not have functioned without their administrative pro-cesses, and it would be valuable to have studies of them that approximate the level of detail found in analyses of Rome's political structure, but that appears impossible given the paucity of information about the African states.[17] The polities of Central and South America before the European conquest, and political units created by Pacific Ocean cultures, would be similarly relevant, if only we knew more about them.

The view that this wide array of cases should show that administration is the central political process deviates from a dominant intellectual mode. Both academic literature and practical action show a persistent effort to ignore the connection between politics and public administration. For the past hundred years, students of public administration have often failed to see the control problem or have sought to avoid it. Evidence for this lies in the alleged distinction between political decisions and administrative decisions.

For at least fifty years, the terms *policy* and *managerial* have sometimes been substituted for *political* and *administrative*. The presumption is that political (or policy) decisions precede, and are qualitatively different from, administrative (or managerial) decisions, which deal with implementation. The idea is that these are two separate activities, distinguishable in concept and in fact, involving different decisional criteria, skills, and personnel. The substitution of terms changes little or nothing. *Political*, as the word is used in this book refers to the nature of a relationship or action. It does not mean the kind of office from which action is taken. The old idea that the two activities—politics and administration—should be separate is designed to create institu-tions, situations, or processes in which control can be exercised without re-quiring those who oversee these entities to compete for their positions. It means that those who are "in charge" for "administrative" purposes are *in charge*. Their decisions are not subject to controversy on "irrelevant" grounds or to intervention from "politicians."

By the 1980s, the "dichotomy" idea was rejected by many political scien-tists, though not necessarily by most other scholars in administrative studies.

Paul Appleby, Frederick C. Mosher, and others who established policy execution as a part of the concept of administration contributed to a useful innovation. On the basis of their thinking in particular, it has become common to define administration as the execution of public policy. This definition is serviceable, but it traps its users in the mental habits of political scientists who are heirs to the New Deal modifications of U.S. constitutional democracy. Moreover, the definition more or less assumes the United States as we know it in its contemporary federal structure.

But the definition does not guide us to the key forms of action or the sources of power. Administration is not necessarily modern or rationalistic. In many polities decisions are made on much narrower, more particularistic, grounds than the contemporary idea of policy would imply. Public revenue may be treated as a source of the private income of the ruler and the ruler's allies, and the amount of taxation levied may be as much as tax collectors can get. The police may be at liberty to use their arms, clubs, or whips not only for "professional" reasons but to satisfy their own egos, to exact revenge, or to coerce recalcitrant people. Information may be disseminated to those whom the officials want to have it and withheld from all others. These only illustrate the fact that the idea of *policy*, as taught in modern graduate schools, could be sheer absurdity and have no meaning whatsoever in some polities. But these examples are just as much administrative situations or power situations as any characterized in contemporary social science.

There are strong (and perverse) reasons to avoid mixing politics with the study of administration; one is intellectual and the other profoundly emotional. The purely intellectual reason to avoid mixing the study of politics with the study of administration is a desire for efficiency. Scholars do not wish to waste their time. Politics is hard to grasp, beyond a certain basic, obvious level. Political knowledge, as distinct from opinion and prejudice, is still extraordinarily primitive. The difficulty of achieving political knowledge is well known to political scientists. Their workaday world contains an array of apparently cogent but contradictory hypotheses.

Experience is valuable and often superior to the kind of learning that people acquire in colleges and universities.[18] Yet even experienced people in high positions, whether public or private, show the limits of what they have learned both in their actions and in their recitations. In their memoirs or oral histories of their public careers, men and women of experience, wittingly or unwittingly, focus on their own mental states. They offer reasons, rationales, and rationalizations for their actions or the actions of others. Moreover, on the basis of their sophisticated choice of strategies, it is frequently impossible to distinguish those who lose from those who win. That is why, in recapitulating their actions, they are likely to emphasize intangibles like luck or timing. Official memoirs or oral histories are not very informative about what strategy works and why it works, although they may tell much about the actions of particular persons. Seldom do their explanations exhibit internal power and coherence.

If one seeking to understand public administration must have an equivalent to the *Physician's Desk Reference*, then political science is not what is required. Those with such a need often prefer to learn something that can be reduced to an elegant and powerful formula. Once learned, the applicability of such formulas to politics is not obvious in specific situations. School-taught political science and experiential learning thus find competitors in organizational theory, administrative science, and management science (see chapter 2).

People might wish to avoid politics not merely because it is difficult to understand but because many find the subject disturbing. The fear is not that they will fail to understand; it is that they will comprehend and find what they comprehend deeply objectionable. "Politics," it is often said in American folklore, "is a dirty business." If the folklore exaggerates, politics nonetheless can be conceived, in Reinhold Niebuhr's terms, as morally ambiguous, never wholly good. As Hannah Pitkin says, politics attracts but it also repels.[19] Knowledge of politics is for many people the forbidden fruit, possession of which touches the psyche in important ways that we want to avoid. If one must be sure that one's actions are more likely to have good, just, or rational results than to be distorted or contradictory, then politics is also to be avoided.

Paradoxically, many people who are interested in politics avoid knowledge of administration for the same kind of reason. The politics they seek is not that just mentioned, but a more idealized kind. As an ideal, politics entails reasoned discourse among people who share values, moral language, and capacity for action, and who prefer to see each other as members of the same community. Public administration inevitably reveals strains and conflicts, and it raises (at best) morally ambiguous questions. Whose shops will actually be displaced to allow new construction? Whose money will actually be transferred to whom? Who will be water-hosed in the next five minutes if the blocked courthouse door is not allowed to open? Whose application to see a file will be denied then and there? These are the operational details that characterize the administration of public decisions, and they fall within the program and policy frameworks with which public administration is necessarily associated.

However, the efficient use of intellectual resources is only a partial reason why many people avoid the study of politics. To reject the interdependence of politics and administration is analogous to chemists denying oxygen and believing in phlogiston. For students of politics to avoid the study of administration, and for students of administration with other backgrounds to avoid studying politics, yields empirically defective results. It systematically deflects attention from shifts in the actual use of force, money, and information. Wherever parties-at-interest make conflicting claims over the right and ability to control or influence actual-use decisions, there turbulence occurs.

Turbulence comes into play when we speak of information as a social resource. Information includes not only sheer facts but also the communication of values. It also entails the use of those facts—filtered through values—as a basis for decisions. Information is both factual and symbolic. Information may be conveyed as a product to be absorbed and used as the receiver permits. Information about the population counted by the census might be regarded as a simple factual matter, but it easily becomes symbolic (see chapter 7). Indeed, a vast proportion of information is intended to arouse emotions that sustain or undermine someone's power to control. This is a source of very great turbulence.

Turbulence is more visible in decisions about the actual use of money. It is most readily manifested, logically, where the largest sums are spent. In the contemporary United States government, this is chiefly in procurement, especially for the Department of Defense, and in the grant and subsidy programs for the civilian sector. In recent times, there can hardly be a country in the world without some analogous experience.

In virtually all nations, turbulence manifests itself in controversies about the use of force to defend and sustain the existing elites. It is easy for political scientists to conceive this in collective terms, such as a ruling social class or some other defined group. Rebellions are part of our thinking. But for much of the world, perhaps most of it, the corollary is that turbulence is expressed in dangers to, and defenses of, the persons of the incumbents of the moment. The inability of the administrative system to perform at this level is indicated when a head of state is assassinated, as in the cases of Egypt's President Anwar Sadat or India's Prime Minister Indira Gandhi. The French administrative system evidently performed very well against the many attempts made on the life of President Charles de Gaulle between 1958 and 1968. Unlike Sadat and Gandhi, de Gaulle lived out his time in retirement and died the natural death of an old man.

On the whole, in today's constitutional democracies, force for elite protection is almost a nonissue, compared to many countries in the Third World.

Sweden is deemed to be one of the most consensual countries in the world. Perhaps such a high degree of consensus explains how Prime Minister Olof Palme could have been vulnerable to assassination. Apparently, he was accustomed to moving about freely, with minimal protection. Indeed, the prime minister was urged by friends to be more cautious, but he discounted the warnings.[20] Palme's murder has never been solved, despite all the resources of the Swedish government. But because the event was so unusual, assassination of the prime minister has not yet been seen as a systemic threat, an event likely to recur. In that context, no administrative change has yet occurred and Swedish prime ministers have gone back to playing a very public role with little security protection.[21]

The problem of elite protection is illustrated by the simplest of cases. In 1974, my wife, son, and I could stand immediately in front of No. 10 Downing Street and take pictures. In 1992, with the fear of terrorism and after attempts on the lives of British officials, we tourists could only stand behind high iron gates at least fifty yards away, where Downing Street joins Whitehall. The protection of the person of the head of government is a good indicator of a nation's sense of threat. We may presume that the administrative system for protecting the head of state becomes more complex over time, once the probability of danger is taken seriously, becoming more intense each time there is some perception of threat, never returning to the status quo ante.

The presumption of a public threat to the chief executive is obviously greater in the United States. There is no presumption of any broad popular disaffection in the population that would put the president in physical peril. Yet there is a recognition that rare deviants and conspiracies of the bizarre can also produce death in this high place. Over the years, with the history of U.S. presidential assassinations, there has come to be an elaborate protection system for the president.

Turbulence, to restate, is to be understood within the argument that administration is central to politics. The essays that follow discuss the interplay between continuity and disruption—turbulence—at three levels.

The first level is conflict and disruption in the intellectual history of public administration: the conflict between concepts of politics and of efficiency and the use of influential theoretical work from engineering (chapter 1); and the flow of intellectual energy into the theory of organization, the seminal contributions of earlier political scientists (Mary Parker Follett and John Merriman Gaus), bureaucratic theory largely imported from sociology, and management science (chapter 2). The second level deals with conflict and disruption on a second level—that is, attempts to control disruption in thinking about the practical conduct of administrative government (chapters 3, 4, and 5). Administrative theory is not merely an exercise in scientific theory, nor a practical inquiry into "how to do it." Theories of administration are also constantly associated with political dogma—sometimes in support of dogma, at other times to escape one dogma in the interest of another, manifest in the development of the concept of executive leadership—presidential leadership—in U.S. government (chapter 3). Chapters 4 and 5 deal with the problem of dogma in the U.S. administrative law process and its functions (chapters 4 and 5).

The third level considers external factors that produce disruptions in administration: physical technology, which is simultaneously a more profound source of disruption in administrative practice and a means by which people seek to impose continuity (chapters 6 and 7) and the conflict and adaptation of groups under ethnic plurality. Ethnicity is one of the most profound and recurring sources of disruption in the body politic, and thus one of the most critical facets of current administrative practice, a problem that has been gravely underestimated both by those who study public administration and by practitioners (chapter 8).

I
Intellectual History

1

THE "ACCUMULATED WEALTH OF CONCEPTS, QUESTIONS, AND GENERALIZATIONS"

Why "Old" Public Administration Should Be Studied Anew

This chapter is predicated on the conviction that because administration is central to the political process, there is a significant need for a political theory of administration. I will argue three points. First, political theory in the grand tradition is potentially useful as a source of guidance for empirical work in public administration. Second, the writings of the founding generation in American political science, notably Woodrow Wilson and Frank Johnson Goodnow, contain key themes from which significant hypotheses may still be derived. Third, the politics-administration dichotomy described in the introduction reflects a loss of self-confidence by political scientists and a surrender of the field of public administration to encroachments from other, less adequate, intellectual traditions—notably engineering, and chiefly Taylorism—on public affairs.

Phrased in a single sentence, my thesis might be: Old books should be read as a part of the search for new knowledge. The work of one's predecessors is to be taken seriously if one believes that a discipline is based on a framework that invites investigation that can move our understanding to some level not yet attained. But one must always remember that the search for the new sometimes has disabling effects.

What is the scientific imperative that drives people to scorn complacency and to quest for new knowledge?[1] Why is it so urgently necessary to be on the cutting edge of research? The answers are various: ambition for fame, even fortune, insatiable curiosity beyond explanation, the desire to reduce human ignorance, and the desire to do some good in the world.

Political scientists are ambitious to do something permanent and to leave a living name behind them. A driving intellectual force that defines the modern world is to emphasize the new, the original, the current and timely. Especially in the past forty years, political scientists have allowed their inquiries to be disrupted by this pressure—largely to their intellectual loss. When a nascent literature on the politics of administration showed itself, students of public administration confused the new with the fundamental and, in search of novelty, prematurely abandoned lines of inquiry that might have proved fruitful if pursued. They would have served the discipline better by making sustained use of what Charles Lindblom calls "the theoretical richness of [the] discipline and its accumulated wealth of concepts, questions, and generalizations."[2]

Regarding the principles of public administration, little changes. The value of new knowledge is modest. The intellectual products published in the most prestigious journals since 1900 doubtless include many original, thoughtful, informative articles. But if one attempted to measure the change in true knowledge from one five-year period to another, the net increment at each stage would be small.

It is not merely that scientific inquiry is inherently difficult in the social sciences. Rapid depreciation of value and premature abandonment of earlier ideas is the problem. In the world of business, depreciation is the process by which an asset loses its value. Depreciation rates are set under the private system of legislation known as accounting principles, and rates and methods of depreciation are among the most vital of business issues, with profound effects upon income and one's net worth.

For hypotheses about human organization, there is seldom decisive evidence—nothing analogous to Mendel's observations on sweet peas or Harvey's notes on the heart and blood. Social science entails tedious difficulties of definition, observation, and measurement. When difficulties appear, the tendency is to abandon the basic concept and seek another. We might compare this reaction to shifting patterns of cultivation in agriculture: slash and burn, cultivate the new soil for a time, and move on to a new site when that soil is exhausted.[3]

To develop the metaphor of depreciation: the significant problem in public administration research has been a scholarly mentality that often leads to abandoning a given approach before its implications have been fully worked out, its strengths tested to the limit, and its limitations defined. Hence it loses value before its time.

That is why this chapter advocates a more serious use of old books. It is true that intellectual history has an enjoyment value of its own. There is a pleasure in tracing the sources and evolution of ideas, much as a cartographer finds satisfaction in studying old maps, or as those who enjoy restoration take pleasure in antique cars or old buildings. But that is not the main issue here. The old literature is still important in its own right and deserves more intensive study than it usually gets.

The prime task, in our still developing discipline, is to distill central hypotheses into forms that lend themselves to systematic testing. Given the present state of political knowledge, studying the contributions of the founders of our political system is a vital intellectual exercise. Intellectual history enables us to make evolving theories explicit. To the extent that we articulate these theories, thereby making hypotheses more explicit, we can the more subject them to verification or incontrovertible disproof. But, on the whole, this is not how public administration research has developed in the twentieth century.

Nearly everyone quotes (or at least refers to) Max Weber or Herbert Simon, many to Luther Gulick, and virtually every graduate student is taught the debatable proposition that Woodrow Wilson was the founder of academic public administration. What has not yet been achieved is a continuity in stating these central ideas, along with explicit testing to see which central ideas may be rejected. What has occurred so far is a series of changes in fashion, a series of disruptions as new words (and sometimes new concepts) come into the lexicon.

Because of the premature abandonment of successive approaches, the literature on administration contains four main strands that emphasize, respectively, *politics, organization, management,* and *bureaucracy.* The central recurring conflict in these twists and turns is between understanding administration as a problem of efficiency and as a problem of politics. The emphasis on efficiency takes for granted that issues about the values and interests that dictate a given course of action have been settled, so that administrative questions are merely instrumental. Enhancing social cohesion and resolving disputes, for example, are not a part of the calculus.

In the twentieth century, the academic disciplines that study efficiency—above all, engineering and economics—have gradually encroached upon the realm of politics in approaches to public administration. In the end, however, the elegant disciplines of engineering and economics do not offer political science much guidance. Those who attempt to work from the models they provide have only two choices: first, to maintain the coherence of a model by excluding from analysis many external factors; second, to create some modifications so as to allow a model to take account of contradictory demands—which is to say to create their own political theory. This is what happened as the advocates of seeking efficiency overcame those who sought a politics of administration.

The first wave of specialists in efficiency were replaced by those for whom public administration became the study of organization theory, bureaucracy, and management. A powerful tension exists between an empirical political theory of administration, in which one is willing to subject one's thought to a discipline of disproof, and a dogmatic approach to administrative theory. The consequence is that our products are like James Shirley's flowers of the spring: they are set, they grow, and they turn to earth. Thus, my argument in this chapter and the next is the intellectual and practical need for emphasizing the indissoluble connection between administration and politics. In studying administration, like other aspects of politics, we lose our bearings when we fail to ask: how do human beings organize power? The rest of this chapter describes the threads of inquiry in which that question is present.

Political Theory and Administration: The Classic Literature

A first source of concepts, questions, and generalizations is political theory in the grand tradition, which claims to offer some understanding of politics that does not depend solely on the laws and culture of a particular time and place.

Political theory long continued to be a central field of required study. As late as the 1950s, virtually all American doctoral candidates in political science had to pass the theory examination. Political theory might have been predicted to play an important role in guiding scholarship as an obvious source of hypotheses for the scientific study of administration.[4] Since so many classic theorists of the past—unlike today's political scientists who live under democratic governments—lived in peril and in fear of autocratic rulers, they might be expected to take note of the mechanisms of power—notably of executive action, whether in a monarchy or another form of government.[5] People often are able to draw deeply upon their own experience and observation.

Commentators have generally addressed the classic studies of politics by asking two questions. First, under what conditions of obligation should people submit to constituted authority? Second, how should just rulers govern themselves as they impose burdens and assign benefits to people over whom they claim to have authority? Yet commentators on political theory have generally given only modest attention to the mechanisms of power. Insofar as they have addressed the issue, they devote much attention to representation and somewhat less to executive power, in general terms.[6] Because students of political theory showed no interest in the problems of the actual world around them, it was only natural that more empirical researchers felt they could ignore theory. This, in fact, is what happened. And if our disenchanted professors told us that political theory provided no help in the study of practical politics, we were inclined to believe them. Novices in an *empirical* political science in the 1950s and 1960s were schooled to see political theory as useless.

Charles S. Hyneman's attitude is a useful point of reference. Hyneman, a professor at Northwestern University in the 1950s, had taught at Louisiana State, the University of Illinois, and Indiana University. Hyneman made thoughtful contributions on American foreign policy, the administrative process in the federal government, political pamphleteering, the role of the Supreme Court, and the requisites of a *science* of politics.[7] Hyneman doubted that "dead men" could teach much to students aspiring to a political science. He meant that the grand theorists did not provide principles that were analogous in their intellectual function to the explanatory principles of physics, chemistry, and biology.

The idea that political theory is largely irrelevant to a true science of politics is not new. Consider the ideas of Sir Henry Taylor, a poor young man of the rural gentry who was hired at the British Colonial Office in 1823. He was very successful and remained there forty-eight years.[8] When still a rather young official, he wrote that the "art of exercising political functions" had not received much attention from "professors of politics."[9] Taylor probably did not mean that the books on political theory were not rigorous, for it is not clear that he was very familiar with theory. He probably meant that "professors of politics" did not offer much enlightenment on how to handle practical affairs. One can easily guess why he felt this way. For him, exercising political functions entailed dealing with sugar planters and the fractious colonial legislatures in the West Indies, combatants in the language controversy in Canada, or the owners and captains of slave ships at a time when the British government was seeking to suppress the slave trade.

By any reasonable standard, Taylor must have known that it was untrue that professors of politics had failed to study the "art of exercising political functions." Plato, Saint Benedict, Machiavelli, Bodin, Hobbes, and Rousseau all provide clues that the empirically minded scholar might benefit from studying political theory. "It's obvious to anyone that legislation is a tremendous task, and that when you have a well-constructed state, with a well-framed legal code, to put incompetent officials in charge of administering the code is a waste of good laws, and the whole business degenerates into a farce." So said Plato in *The Laws*, displaying an acute sense of what Pressman and Wildavsky have established as the implementation problem. Plato continues, "The state will find that its laws are doing it damage and injury on a gigantic scale."[10] Plato moves through a step-by-step scheme that lays out the administrative mechanism of his imagined state: the guardians, the highest officials; military officials; a council; an executive committee (in which case he argues that someone must be on duty at all times); priests; expounders of the laws; treasurers; city wardens, market wardens, and country wardens who would more or less be field administrators; and those responsible for education and culture.[11]

Saint Benedict in the sixth century set forth a pattern whereby monks could withdraw from the everyday world, live quietly in common, perform manual work, and pray and contemplate the glories of Christ. The purpose of the monastery was worship, and the abbot was to model himself on Christ. Yet Benedict's legislation for monastic governance could well be found in a modern executive manual or even a modern constitution.[12] The abbot's authority is, in one sense, absolute; but Benedict discusses the absolute authority of the abbot both in terms of the qualities he should have and the form of organization that the monastery should exhibit. The abbot should be "worthy to rule" and not merely "able to preside," which is a statement about character. The abbot should be chosen for life. Otherwise, "the abbot, regarding himself as a caretaker, hesitates to lay down a policy which is likely to be reversed at the next election, or else the monks, regarding themselves as bound in loyalty to their superior only for so long as his term of office lasts, envisage alterations at a determined date."

The abbot's absolute authority, however, must be exercised in the right spirit. The brethren must be called into council to air their opinions for his guidance. A formal set of officials with designated functions run the house: the prior, the cellarer or bursar, the deans, the guestmaster, the porter, and other officials. The deans are the abbot's field officers, but Benedict does not quite solve the problem of division of labor, for he places the deans under the supervision of his bursar. Benedict faces, and is apparently uncomfortable with, the problem of "number two," the prior:

> It is St. Benedict's expressed opinion that peace is more likely to be
> preserved when the place is under a number of deans, all on a equal

footing of authority, than when a single deputy rules in the abbot's name. When the power is evenly distributed there is no competition and no one monk will be proud. The abbot's deputy, on the other hand, is tempted to use his authority either arrogantly or subversively. A man who is a substitute will often want to go beyond the one for whom he is doing service, and if this is not his temptation he may want to undermine the influence of the man whom he is meant to represent.

The same issues come up sometimes in secular political theory, especially from the sixteenth century onward. In the 1520s, Machiavelli discussed the dynamics of the relationship between the prince (chief executive) and his secretaries or ministers, anticipating a modern level of interpersonal psychology as applied to problems of bargaining and command.[13] He thus considers such questions as the prince's need to find ministers who will concentrate on the prince's interest, not their own, and the importance of retaining the ministers' fidelity. Of course, one might expect Machiavelli's recommendations to be more calculating, more cynical, than those of Benedict. The prince (chief executive) should, Machiavelli advises, ensure a minister's loyalty by "honoring and enriching" him, by doing him kindnesses, and by assigning to him responsible tasks. If these things are done, the minister's own self-interest will bind him to the loyal service of his prince. Machiavelli also discusses the problem of securing the loyalty of military commanders in the field; he suggests that commanders should be punished lightly or not at all, even for serious errors, so as to relieve them of anxiety about their own exercise of authority. He recommends creating a structure in which magistrates are not able to veto the conduct of the public business; he suggests creating a unity of command; and he proposes placing advisers at risk when they are prominently and uniquely identified with any specific or unusual policy, in case it fails.

About fifty years later, in 1576, when the French writer Jean Bodin approached administration from the standpoint of what the prince (or chief executive) should do, he discussed the necessity of delegation. Whether or not the prince had a council and an assembly of the estates—which he should have—it was indispensable that he have magistrates: "When we say that the force of law lies in the fact that it commands and prohibits, permits and punishes, we are speaking of the magistrate, rather than the law, which is silent. The magistrate is the life of the law because he accomplishes these things."[14] Thomas Hobbes takes the necessity of delegation for granted and discusses the structure within which delegation works.[15] At once, he makes a distinction between the "public ministers of sovereign power" and the personal servants of the ruler—between those who carry out orders and those who merely advise.

In the eighteenth century, Jean-Jacques Rousseau's discussion of *magistracy* appears to encompass virtually all governance. Yet he also asserts that the responsible magistrate is to carry out laws, not to make them. If "the magistrate wants to make laws . . . disorder succeeds regularity; and as force and will can no longer act in concert, the State is dissolved, and must of course fall into despotism or anarchy."[16] This view broadly anticipates the ideas of Hannah Arendt in our own time.

Political theorists are worth our attention because they may be a source of guidance as we formulate our ideas for modern study. As these examples illustrate, my reading of Plato, Benedict, Machiavelli, Bodin, Hobbes, and Rousseau leads to the recognition that there has long been much implicit theory and some explicit discussion of structure and implementation, bargaining and command, delegation, structure and classification of functions, and self-restraint on the part of administrators. These are all crucial issues in the study of contemporary administration and administrative theory.

Fifty years after Taylor, Woodrow Wilson made a remarkably similar claim. Since administration is "government in action," one might expect it to have "arrested the attention and provoked the scrutiny of writers of politics very early in the history of systematic thought." Wilson said, however, "No one wrote systematically of administration as a branch of the science of government until the present century had passed its first youth and had begun to put forth its characteristic flower of systematic knowledge."[17]

Within the methodologies that he himself had adopted, Wilson's statement that no one had studied administration before was wrong. If we use the word *systematically* as applied to today's social science, then Wilson's statement of a century ago might make sense. That criterion would require us, however, to ignore Wilson as well. Succeeding scholars have accepted the error at face value; anyone who takes Wilson's words seriously, in this respect, will be misled. The study of administration in the United States developed with little explicit reference to European political theory, but it is incorrect to say that there was nothing in past theory that is relevant to it.

The Misuse and Abandonment of Wilson and Goodnow: *Politics* and *Administration* as Distinction, Dichotomy, and Cliche

If the study of public administration developed without reference to European political theory, it did not spring *de novo*, without the influence of

European institutions or ideas. The American Framers consciously rejected European institutional models.[18] But the Framers' attitude was not persuasive to the founding generation of U.S. political scientists.[19] Young scholars went to Europe, much as Third World scholars came to the United States after World War II. They consciously advocated adopting large parts of the European method as they saw it, being convinced that European models could be integrated into American institutions. The effort to do so forced them to think about and formulate the relationship between politics and administration.

Politics and administration are different, to be sure. In U.S. politics the distinction between the two activities soon came to be regarded as a dichotomy, and in any event the dichotomy became a cliche. This process is reflected in the original work of two major figures, Woodrow Wilson and Frank Johnson Goodnow, and in the misuse and eventual oblivion to which their works have been relegated.

FIVE INTERSECTING THEMES OF WILSON AND GOODNOW

Woodrow Wilson and Frank Goodnow stand as two landmark figures in American academic public administration, as they were also seminal figures in the study of political parties, which they regarded as integrally related to administration.[20] The source of the alleged dichotomy, from which political scientists have spent so much energy trying to recover, is attributed to both Wilson and Goodnow, but it is properly rooted in neither. Neither Goodnow nor Wilson conceived of an absolute separation of politics from administration. The genuine substance of the work of Wilson and Goodnow was soon abandoned, and the substantive implications of their work have never been fulfilled in scholarly research.

Intellectual work is not merely an abstract exercise; it is also a venture into social networks and concrete history. Goodnow and Wilson were chronological and intellectual contemporaries. Wilson commands far more attention as a student of public administration than as a scholar. After studying law at the University of Virginia, Wilson went to Atlanta for a year to practice law (1882–1883). As a lawyer, Wilson was a failure. He returned to graduate school at Johns Hopkins, taught briefly at Bryn Mawr, then at Wesleyan in Connecticut for two years. In 1890, he became a professor at Princeton.[21] He remained there for twenty years until he was elected governor of New Jersey.

Goodnow is not well known today, but in his lifetime he was a commanding academic figure. Goodnow received a law degree from Columbia in 1882, the same year Wilson left Virginia. His start seems to have been more successful. For a while he worked with John F. Dillon, the great legal commentator whose name endures today in Dillon's Rule—the principle that the state government has unlimited authority over local governments. Goodnow became a pioneer in the study of administrative law and municipal government (or, as it would now be termed, urban government).[22]

Goodnow joined the Columbia faculty, where he remained until he became president of Johns Hopkins in 1914. He continued to teach for the rest of his active professional life, even while university president. His academic work made him a giant in the field of public administration.[23] Austin Ranney, although emphatically disagreeing with Goodnow's concept of the political party, pays tribute to his influence, calling him a "scholar . . . whose ability and industry have won for him the admiration of all subsequent generations of political scientists."[24] Dwight Waldo refers to him as "the Father of Public Administration."[25] Alice B. and Donald C. Stone write of the early years:

> There were as yet few administrative concepts, doctrines, or recognized principles and practices; there was no system of administrative analysis; there were no textbooks. But we had an indefatigable scholar at Columbia University, sometimes referred to as "Father of Public Administration," because of his prolific writing and ardent teaching.[26]

James Hart, and George W. Spicer, Marshall E. Dimock, and Pendleton Herring were among Goodnow's students. Remarkably, neither Wilson's public papers nor Goodnow's book shows any sign that the two men had direct contact, except once. (Goodnow had somehow become involved with Chinese affairs, and once visited Wilson, with a partner of Alexander Brown and Sons, to discuss a loan to China.)[27] Goodnow, at Columbia, would naturally have known of Wilson's article published in *Political Science Quarterly*. For his part, Wilson learned about Goodnow not later than 1888. Both men were well enough connected to be invited by James Bryce, in 1888, to write supplemental chapters for *The American Commonwealth*. When Bryce told Wilson that Seth Low and Frank Goodnow had also agreed to write chapters, Wilson declined as too busy. When Wilson drafted a review of the volume for *PSQ*, Munroe Smith felt it necessary to prod Wilson to mention the Low and Goodnow contributions as a diplomatic gesture.[28] Outlines for his lectures given at Hopkins show a substantial reliance on Frank J. Goodnow's *Comparative Administrative Law* (1893).

By the same token, when Goodnow's book was published in 1900, it made no reference to Wilson, though it would have been incredible for a member of the Columbia faculty, so interested in administration, not to have heard of it, and improbable that he would not have known of Wilson's courses taught at Hopkins. Goodnow was the first president of the American Political Science Association. Five years later, Wilson held the same post.

Wilson expressed a great interest in administration while teaching at Bryn Mawr College.[29] However, his knowledge was bookish and academic, not practical. He knew that in both Germany and France public administration was more professionalized than in the United States. He was determined to go abroad to study how public administration actually worked, despite the difficulties of finding a means of support and of assuring that he would have a teaching post when he returned—a matter his father very much emphasized. In December 1886, he appealed to Herbert Baxter Adams, who had helped him in negotiating his doctoral travails at Hopkins.

> I am thinking very seriously of going to Europe next summer to stay two, or it might be three, years and see the constitutions of the Continent *alive*. . . . I *must* learn German as it cannot be learned from books, and I must see European politics and administration as no library can show them to me. . . . I have learned . . . all that is necessary to know about what that autocratic person the French *Prefect may* do. . . . What I want to know is, what the Prefect does do.

Wilson's "The Study of Public Administration"

Wilson's celebrated paper has a history. It seems at first to have been a "job talk." For about a year, Wilson had been in contact with the new president of Cornell, Charles Kendall Adams, about a teaching position. When Adams invited Wilson to give a lecture to Cornell's History and Political Science Association on November 3, 1886, Wilson delivered the essentials of the now famous text.[30] He set forth the theme well known to political scientists today: the problem of modern politics is not so much how to make a constitution as to run one.

As much as anything, it was a reformist tract for the times.[31] The *New York Evening Post* the next day reported:

> Prof. Woodrow Wilson read a very able paper on "The Study of Administration." Prof. Wilson outlined the history of the study, showed how it was a comparatively new development in political science, very cogently presented the necessity and value of such study, and indicated the means by which it ought to be carried on.

Five days later, Edwin R. A. Seligman, an economist at Columbia and an editor of the *Political Science Quarterly*, wrote Wilson about publishing his lecture. (Even then, new journals needed material. Seligman, an entrepreneurial scholar with wide civic interests, was not slow.) Wilson accepted. With modesty, or with a sense of self-protection, he said, "I did not prepare it with any thought of publication, but only as a semi-popular introduction to administrative studies, treating of the history of the Science of Administration, of the conditions of the study, and of the needs for it in this country; the methods proper to it &c."

In the words of Jay M. Schafritz and Albert C. Hyde, "While ["The Study of Administration"] attracted slight notice at the time, it has become customary to trace the origins of the academic discipline of public administration to it."[32] This linkage first emerged in the 1970s with Vincent Ostrom's use of Wilson as a foil for his own emerging arguments against "bureaucratic" administration in favor of "democratic" administration.[33] (Dwight Waldo, a careful student of these matters, points to such a discussion in the early 1940s.) This attribution is scorned by Paul P. Van Riper, who derides the idea of Wilson's intellectual or practical influence on public administration. He notes that of "the four public administration textbooks written prior to World War II by Leonard White, W. F. Willoughby, John Pfiffner, and Harvey Walker, only White cites Wilson's essay."[34]

Although Leonard D. White observed, in the first edition of his textbook (1926) that the future president of the United States never returned to his researches on the subject, he was mistaken in the biographical particulars.[35] Wilson was very much interested in administration and continued to develop his ideas on the subject. Wilson regularly lectured on public administration at Johns Hopkins, while he taught at Bryn Mawr, Wesleyan, and Princeton, and he may have continued to do so as late as 1896.[36]

Yet Wilson's contribution had no impact on the field until the past quarter century, more or less. Apart from a few people who wrote to Wilson just after his article was published, no one appears to have read or remembered it.[37] William F. Willoughby obviously had an opportunity to know of Wilson's interest in administration. Willoughby and his twin, Westel Woodbury Willoughby, were graduates of Hopkins. Wilson prepared public administration questions for Westel Woodbury's Ph.D. preliminary examination. Moreover, in a collateral book, William F. Willoughby devotes much attention to Wilson's views on constitutional government, the character of parliament, the president's second term, and the president as a political leader.[38] If he ignored Wilson on administration, he must have done so consciously.

Wilson's paper has received wide discussion—and possibly too much credence. If one took at face value his letter to Seligman, one might call it slight and let it go at that. Quite possibly, an editor might be tempted to say to Professor Wilson, "Revise and resubmit."

Nonetheless, given the scholarly attention it has received since the 1970s at least, we may discuss what it does and fails to do. Wilson's published work on administration is limited to this small paper, and it is best analyzed as a source of guidance toward useful hypotheses. What ideas does it contain that might contribute to a political theory of administration? Certain academic-rhetorical rituals seem to be almost mandatory. Wilson explained, for instance, that a "science of administration" had not been forthcoming earlier—as nothing appears before it is needed—because the government and the economy had once been more simple.

"The Study of Administration" anticipates the future in that it proposes something akin to what we now would call a school of public policy or public administration. It specifically advocates what other Princetonians would call "education for the public service."[39] Wilson foresaw the time when no "college of respectability can afford to do without a well-filled chair of political science," but education alone would not create a "competent body of administrators."

> It will be necessary to organize democracy by sending up to the
> competitive examinations for the civil service men definitely prepared for
> standing liberal tests as to technical knowledge. A technically schooled
> civil service will presently have become indispensable.

One could interpret the essay as explaining the context in which this new body of professional public officials should be understood. But the article's contradictions and unresolved problems are notable. What is "administrative study" to do? At several points, Wilson assigns to scholarship in administration tasks that go far beyond educating officials. "It is the object of administrative study to discover, first, what government can properly and successfully do, and, secondly, how it can do these proper things with the utmost possible efficiency and the least possible cost of either money or of energy." To determine "what government can properly and successfully do" calls for a normative theory of government functions, both as to what is "proper" to government and the measure of "success." Moreover, the formulation does not show any awareness that "energy" and money may be approximately fungible, that is, in actual behavior one may yield the other. In any administrative exercise, officials may find it easier to persuade people to cooperate in a public project if they have the cash with which to pay them.

"The object of administrative study," writes Wilson, "is to rescue executive methods from the confusion and costliness of empirical experiment and set them upon foundations laid deep in stable principle."[40] As noted, Wilson's treatment of intellectual history is striking for what it ignores about political theory. Moreover, Wilson could be faulted for less than rigorous logic. Clearly, he had made the value judgment that the United States as he knew it needed a different form of administrative practice. Moreover, he was sure that administration as conducted in France and Prussia was vastly superior to that in the United States. But his method in coping with possible difficulties was essentially that of the rhetorician, ridiculing difficulties or affirming that they could be solved by faith or future study. Wilson lays down the doctrine that "for all governments alike the legitimate ends of administration are the same," and consequently the measures found in one can be used in the other. In this manner, the rhetoric then turns to "filtering away foreign gases," to ignoring the foreign political principles of France or Prussia and focusing only on their administrative methods. This overlooks the fact that some administrative methods, such as the prefectoral system, were chosen for political (*control*) purposes; yet Wilson stated that he did not care "a peppercorn for the constitutional or political reasons Frenchmen or Germans give for their practices when explaining them to us," being willing only to borrow the technique when one sees "a murderous fellow sharpening a knife cleverly."[41] Such rhetoric is adequate to rally the believers and to keep one's opponents off balance in a debate, but it has nothing to do with proving the validity of the argument advanced or taking its difficulties seriously.

In dealing with politics and administration, Wilson leaves a contradiction so profound that one wonders what the discussion following that evening's lecture at Cornell may have been. The late twentieth-century political scientist may legitimately find Wilson fuzzy on the *politics* he has in mind. It is not difficult, at times, to perceive that Wilson means corrupt politics—namely, the self-enrichment of officials and political bosses.[42]

Bosses, who controlled party mechanisms and coordinated how various officials used the power of their offices, were sometimes well-educated persons of elite social background; but others had little schooling and came from impoverished backgrounds. The secret to their success was control over the nominating process, which meant control over the party machinery leading to nominations. Officials whom a boss had put in office were under great psychological pressure and often were simply expected to use their discretion over the public payroll to employ persons, regardless of their competence, who could help deliver the vote. They similarly abused public purchasing power and were responsible for many other corrupt practices common in the late nineteenth century.

This was the kind of politics that Wilson explicitly sought to eliminate. At other points Wilson seems to mean by *politics* something more akin to the neutral usage familiar to present-day political scientists. When Wilson says that his real objective is to cleanse the moral atmosphere of official life, he presumably means to overcome corrupt politics. He cannot mean the same thing when he says that although politics should not be allowed to manipulate the offices, politics should be allowed to set the tasks for administration.

How far can one separate politics from administration, and what does Wilson mean by these terms? Wilson seems to think that he is being very clear: "The field of administration is a field of business. It is removed from the hurry and strife of politics; it at most parts stands apart from even from the debatable ground of constitutional study."

By no illustration does Wilson indicate what he means. His definition of *administration* refers to carrying out laws with efficiency and dispatch. This implies that administrators take merely subordinate action in which their discretion is fairly narrow. The law exists, in effect, and the administrator's task is to find means to carry it out. But the broad language about carrying out existing law must be understood against the facts of practice. The most urgent administrative issue of Wilson's time concerned personnel, not the substance of policy.

Wilson's audience knew that employees in the Customs Service and the Post Office, the largest employers in the United States government, were regularly turned out when their sponsors' parties lost the presidency. One might think of the work of the Customs and the Post Office as "removed from the hurry and strife of [partisan] politics," rendering patronage inappropriate. But his audience knew the reality. They could also have known of controversies about the use of the western lands, and in these disputes substance was deeply involved.

Moreover, what Wilson gives with one hand he seems to take away with the other. Having limited administration to merely carrying out the law, he then links it to lasting political truth. The field of administration, he said, is "at the very same time raised very far above the dull level of mere mechanical detail by the fact that through its greater principles it is directly connected with the lasting maxims of political wisdom, the permanent truths of political progress."[43]

Politics should set the tasks for administration, but should not be allowed to manipulate its offices. The source for this, he says, is Johann Kasper

Bluntschli, a Swiss-born German scholar who had been publishing since the 1850s. Bluntschli, says Wilson, would hold administration separate both from politics and from law. "But we do not need German authority for this position; this discrimination between administration and politics is now, happily, too obvious to need further discussion."[44]

Wilson, like most other important students of politics at that time, placed a great value on comparative studies. France, Germany, Britain, and the United States were reasonably well known to most people who wrote about political science. Wilson advocated comparative studies because they would help us "rid ourselves of the misconception that administration stands upon an essentially different basis in a democratic state from that on which it stands in a non-democratic state."[45] Restatement: It is a misconception that administration stands upon an essentially different basis in a democratic state, compared to that in a nondemocratic state. Or, administration is administration and is essentially the same, whether the state is democratic or not. However, that stands in bold contradiction to Wilson's statement on the very next page: "Our own politics must be the touchstone for all theories. The principles on which to base a science of administration for America must be principles which have democratic policy very much at heart."[46] It seems implausible to speak of political principles on which to base a science of administration and, at the same time, to speak of administrative techniques as if they have no more political significance than knives.

Unlike most of his contemporaries interested in the practicalities of reform. Wilson attaches extraordinary importance to public opinion as a force behind positive change. The internal conflicts in Wilson's paper are repeated in his views on this issue. The best administration had so far been found in governments with a history of absolutism, but Wilson's confidence that professional administration and democracy could be reconciled was merely stated, not argued. He merely states that he would prefer American politics *and* administration than Prussian politics and Prussian skill?

Moreover, the constitutional and administrative spheres must be distinguished, Wilson says, though they are not easy to define. Thus, he criticizes the view that liberty depends more on sound administration than on a sound constitution. Wilson's definition of public administration as "detailed and systematic execution of public law"[47] is but a "roughly definite" criterion by which to divide the province of constitutional law from that of administrative function. Administration and proper distribution of authority are linked, and if administration can reveal its guiding principles, it will have done constitutional study a service. Cannot the administrator's choice of methods frustrate the law? In contrast to Goodnow, Wilson never admitted this possibility. When he says that "the administrator should have and does have a will of his own in the choice of means for accomplishing his work,"[48] Wilson seems never to imagine the unlimited discretion that this choice permits.

One of the more significant features of the essay is Wilson's recognition of the interest of the official: How can the interest of the official be made to serve the public? If we solve this problem, we shall again pilot the world. Though he offers no guidance, Wilson is decades ahead of the public choice theorists in articulating the problem.

GOODNOW'S POLITICS AND ADMINISTRATION

Frank Goodnow was, on the other hand, a major figure in the public administration studies of his own time. No one was more identified for a time (erroneously) with the idea of a simple dichotomy between politics and administration. The late V. O. Key once wrote that Goodnow as scholar had been almost too successful: the "necessary compression" of the central idea into a "convenient phrase, 'politics and administration,'" he said, "induced intellectual compartmentalization" to the extent that the "monographs of a generation" have been assigned to pigeonholes marked *politics* or *administration*.[49] This pigeonholing could only detract from careful analysis of the logic of Goodnow's argument and from developing and testing propositions in the search for an empirical political theory of administration.

In *Politics and Administration* (1900), Goodnow touched upon at least four points that are very important to political science as a discipline and to public administration as a field within the discipline.

First, Goodnow tried to show "that the formal governmental system as set forth in the law is not always the same as the actual system."[50] His express language, therefore, and the context of his writing negates the persistent claim that political science before World War II focused exclusively upon the formal-legal attributes of states. Goodnow had some shadowy concept of theory, to infer from his work, but quite limited concepts of methodology. To read him is to read exposition, including his conclusions, but one finds few rules for interpreting evidence, let alone rules for designing an inquiry and assembling data. The real difference one observes in his work is how unselfconscious, compared to those in recent years, political scientists were about scientific criteria and methods of verification, notably quantitative methods that were then nascent in the other social sciences. The one thing that Goodnow's work was *not*, in any serious sense, was formal-legal.

Goodnow was nearly fifty years ahead of the discipline in adopting functionalism as an explanatory principle. He believed that political arrangements are a function or result of human needs. Subject to "the degree of intelligence" and "ideas of right and wrong"—which taken together may be regarded as political culture—similar peoples, at similar stages of development, will create similar institutions. Functionalism arises from the idea that political institutions cannot be explained solely, or even primarily, on the basis of their prescribed legal powers and responsibilities. Functionalism assumes the idea that there are important human needs and that the behavior of institutions, including illegal or objectionable institutions, can be explained in terms of how they fulfill them. Political scientists after World War II were inclined to think of the political machine—an institution generally deemed disreputable—along lines described by Robert K. Merton. The function the machine performed, said Merton, was to organize and humanize the delivery of services that immigrant populations needed, services the formal government system did not provide as well. For a time, political science was saturated with references to manifest (prescribed) and latent (real) functions. Functionalism also introduced the idea of basic necessities in the political system (functional requisites).[51] This conception was crucial to the work of Gabriel Almond and G. Bingham Powell in comparative politics.[52] While latter-day political scientists borrowed functionalism mainly from sociology, its essentials were present in Goodnow's book published in 1900!

Goodnow develops an argument of considerable elaboration and subtlety on the two primary functions or activities made explicit in his very title.[53] The breadth and purport of these functions should be noted, though they cannot be discussed in detail here. Politics determines the "state will" or, in contemporary language, public policy. Administration is the execution of that will. The state will is, in effect, expressed in legislative decision. The point was not to separate politics from administration but to recognize government tasks and powers more realistically than the separation-of-powers concept does. "It is easy to conceive of a condition, in which the authorities provided for the execution of the law may refuse . . . to execute it. This executive function must therefore of necessity be subordinated to the function of politics."[54] Goodnow is the premier advocate of the political scientist's theory of governance. This theory effectively repudiates the idea of a hermetic separation of powers found in law school political theory. These functions or activities cannot be segregated and assigned to specialized institutions.

Goodnow also asserted that the state, like a person, must make up its mind or determine its will. Goodnow expressly draws a human analogy.[55] This simple formulation contains a kernel that Herbert A. Simon rediscovered and independently articulated more than four decades later. Simon's concept of decision making shifts from decision making to problem solving, and from problem solving to inquiring into the cognitive basis of administrative decision making.

Goodnow embarked on what we call *policy analysis*. He set out "to indicate what changes [would] make the actual system conform, more closely than it does at present, to the political ideas upon which the formal system is based."[56] In that respect, Goodnow's book essentially advocates two major structural reforms: greater centralization of state administration, "following the model of the national administrative system," and placing the political party—then an informal private entity—under public control. Goodnow ceased to write much about administration after this book, devoting more effort to texts on municipal government, to casebooks on administrative law, and increasingly to public affairs and university administration.

The Five Interconnecting Themes

Although scholarship on these matters was only just developing, five important themes may be derived from the works by Wilson and Goodnow, just surveyed, that offer some potential for a political theory of administration. These are the permanence of politics; the importance of culture in determining a given administrative system; the influence of public opinion on its evolution; the critical nature of decision making; and the hope of discovering the principles of sound organization. Political scientists writing about administration have not yet, however, crystallized these themes into theory, and have even been obstructed by the search for novelty—and especially by the impact of scientific management and the engineering profession on administrative thought.

THEME 1. THE PERMANENCE OF POLITICS IS THE CONTEXT FOR ADMINISTRATION

A theme inherent in the work of both Wilson and Goodnow is that whereas politics sets the tasks of administration, it should not be allowed to manipulate administrative offices. The idea is often missed both because Wilson's work on administration contains paradoxical statements that go both ways. Wilson simultaneously emphasizes the *nonpolitical* character of administration and uses arguments that necessarily imply that the *political* is essential to administration. Wilson's inherently political logic is not dismissed by referring to his desire to overcome the patronage politics practiced overtly in the

United States in his time. It is true that administrative discretion was used to enrich politicians of the dominant party, or their allies. And it is true that this is the kind of politics Wilson wished to eliminate. But to exclude partisan enrichment would not end the more pervasive social conflict, and nothing he says implies that he thought it would. Insofar as pervasive social conflict remains, politics remains and must be accepted in relation to the administrative process, as a result of his logic, even when he uses words that might otherwise mean something different.

To affirm the permanence of politics as a context for administration means—to repeat—that politics should set the tasks for administration but not manipulate the offices. This stipulation would not make sense if the politics-administration separation, later so strongly asserted by reformist business and civic leaders, had been achieved. Such a separation would negate the potential dominance of politics over administration. To say that politics should be allowed to set the tasks for administration implies that a professional administration cannot be immune from political influence. The idea that politics should be allowed to set the tasks for administration but not maneuver the offices can only be addressed to those who seek to control the role of politics. As Wilson was not writing about a dictatorship, one can assume that he was writing advice to the public or to contending parties about how they ought to agree.

Wilson's language makes best sense if we rephrase it to say: competing social groups ought to agree to limit their competition to policy (tasks of administration). If, like Montague and Capulet, they will not agree, or cannot take the risk of agreeing, then it is fruitless to speak of what politics should not be allowed to do. The real objective, Wilson says, is to cleanse the moral atmosphere of official life. Goodnow's recognition of the permanence of politics is much more elaborate. His real objective is to show that "the formal governmental system as set forth in the law is not always the same as the actual system."[57] Political arrangements are a normal human function. This argument is either psychological or biological. In 1900 Goodnow declared his intention "to indicate what changes [would] make the actual system conform, more closely . . . to the political ideas upon which the formal system is based."[58]

THEME 2. ADMINISTRATION MUST BE INTERPRETED CULTURALLY

The European science of administration (or professionalized administration) had been created to serve monarchs. This was well known to early U.S. political scientists. Wilson particularly recognizes, if imprecisely, that the professional administration he admired was best suited to German political culture. It might require adaptation if applied to American political culture.

Wilson uses somewhat grandiloquent terms to express this idea: "We can borrow the science of administration with safety and profit if only we . . . filter it through our constitutions, only . . . put it over a slow fire of criticism and distil away its foreign gases."[59] What Wilson meant, says James Stever, "was that cameralism (the school-trained bureaucracy that supported German absolutism) could be wrenched out of its Germanic intellectual context and grafted onto the American political system."[60] (Wilson's notes also show his attention to French administration.) We can imagine the main point if we imagine Wilson in a debate with others more skeptical. If the skeptic says, "We don't want to borrow those administrative methods because they will pollute our political process," Wilson would answer, "Yes, we do; if only we will do this or that, then all will work out well." A dissenter might even argue that a highly professionalized administrative establishment could, in itself, become a substantial power force, apart from other forces in society.

The underlying problem regarding cultural context became very important after World War II, when comparativists—stimulated by the United States' foreign aid interest—sought to study administrative reform in a variety of countries around the globe. It includes such questions as whether a "professional" police training program, transposed from the United States with its array of cultural constraints, would yield vastly different results in another country, with a different cultural pattern. Wilson seems not to be aware of the paradox of advocating "one rule of good administration" suitable for all governments, and of the necessity of cultural conformity for an effective administrative system. But it is present in his work and might well have been developed by a systematic exegesis from Wilson's contribution.

Goodnow's recognition of the importance of cultural context is based on an interpretation of the U.S. administration he observed, as well as more abstract observations. Goodnow surely advanced an inchoate *cultural* hypothesis when he referred to the "strong mayor" concept as an expression of "the one-man idea in this country," a pattern he thought was also manifested in corporate and college presidencies.[61] That was an interpretation of the United States at the time. But his more abstract interest in culture is deeper and explains, for him, how groups will act politically. Subject to "the degree of intelligence" and "ideas of right and wrong"—or, in contemporary terms, political culture—he hypothesized that similar peoples at similar stages of development will create similar institutions. The implicit recognition of the importance of culture, both in Wilson and in Goodnow, became explicit for a relatively brief period in the 1960s and early 1970s, when political development and development administration were subjects much encouraged by the grant-providing organizations.[62] Scholars of administration of nearly all methodological persuasions have been slow to recognize the significance of culture. It is patent, by now, that the concept of the president as embodying of something akin to the "general will" is not an expression of reality. Indeed, the expectation of executive leadership may have some broader cultural significance. On the whole, the discipline has regressed to the norm, so that studies that explicitly address the importance of culture on administrative patters have receded from view.

THEME 3. PUBLIC OPINION IS A DOMINANT FACTOR IN ADMINISTRATION

When Wilson asks what forces prevent "naturalizing" the administrative skill, he speaks as if administrative skill were as "foreign" as the immigrant. His thesis is that it also has to be naturalized. The obstacle to such naturalization is principally popular sovereignty.[63] In a long discussion of public opinion, he said one must persuade people to want change and to want the particular change one proposes. Reform is slow, for wherever public opinion exists, it must rule. Public opinion is slow to change in any event; nothing can be done hastily, since public opinion cannot be disregarded. This presents at least a potential hypothesis about the necessity of social support for administrative reform.

When *popular government* still had some evocative meaning, *public opinion* also had meaning. If Wilson could see that public opinion was slow to change, he might also have seen public opinion as the great hydraulic force that moves society in ways still uncaptured by modern survey analysis. Public opinion is much more than the current and measurable responses of individuals to interview questions. The really important questions are not on the survey instrument, but are asked in political nature—everyday life—by real events. When questioned, individuals offer favorable or unfavorable reactions, or merely remain inert. How or whether they react is the important issue, when, why, and in what ways. Do people approve or disapprove of what they hear or see about how some administrator is behaving? Do they care? Do they dare care?

Public opinion, if one followed Wilson's observation to its full extent, obliges the scholar to inquire into the depths of popular culture and what it means to public administration. Deep values and attitudes, volatile if inarticulate, may produce vast and dramatic political consequences. Wilson's biography is that of an intelligent young man who would have to deny his own experience to avoid seeing potentially measurable indicators of legitimacy, consent, acquiescence, or rebellion in the face of political realities.

Wilson was born in Virginia three years before the Harper's Ferry uprising, and spent time in North Carolina, Georgia, and South Carolina. He was eight years old when the Civil War ended. As a boy he lived under Confederate influence and through the period in which the Freedman's Bureau still played a role in the South, and he witnessed the efforts of the white southern elite to frustrate it. It was not hard to see how public opinion could grant effective permission, or even demand, administrators of the law (the police) to negate by nonenforcement what the courts said were defendants' rights.

The potential interconnection between public opinion and the success of public administration is one of the most profound realities to which political science may yet direct new attention. In his perceptions of culture, political dominance, and public opinion, Wilson touched fundamental issues that have yet to be formulated and explored in political science. The "unphilosophical bulk of mankind" must be persuaded to trust officialdom. *Trust* is strength and "as it is the office of the constitutional reformer to create conditions of trustfulness, so it is the office of the administrative organizer to fit administration with conditions of clearcut responsibility which shall insure trustworthiness." This is necessary to one who writes, "Large power and unhampered discretion seem to me the indispensable conditions of responsibility."

Trustworthiness must be disclosed and rewarded by the public, Wilson believed. Public opinion plays the role of authoritative critic in the conduct of administration. This is very important in a democracy. As sovereigns are always suspicious of their servants, a sovereign people are more so. Political education is part of the necessary process, but if "we are to improve public opinion which is the motive power of government, we must prepare better officials, as the *apparatus* of government." The corps of civil servants to be produced "must at all points be sensitive to public opinion." Wilson emphasizes,

> If comparative studies of the ways and means of government should
> enable us to offer suggestions which will practically combine openness
> and vigor in the administration of such governments with *ready docility to
> all serious, well-sustained public criticism*, they will have approved
> themselves worthy to be ranked among the highest and most fruitful of
> the great departments of political study.

THEME 4. DECISION MAKING IS A CRITICAL ASPECT OF ADMINISTRATION

The decision-making theme is implicit in Goodnow in ways that anticipate the cognitive work of Herbert Simon. *The state, like a person, must make up its mind or determine its will.*

> Whatever may be the truth or error in this conception of the state, it is still true that political functions group themselves naturally under two heads, which are equally applicable to the mental operations and actions of self-conscious personalities. . . . The will of the state or sovereign must be made and formulated before political action can be had.[64]

Many decades later, Herbert A. Simon rediscovered the same relationship which he then turned into problem solving, and then into an inquiry into the cognitive basis of administrative decision making.

THEME 5. ADMINISTRATION INVOLVES CENTRAL PRINCIPLES THAT IT IS THE BUSINESS OF SCHOLARSHIP TO EXPLORE

Wilson speaks of finding "one rule of good administration for all governments alike." Efficiency requires sound organization, which the study of administration must attempt to discover. Goodnow had touched on this issue mainly by referring to administrative activities from which politics should be excluded: statistical and scientific work, adjudication, and so on. Wilson is clearer, though not definitive, in his discussion of administration. He refers to carrying out laws with "efficiency and dispatch." However, his conception of administration is not narrow; it is perceptive and interesting, and much of what was later written is consistent with it. When Wilson speaks of the possibility of finding "one rule of good administration for all governments alike," he seems to intimate that administration is a purely technical activity with one true way. The province of administration is business, not politics, and civil service reform is but the first step. It is not clear what the indicators of *business* are, in contrast to the indicators of *politics*.

"Sound organization" for the conduct of public "business" might have been a cliche for political debate, but the theme was not developed seriously in political science until nearly forty years later. Wilson's statement is the first example I have seen of a concept of either an objective standard or an implicit theory of organization. If followed to its logical end, the concept of sound organization for the conduct of public business would probably yield something like the organizational concept that William F. Willoughby articulated in 1927 and again in 1937.[65] To call administration *business*, however, implies that Wilson assumed a sensitive connection between politics and administration.

The Dichotomy, Principles, and Management: White and Willoughby

An interesting problem in formulating a theory of administration is whether *principles* are like hypotheses subject to further testing, or whether they constitute precepts for action. Even if one accepts the latter definition, the question is not closed unless principles can be treated as dogma not open to doubt. Action must take place, and a legitimate question is whether all who act are as well off without thoughtful scholarship as with it. Indeed, some practitioners tend to adopt principles as unchangeable rules by which all other decisions are measured. This is not inherent, however, in any analytical scheme, but in other bases for belief. It is at least correct to say that the work on empirical principles was as well founded as any other empirical work of the generation under discussion.

Two theorists who were much concerned with principles were Leonard D. White and William F. Willoughby. Both were aware of politics and its relevance. Each was constrained, however, by a focus on principles that would govern the internal structure and direction of an administrative organization. Each began to develop the same problem that Wilson had anticipated but not developed: what is required for sound organization? The paradoxical feature of Wilson's paper, which points to politics, is that his ideas also point to the emerging concept of *scientific management*.

Leonard D. White overshadowed all others in his generation except for Luther H. Gulick.[66] White's primary emphasis lay in his effort to create some type of administrative theory that would reveal the pattern in the work of a busy agency. White said that his formulation of administration "leaves open the question to what extent the administration itself participates in formulating the purposes of the state, and avoids any controversy as to the precise nature of administrative action." What truly concerned White was the aggregate of routine and the magic and mystery by which a rational result emerged. His significant contribution was to create an administrative theory that did not depend on the findings of law. At the least, this was a search for principles by which action could be anticipated and, if anticipated, also guided to an extent. In the 1926 edition of his textbook, he choses as an imaginary setting a big-city health department: "Business commences at nine o'clock. . . . A steady stream of business develops; telephone calls from citizens, from field inspectors, and from special detail; window calls on a great variety of topics large and small;

telegraphic reports from a neighboring city in which an epidemic is threatening; conferences within the bureaus; conferences between the bureaus."

All this seems, to the uninitiated, a mass of confusion. But there is pattern. Work is segregated by type and assigned to people with the right training for that work. Some kinds of inquiries and complaints are given a standardized handling. Others are referred to some higher authority. Important matters are referred to people at the highest levels. "Thus proceeds in an orderly fashion all the complicated business of the office; some spend the day making out forms, others filing correspondence, others dictating correspondence, making bacteriological analyses, inspecting ventilation systems, granting licenses, mailing blue prints."[67] White expressly left open the question "to what extent the administration itself participates in formulating the purposes of the state, and avoids any controversy as to the precise nature of administrative action."[68] Except for an occasional article, White wrote at the descriptive level. His textbook was very informative about the U.S. government. The analytical understructure was somewhat less clear, and as time passed the material in his discussion appeared obsolete.

William F. Willoughby was more expressly normative and formulated more clearly the standards and criteria that he deemed relevant. Whether one regards Willoughby's formulation as more or less abstract, it answered the following question—though it is not clear that he would have chosen the question: If you were responsible for setting up a government agency, what actions would you have to take and what contingencies would you have to prepare for?

Marshall Dimock commented in 1937 that the underlying objective of Willoughby and others who shared his approach was efficiency.[69] In the same year, William F. Willoughby summarized his conception in a *festschrift* dedicated to his twin, Westel Woodbury Willoughby. Some general principles can attain the result of efficiency in administration. They are "analogous to those characterizing any science, which must be observed if the end . . . is to be secured; . . . these principles are to be determined, and their significance made known, only by the rigid application of scientific methods."[70]

Those trained in modern political science may find this unexceptionable, with methodological reservations about the "scientific" methods to be "rigidly" applied. Why there is some room for debate is shown in Marshall E. Dimock's further summary.[71] The "ideas of those who have developed this approach to public administration," he wrote, "have been influenced primarily . . . by the ideas of the Taylor Society and of those concerned with industrial management." This was what people came to call *scientific management*. (The Taylor Society, originally the Society for the Promotion of the Science of

Management, was formed in 1911 by Frank Gilbreth. Still later, it became upon some merger the Society for the Advancement of Management.) Those "who have taken this approach to the problem of public administration appear to believe in the possibility of formulating general principles relative to administration with the resulting simplification and formalization of the subject matter," wrote Dimock.

This comment reflects the basis for separating politics from administration. Scientific management was itself an approach to organizing power in the private government of the workplace. Early in its influence, it was known as Taylorism, reflecting the work and influence of Frederick Winslow Taylor (1859–1915). The "father of scientific management" was a practical manager and organizer. The folklore is that Taylor was not healthy as a teenager, and so went to work as a draftsman rather than going to Harvard.[72] Schachter challenges this account: if his eyes were too poor for college study, she asks, how could he go to work as a draftsman, where close attention to detail involved intense eye concentration? She concludes that Taylor simply did not want to go to college. In any case, after an apprenticeship as a pattern maker and machinist, he worked in the steel industry in the late 1870s, a period of great labor unrest and declining profits.

Taylor went to work about the same time Woodrow Wilson entered Davidson College. In the early 1880s, when Wilson and Goodnow were in law school, Taylor was a foreman faced with problems of everyday shop management. Concerned by the wage-rate system, he became interested in piecework, or the practice of paying employees by unit of product rather than by the hour. Industrial practice had always been determined by "the great mass of traditional knowledge, which in the past had been in the heads of the workmen, and in the physical skill and knack of the workman, which he has acquired through years of experience."[73] Taylor's central strategy, in contrast, was a "deliberate gathering in on the part of those on management's side" of all this traditional craft knowledge. Taylor believed that a science should be developed to replace the old rule-of-thumb knowledge of the worker. Taylorism, scientific management, was a prescriptive approach to organizing power in the private government of the workplace. The concept was that "of setting a measured standard of work for each man to do each day"—the task idea. This was at the core of what later came to known as time-and-motion studies.

Taylorism became particularly unpopular with workers. They disliked the idea of a "speedup" and were offended at the idea of measuring every gesture and movement in the performance of work. Taylor always insisted that time-and-motion study was a mere technicality, not the essence of scientific management. Taylor's "scientific" management recognized the consequences of the division of labor: his effort to centralize knowledge was designed to overcome the power that the division of labor allows lower-level functionaries.

Taylorism did not pay much explicit attention to American public management. Taylor wrote little about public administration and refused virtually all invitations to address such problems. Therefore, any interpretation of his ideas about the public sector must be inferred from his work on industrial management. Schachter discovered only two sources giving direct evidence of his perspective on public management.[74] James Clay Thompson and Richard F. Vidmer explain this as a result of resistance by public employees.[75] This may be doubtful, however. There may have been some congressional districts in which government employees were numerous enough to block the adoption of Taylor methods by the whole. However, there must have been other considerations, because unions—particularly public employee unions—were not strong between 1900 and the 1930s. Taylorism was probably distasteful to two more important groups: bosses of local political machines, who had representatives in Congress, and business firms (often boss-connected) that sold goods and services to the U.S. government.

In 1911 the army chief of ordnance sought to introduce Taylor's system at the arsenal in Watertown, Massachusetts, and provoked a strike. The strike led to a hearing before a special House of Representatives committee convened to investigate the social impact of shop management systems. Taylor rigorously defended his system before the committee. In correspondence with the Watertown authorities, Taylor reminded them that "efficiency, narrowly construed, would not lead Congress to support changes so much as would worker satisfaction with the new system expressed at election time." The other specific reference is a manuscript entitled "Government Efficiency," which discusses personnel selection. The essay "favors 'merit' over spoils systems, which he equates with loafing and fear of change."[76]

The application of Taylor's ideas to public administration also comes through Morris L. Cooke, an engineer whom Schachter calls Taylor's intellectual deputy for public administration, and through the New York Bureau of Municipal Research, where educated young people learned to apply Taylor's principles to municipal administration.

Conclusion

Scholarly inquiry into public administration has grown too far removed from its own intellectual history. "Old" public administration is valuable not necessarily because it is correct. It is valuable because it contains most of the ideas now present in scholarship, even if they have not been systematized or tested to the full.

Rediscovery, codification, clarification, and testing are signifcant parts of our present task. Reconsidering the relationship of political theory to administrative theory is an important step. In the vast body of political theory cannot we find important points that may help to structure our thinking about administrative relationships, as do the fragments from Plato, Benedict, Hobbes, Bodin, and Rousseau? Among our more immediate predecessors, can we not abandon the shallow conception that the dichotomy between politics and administration comes from Wilson and Goodnow?

If Wilson's latent theory, though expressed in a fragmented and journalistic way, had been crystallized, politics would logically play a central part in that theory. The same is even more true for Goodnow's latent theory. A Wilson model, conditioned in public opinion and culture, would have led to a different research agenda from that of Goodnow. A model based on Goodnow's ideas could not have ignored public opinion, but it might have been more oriented to the sources of executive power, to executive direction of bureaucracy, and to mechanisms for assuring the exclusion of external demand from those functions. Either model, however, would have focused on the exchange between the administrative entity and the rest of society.

The five themes discussed in this chapter have long existed in the literature, in certain variations. Each has been subject to debate and research and to disruptions or challenges from outside the community of political science. Of all the themes found in Wilson and/or Goodnow, the idea of principles caught on most firmly. In the years between 1900 and World War I, public administration literature seemed more or less implicitly to adopt the idea that one can discern principles by which to anticipate action, and therefore, to guide it. In the last thirty years, however, the idea of principles has had a notably bad press. Leonard D. White and William Franklin Willoughby had much to do with the principles idea. However, each constrained this inquiry by assumptions that focused on principles for the internal structure and direction of the administrative organization. In this respect, each began to develop the same problem that Wilson had anticipated but not further developed; namely, what is required for sound organization? The paradoxical feature of Wilson's essay, which points to politics, is that his ideas imply a kinship with the emerging ideas about scientific management.

Scientific management, adopted by some political scientists and given great public credence, helped to change the language and mental habits of students of public administration. It helped to create and sustain the idea of a dichotomy between politics and administration. The cultural resistance to politics as both dirty and inefficient expressed a prejudice strongly shared both by the elite and the mass public.

Taylor's concepts, translated through Willoughby's work, are a variation on the concept of principles in administration outlined by Wilson. They highlight the concept of administration as an autonomous activity having nothing to do with politics. Taylor's ideas amounted to a virtual preemption of administration by those who chose to study matters other than politics, or a virtual removal of politics from the study of administration. There, not in the work of Wilson or Goodnow, is the origin of the famous dichotomy as an intellectual proposition. In direct opposition was the *politics of administration*, a logical refinement of the partially implicit, partially explicit theme of the primacy of politics. The ideas of a politics of administration, asserted and reasserted boldly from time to time, has never been persuasive in the field of administration any more than a concern with administration has established a secure place at the center of political science. Other approaches to administration have preempted politics over the past forty years. Or, to put it in another perspective, political science has surrendered the study of public administration to other modes of analysis.

WHY AND HOW POLITICAL SCIENCE SURRENDERED THE STUDY OF PUBLIC ADMINISTRATION

If political science, as a discipline, takes seriously the study of how power is organized—the study of politics—it must necessarily give a central place to administration. It will require an empirical political theory to describe and explain administration as the lifeblood of power. Moreover, at one time political science might be thought to have started down this path. But knowledge gets lost, or at least forgotten, and some of the knowledge worth reclaiming is set out in old books that are no longer read. The recovery of lost knowledge is one reason to attempt to work out from the "accumulated wealth of concepts, questions, and generalizations."[1]

It was never possible, even in the terms of Woodrow Wilson and Frank Goodnow, to have a strict and total separation of politics from administration. The clues, latent or explicit in the work of Wilson and Goodnow, for a brief moment yielded a "politics of administration," a logically inherent refinement. (The contemporary version, grounded in economics and protected by mathematics, is known as *principal-agent theory*.)[2]

The discovery that administrative discretion is important, for example, can be placed in a chain of reasoning that proceeds, incrementally, from Goodnow. Administrators can, he said, negate the will of the state by nonexecution. Therefore administration must be subject to political authority. In the 1930s and 1940s political scientists began to build both a concept and a set of empirical studies of the politics of administration. The pivotal writer was

E. Pendleton Herring, who brought his conception of group politics into the study of administration. "We assume," he wrote, "the possibility of achieving a balance of forces, social and economic."[3] This statement contains a cultural assumption, though Herring did not use that language. That is, the values implicit in Herring's formulation leave room for the possibility of finding other results. "Whether this process becomes anything more than political jugglery depends upon the standards of justice that are accorded general acceptance by the community." Will social opportunity and loyalty to the democratic process outweigh opportunities and immediate self-interest? Thus Herring recognizes the relevance of value choices made by administrators.

> Intrinsically, this is a question for statesmen, but officials can affect in some manner the turning of the scales. The administrative branch of the government cannot maintain a balance in a dynamic society but it can do much toward clarifying and effectuating the purposes declared by our legislators.[4]

Herring proceeds to an empirical analysis of traditional, regulatory, and special interest agencies within the U.S. federal administration. Among the first include the Internal Revenue Service, the State Department, and the Tariff Commission, later called the International Trade Commission.[5] In the second group, Herring includes the Federal Trade Commission—about which a major controversy had just been decided as to presidential powers—the Federal Power Commission, and the Interstate Commerce Commission, which later was the basis for a famous article by Samuel P. Huntington.[6] Herring's analysis thus extends Goodnow's reasoning when he says that "the course of administrative action is not chartered by dead reckoning with statute books as the only point of reference."[7]

This chapter cannot provide the deserved treatment of the politics of administration concept as it emerged in the 1930s. The idea had substantial potential, even on issues still poorly developed today. The chief point is that this literature, based essentially in a group theory of politics, opened major paths that have yet to be completed, many of which were scarcely begun. It illustrates what we have called metaphorically "excessively rapid depreciation," or the result of "shifting cultivation." As a prime illustration, the phenomenon of field administration is inherent in any hierarchy. Decision making, and external responses to decision making, take place not only at the most central point of authority, but at successive points down the line until one deals with the Nth clerk, or truck driver, or police officer, involved. In the 1930s and 1940s, the politics of administration, or field administration, had begun to interest scholars. Empirical work of more recent vintage is sparse, except for studies conducted under the rubric of implementation.[8] The essential conceptual issues thus have lain dormant in the literature of political science for at least four decades. James W. Fesler's work continues to receive some recognition.[9] Schuyler C. Wallace, David B. Truman, and Earl Latham and colleagues, in a remarkable research memorandum, anticipated in the 1940s virtually all that appears in the new literature of policy analysis or policy implementation.[10] Yet the striking thing is that the work of all these scholars, oriented to politics, has largely been by-passed, as students of administration have gone on to other interests.

Political science thus surrendered the intellectual initiative in studying public administration and surrendered the opportunity and challenge to bring its perceptions to bear on important public problems. In consequence, intellectual dominance moved largely outside the discipline, to work on organization theory, bureaucracy, and management.

Why Did Political Science Cease to Study Administration?

The reasons for this surrender are twofold: one is essentially pragmatic, from outside academic life, and the other goes deeply to the psychology of the discipline. Political science in this century has largely been captured by the needs of undergraduate teaching. That usually means repeating material found in books. The emptiness this can lead to is what Woodrow Wilson recognized when he sought to study in Europe in 1886: "What I want to know is, what the Prefect does do."

If a scholar has an idea but lacks the resources to follow the idea, the idea will languish. If some social interest has a need and is given the means to gratify it, scholarly resources will flow toward meeting that need. If the scholarly resources in a discipline are devoted to some other field, new resources will flow to competing scholarly groups.

In political science between the two world wars, there was rather little research devoted to creating new knowledge. Creating new knowledge demands new ideas and new data. Research requires time, books, papers, equipment, and travel. Money generally was not available for research on administrative questions. Political scientists interested in learning more about public administration could achieve desired results not by pursuing their intellectual interests, but rather by redefining their interests in terms that public officials or private interests could accept and sponsor.

Targets of opportunity existed where some group had an action project it wanted to advance. Alice B. Stone and Donald C. Stone report that by 1894 "there were eighty-four citizens' associations and clubs in different cities attacking general deterioration or specific abuses," and from these groups emerged the National Municipal League, "the strategy center for many municipal reforms in the subsequent decades."[11] If, for example, there were some local campaign to install a city manager plan, and if a local professor could be found who could summarize the texts, collect statutes and statistics, and write a supportive pamphlet, then that person could find some modest support. In a handful of cities, the local organization developed a close relationship with a local academician. So it was with the Detroit Bureau of Governmental Research, with which the famous Lent Upson had a close relationship.[12] So it was also with the Cleveland Foundation and the Citizens League of Cleveland, with its relationship to A. R. Hatton, a political scientist at Western Reserve University.

While these matters were very important, they did not always lie within the range of issues that commanded the broadest intellectual interest. In some cases, moreover, severe intellectual analysis would have been unwelcome. Those who sought to clean up local corruption by installing a city manager surely did not desire analysis of the kind later inspired by Robert K. Merton, to the effect that there some functional utility to the political machine as a device of social integration.[13] Opportunity played an important role. Rowland Egger mentions a "privately financed investigation by an ad hoc Commission of Inquiry on Public Service Personnel [that] conducted extensive research and held a series of public hearings in 1933/34."[14]

About the same time, the Social Science Research Council created a Committee on Public Administration to improve academic research and bring it into more operational contact with working public administrators.[15]

> Notable studies of city-manager government, of grant systems in the United States and Canada, of social security administration, of Federal work relief, of agriculture and public administration, and of education and public administration were planned and funded by the Committee. A highly provocative series of monographs on the scope and methods of research in public-personnel administration, administrative law, the administration of public tort liability, and NRA code administration had great influence on research subjects and methods in the academy in both the Second New Deal and in the postwar periods.[16]

When practical incentives disappeared, support for research disappeared. There has, for instance, been no support since the 1940s for a research program that would have capitalized on the work of the Committee on Public Administration.

The psychological reason was more important. The shift to new nomenclature often entailed the pursuit of ideas, meritorious in themselves, that were increasingly far removed from the core problem of political science: observing, explaining, and anticipating the organization of power. The reason for the shift was that many political scientists were growing ashamed of themselves. They experienced a failure of will to work out their intellectual problems, on their own, to the end. Critics within the discipline taught newer political scientists to believe that they were not *scientific* in a way that commanded respect. Knowledge sought by political scientists was central, David Easton wrote in the troubled postwar era, to solving the "present social crisis." Accordingly, political scientists

> might well set modesty aside and confess to a belief in the transcendent value of their research, in that of all the social sciences, for the destinies of man. Yet, in the light of what society demands from them and of what is in fact possible for political science, they would be compelled in equal honesty to set all pride aside and confess than in its achievement in research American political science has grave difficulties measuring up to the tasks imposed upon it.[17]

Easton was perhaps only the most influential among the many internal critics who challenged existing concepts about how knowledge was acquired and offered new formulations about how it could be expressed to attain intellectual legitimacy. The underlying idea that there was something of transcendent value in the discipline was virtually buried in the avalanche of self-criticism concerning "the disappointing results of a discipline already twenty-five hundred years old." Easton goes on,

> It has not been until quite recently, with a few notable exceptions, that a limited number of political scientists have undertaken to re-examine the conception of science in political research. In terms of a sophisticated understanding of the prerequisites for scientific research, political science is probably the last of the social sciences to feel the effects of scientific reason in its most developed form.[18]

When the hallmark of approbation became *sophisticated*, a sense of collective embarrassment saturated the discipline. The "sophisticated" looked down on their "unsophisticated" colleagues, outward to other colleagues who were similarly sophisticated, and upward to the more prestigious disciplines. The unsophisticated were sullen and resentful, and each refused to learn much from the other. The loss of internal self-confidence left the newer generation of political scientists naked on the academic prairie, exposed to the cold winds of external criticism.

The same year that Easton's book was published, Kenneth Davis carpet-bombed public administration and particularly the teaching of administrative law within the field of public administration.

> The texts on public administration that include substantial discussions of administrative law show rather clearly that the textwriters have developed no such basic understanding [of the subject matter]. The resulting summaries are in a fundamental sense seriously misleading. The proportion of misinformation is exceedingly high. Even the most elementary ideas are often flagrantly in error.[19]

Because there was no clear, comprehensible, powerful reply to these charges that could be aligned with the newer political science, no new assistant professor of political science knew how to engage in effective debate with a new assistant professor of law.[20]

Oskar Morgenstern wrote in 1959, "Political scientists have spent much time and effort to produce a body of knowledge that is singularly unsuited to guide us in the present dilemma of our life—a body of knowledge that is a peculiar mixture of constitutional law, history and description of political institutions of all kinds, everything generously sprinkled by strong opinions and value judgments."[21] Political scientists, in the interest of dissonance reduction, could have ignored the criticism from the economist Morgenstern: "Of the social sciences only economics has so far achieved a modicum of operational value."[22] Morgenstern was correct in saying that "political science does not offer a *systematic* body of such rules applicable to the present circumstances"—it is not, as one says, operational—but to offer economics as an alternate model is debatable. One can agree, however, with his statement, "So far political science has not even abstracted the counsels given by Machiavelli in order to discover whether a consistent system of rules of behavior could be constructed on that basis."

In face of such criticism, it is not surprising that the discipline did not know what it was doing. Lindblom did not exaggerate much, if at all, when he asked if anyone's self-esteem was better disguised than a political scientist's.[23]

Political scientists who provided the dominant intellectual leadership in the 1950s almost seemed to accept the idea not merely that anthropology, economics, psychology, and sociology contained useful material, but that they were better in fundamental theory, data, and methods of inquiry. This disability of the will was powerfully evident in public administration, where at that moment there were strong pragmatic and intellectual outside challengers. In the end, however, political scientists ignored their own major problems. Ultimately they arrived at the same problems by other and no more productive intellectual routes because they were fundamental, and scholars in other disciplines were forced to deal with them too.

How Organization Theory Was Surrendered

In any discipline, some questions and methods are mandatory, some permissible, and some prohibited. When the mandatory and the prohibited, together, preclude attention to matters that seem compelling to the rest of the world, a discipline surrenders some of its capability. The first area in which political science's surrender of intellectual initiative is now called organization theory. *Organization theory* embraces the theories, speculations, propositions, and data undertaken to describe and explain the organization, whether public or private. Psychologists and biologists, energized by plant needs during World War I, had begun to study fatigue, morale, and interpersonal cooperation. These studies were the seeds of what became the *human relations* school of organization theory. The kind of organization theory to which I refer comes out of various strands of work dating from the 1920s and before. It got its strongest attention in the 1950s, and especially in the 1960s, often being adopted by scholars of a behavioral disposition. Organization theory, as introduced by Herbert Simon, became the means by which the newer political science deemed something that had been in the old, "outmoded" public administration. Simon is specifically cited by David Easton as among the "limited number of political scientists [who] have undertaken to re-examine the concept of science in political research."[24]

Political science already contained the foundations for a theory of organization, and there is no compelling reason why organization theory should have developed elsewhere. The idea of a theory of organization is foreshadowed in Woodrow Wilson's article on administration. This latent concept never matured within the disciplines. But it developed, along independent lines, not from political science but from engineering. Engineers like F. W. Taylor began to state "principles" of administration or organization. The works of Mary Parker Follett, John Merriman Gaus, and Luther H. Gulick were even more directly relevant.

In the 1950s, Follett and Gaus were largely ignored, and Gulick's work was, at least for a time, repudiated as having been demolished by Herbert A. Simon.[25] By the time political science absorbed the impact of Simon's thought, the organization theorists' interest turned away from all politics except the micropolitics of the organization. Rather than maintaining a linkage between the two questions, organization theory tended—because of the powerful stimulus of Herbert Simon—to turn entirely to decision making within the organization, and to the competence of the decision-making *person*, which means to the cognitive processes of the mind. As a matter of science, the elegant and demanding problem to which this leads, and which Simon found it more productive to follow, lies in information, intelligence, and the replication and extension of intelligence—to wit, computer science.

MARY PARKER FOLLETT AND JOHN MERRIMAN GAUS

The intellectual origins of Mary Parker Follett (1868–1933) lay in the boundary zone between history and political science. She wrote her first book, on the Speaker of the House of Representatives,[26] when political science was still emerging as a separate field of inquiry. It is still respected by scholars who now work in a very different style.[27] The introduction, by the famous historian Albert Bushnell Hart, reflected his support for her aspirations. Yet Follett never held an academic post. Academic posts were generally scarce, especially for women, except in women's colleges, and the higher education community was much smaller than it is now. Possibly she did not want one. Henry C. Metcalf and Lyndall Urwick showed their admiration for Follett's far-ranging style in a posthumous appreciation:

> Her first publication was the pamphlet on *The Speaker of the House of Representatives*, (1909), but her main work, *The New State*, did not appear until 1920, to be closely followed (1924) by a masterly treatise in a parallel field under the title *Creative Experience*.
>
> Miss Follett had now reached the front rank of political scientists. *The Speaker of the House of Representatives* had carried an Introduction by the well-known Professor Albert Bushnell Hart. *The New State* was reviewed in learned journals the world over, and brought her national and international recognition. It led to her friendship with Lord Haldane, the English statesman and philosopher, and with other distinguished philosophers and political scientists.[28]

Metcalf and Urwick's placement of Follett is, perhaps, not quite correct. She was a celebrated figure in the world of affairs. But it was possible for later political scientists to lose sight of, rather than to capitalize on, her work exactly because she was a marginal figure in political science. Her marginality seems similar to that of Peter Drucker, who wrote somewhat unhappily of his career in political science and what he saw as the generally negative reception to his joint interest in economics and politics, especially in *The Concept of the Corporation*. He recalled, "The highly sympathetic reviewer in the *American Political Science Review* ended by saying: 'It is hoped that this promising young scholar will soon devote his considerable talent to a more serious subject'; and when the American Political Science Association next met, I was not reelected to the Committee on Political-Theory Research."[29] Follett was also soon outside the mainstream of political science. Like Drucker, she became quite famous in the world of practical administration, especially in business. Follett spent some time at a settlement house in Roxbury, a poor Boston neighborhood, just before World War I. This led to Follett's becoming a member of a vocational placement board created by the Boston School Board. In turn, she became a member of the Minimum Wage Board of the Women's Municipal League, where she "represented the people and worked in close association with both employers and employed."[30]

This may have been how Follett started her association with business firms, presumably as a consultant, to which she refers frequently. At that time, ideas about business management were based in the old idea of prerogative, or leadership reflecting a will uncontrolled by any other will.[31] The boss was the boss. Follett's original contribution was to bring to business problems a concern, reinforced by the developing field of psychology, with human relations. She saw that control was coming to mean control of facts rather than control of human beings. This implied that greater power would be based on knowledge, not merely on holding a position that allowed one to give orders. Follett also stressed what she called correlation of many controls, rather than superimposed control. Finally, she saw that coordination is a continuing process, not a mere event or action: "In seeking for leaders we are not seeking first the ability to dominate people."[32]

Follett's spirit of innovation leads her in a methodological direction, but she is also concerned with substantive issues now dealt with as *organization development*. How does one acquire the knowledge that allows one to make short-run proposals for constructive change in organizations? The substance of Follett's proposals is less important than her concern with participant observation. "It is seldom possible," she said, "to 'observe' a social situation as one watches a chemical experiment; the presence of the observer usually changes the situation."[33] She thus proposes a method of research for improving situations, not merely for clarification: "We need then those who are frankly participant-observers, those who will try experiment after experiment and note results, experiments in making human interplay productive." In the clearest spirit of what we have come to call organization theory, she puts this proposal on a very broad scale. It should apply "in industry and business, in legislative committees and administrative commissions, in trade unions and shop committees and joint boards of control, in athletic committees and college faculties, in our families, in parliamentary cabinets and international conferences." At the same time, she argued for working out the relationship between quantitative and qualitative analysis, a relation not always understood in social science. (In this respect, she anticipated an interventionist mode of thinking later presented by Harold Lasswell, though very few political scientists find it attractive.)[34]

John Merriman Gaus, in contrast to Follett, was a major figure in his generation who profoundly influenced political scientists who are still active, among them Alfred Fernbach and Clara Penniman, who knew him at the University of Wisconsin; James A. (Dolph) Norton, who knew him at Harvard; and Charles O. Jones, who knew him in retirement.[35] Gaus, in particular, may be understood as a humane, optimistic, indigenous American democrat. Like others, Gaus took cognizance of the increased delegation of authority to administrators in the United States. More distinctively, he turned toward theory "concerning the motive forces of human behavior which are gradually being revealed to us by the psychologist and the physiologist."[36] He observed, "A theory of organization must include some answer to the question, 'What keeps the people in this organization working together?'" An agreed purpose is central. Gaus also raised the problem of the *constituency*. Everyone with any experience in government now emphasizes constituency, but it was not so significant in the 1930s. Gaus's perception showed originality: a significant part of the relationship between the organization and the citizen who is not a member of that organization is their joint participation in the end result.

Gaus was not consciously methodological; his exposition is deceptively simple, informal, almost conversational, but it masks perceptions of startling power. Yet even Gaus expressly seeks explanatory principles that remain constant in any human setting. He defined a *principle* as a tested hypothesis. To be sure, neither he nor others of his generation thought of principles as absolute. He believed that a principle would be "as useful a guide to action in the public administration of Russia as of Great Britain, of Iraq as of the United States," when "applied in the light of its appropriate frame of reference."[37]

LUTHER HALSEY GULICK

The pivotal essay in the theory of organization was that of Luther H. Gulick, published in 1937.[38] He starts with the proposition that organization is a function of structure for coordinating the division of work. Gulick discusses why work is divided (because people differ in capacities, cannot be in two places at once, cannot do two things at once, or cannot know everything); the limits of division (time, technology, and utility); and the necessity for coordination (the whole is greater than the sum of the parts). He reviews coordination through organization: the principle of the unity of command—on which he lays great stress; the problem of technical efficiency—which entails judgment about what work can be supervised by lay persons and what cannot; the span of control, which is "partly a matter of limits of knowledge, but even more is a matter of limits of time and of energy"; and cautions that experts themselves will be both dogmatic in belief that their "particular technology [is] the road to salvation" and inclined to "step without embarrassment into other areas."

Gulick then considers what organizational patterns are desirable, such as whether the emphasis should be "top down," thus emphasizing the needs of the chief executive, or "bottom up," thus emphasizing the situation of work units and the people in them. Gulick discusses how to aggregate work units, which leads into the question of organizational structure—including horizontal and vertical relationships; organization by major purpose, process, clientele or material, and place or area; as well as the line-staff relationship, interrelation of systems of departmentalization, and interdepartmental coordination.

The most famous part of the essay is also the most criticized. Gulick sets out a concept for organizing the chief executive which, under the acronym POSDCORB, has stereotyped the essay in the minds of succeeding scholars. POSDCORB was one way of framing inquiry into these matters; if the definitions offered by Gulick were treated seriously, and terms operationalized to get some idea of what data would be required, then problems of research design could be faced. Gulick was writing not about all administration or all executives, but about how to institutionalize the job of the chief executive. To do that, it was necessary first to answer the question, "What is the work of the chief executive?" The answer is POSDCORB.

> POSDCORB is, of course, a made-up word, designed to call attention to the various functional elements of the work of a chief executive, because "administration" and "management" have lost all specific content.

POSDCORB is made up of the initials and stands for the following activities: Planning, Organizing, Staffing, Directing, Coordinating, Reporting, Budgeting.

POSDCORB does not offer a priority schedule for these activities, nor does it offer a theoretical explanation about the relationships between them. Nonetheless, it is potentially an extremely useful checklist. Very simply, if POSDCORB were treated not as an article of faith for believers or rejection by atheists, but as a set of provisional hypotheses for ordered inquiry, then the initial questions are apparent. What is entailed in the planning activity of, or on behalf of, the chief executive? It violates good sense to believe that no planning takes place; but who has examined how this is done by, or for, any president of the United States? The same question might be asked about organizing, staffing, directing, coordinating, reporting, and budgeting. Though fragmentary discussions exist for particular activities that might be so classified in particular U.S. administrations, I know of no studies that encompass all these functions for any administration—or any functions over an extended period in any country.

Gulick's essay touches on issues of measurement and organization, structure and coordination, and the holding company idea; then it turns to the important psychological theme of coordination by idea. Gulick thus addresses the psychological requirements for high-level leadership:

> Any large and complicated enterprise would be incapable of effective operation if reliance for coordination were placed in organization alone. Organization is necessary; in a large enterprise it is essential, but it does not take the place of a dominant central idea as the foundation of action and self-coordination in the daily operation of all the parts of the enterprise.

He continues:

> Human beings are compounded of cogitation and emotion and do not function well when treated as though they were merely cogs in motion. Their capacity for great and productive labor, creative cooperative work, and loyal self-sacrifice knows no limits provided the whole man, body-mind-and-spirit, is thrown into the program.

Finally, the essay concludes with a somewhat philosophical excursion into the limits of coordination, including a thoughtful discussion on the risks of authoritarian states, the accretion and loss of organizational functions, and the evolution of government. After this, Gulick never turned sustained attention to developing the ideas in his essay. Administrative practice and not administrative theory became his career.

HERBERT A. SIMON

Gulick's widely cited formulation became the standard against which Herbert Simon contended a decade later.[39] Simon's own scope is, in fact, magisterial. No writer down to 1950 showed a greater command of the preceding literature (though Simon's work has some strange omissions such as little reference to Willoughby, yet considerable discussion of Goodnow). Throughout *Administrative Behavior* (1957), his notes and asides reflect an extremely broad knowledge of legal, historical, and conventional political science studies of the time.

Methodologically, Simon concentrates on "the single member of the administrative organization" in order to study the limits to the quantity and quality of that person's output. In that respect, Simon elaborates on ground identified by John Gaus a decade before. These " 'limits' to rationality with which the principles of administration must deal" include (1) physiology, laws of skills-training, and of habit, (2) values and conceptions of purpose, and (3) knowledge, which must encompass substantially what Gulick encompasses under *cogitation*.

In the very act of proposing a different approach to decision making, Simon's express language continues to recognize "the mechanism of authority" as equally crucial. Latter-day scholars have overemphasized the originality of the idea that human decisions focus not upon optimizing but upon *satisficing*. Lord John Morley quotes Thucydides: "So little pains will most men take in search for truth: so much more readily will they turn to what comes first."[40] Satisficing caught on, one suspects, because its scholarly expression was a revelation of light to economists, who had before been committed intellectually to a perfectionist mode they knew to be unreal, and was attractive to political scientists who had not before had a good exposition of what they knew to be true. What modern social science needs is to establish when satisficing occurs, when people are able to do somewhat better, and what its consequences for decision making are.

Simon's critique is both theoretical and methodological. His theoretical challenge is that the "principles of administration" do not identify the significant variables in administration and the relationships between them. Simon undertakes the task simply enough, by identifying what he regards, correctly, as "the more common principles." Four are particularly important, all relating to achieving efficiency: (1) specializing by task; (2) determining hierarchy on the basis of unity of command; (3) limiting span of control to a small number (say six); and (4) grouping personnel according to purpose, process, clientele, or place.

These principles contain contradictions, according to Simon, so that action based on them could produce results other than efficiency. With regard to specialization, it is not so much that it is internally contradictory as that it is empty. All group effort involves specialization; the question is what particular specialization will produce efficiency.

As to the hierarchical unity of command, Simon attempts to show that some degree of functional coordination is essential, and that this runs contrary to the vertical specialization called for by unity of command. Similarly, if the span of control is narrow, the number of levels through which communications must pass in order to achieve compliance must increase. Again, there is some contradiction. Finally, as to the fourfold basis for the assignment of functions, he is able to show that the terms themselves contain profound ambiguities. The bases for assignment are competitive, and the Gulick formulation does not provide clues to assist the choice. Simon does say of his approach, "If it is a valid one, . . . it constitutes an indictment of much current writing about administrative matters." But he simply does not say, contrary to many contemporary accusations, that he had overthrown or demolished the previous literature, although he maintains it will serve only with a radical restructuring. To the question, "Can anything be salvaged which will be useful in the construction of an administrative theory?" he answers, "Almost everything can be salvaged."

Indeed, he could not logically say otherwise. The limits that Simon specifies are substantially identified by Follett, Gaus, and Gulick. Thomas Hammond's recent critique of Simon may be severe, but his defense of Gulick has merit. Gulick's essay was, as Hammond says, "rich, subtle, sophisticated, and complex . . . showing a clear awareness of the various problems with the principles of administration that Simon pointed out." It is also true that "Gulick himself made 'bounded rationality' an integral part of his treatment of organization."[41]

Simon's own criticism of his predecessors sometimes contains rhetorical overstatement. "Administrative description . . . has confined itself too closely to the mechanism of authority, and has failed to bring within its orbit the other, equally important, modes of influence on organizational behavior." Simon was right to suggest that other "modes of influence" had not been studied with scientific precision. But the way he put it was simply wrong. The language of Gulick, Gaus, or Follett, already quoted, is adequate evidence on that point. Similarly, Simon caricatured, rather than reported, the administrative literature when he said it refused "to undertake the tiresome task of studying the actual allocations of decision-making functions." There is also distortion in his comment that the literature had been satisfied to speak of *authority, centralization, span of control, function*, without seeking operational definitions of those terms. Possibly Simon did not like the way those terms had been examined in the literature. But the "tiresome task" has been undertaken, however incompletely, in the works of Herring, Leiserson, MacMahon and Millett, and others.

At that stage in his thinking, Simon enunciated a "theory of administration [as] concerned with how an organization should be constructed and operated in order to accomplish its work more efficiently." It is impossible to make an exhaustive list of the "factors that determine the level of efficiency which is achieved by an administrative organization." However, the principal categories can be enumerated. "Perhaps the simplest method of approach is to consider the single member of the administrative organization, and ask what the limits are to the quantity and quality of his output." The limits he finds—physiology, values, and knowledge—foreshadow what later became Simon's powerful concentration on thinking and knowing, which led him far from public administration. He is interested in "political" relationships throughout his work, though not always explicitly, as they pertain to authority and communications; organizational loyalties and identification; and the anatomy of organization. Consider the title of the final chapter, "The Business School: A Problem in Organizational Design." Yet, what Simon was concerned with in public administration has largely been left to others to explore. Political science and public administration followed his lead just far enough to isolate themselves from their own intellectual roots and from the problems of power—but not far enough to establish a new domain of inquiry.

The Problem of Bureaucracy

Larry B. Hill argues persuasively that students of politics should "take bureaucracy seriously." Research should start from the recognition that large-scale administrative government is far more significant than is recognized in doctrines and attitudes.[42] Hill recognizes that bureaucracy has not been a domain of serious inquiry. Political science stood at the threshold of its own organization theory, but never generated its own bureaucratic theory. This is surprising because observers of politics were familiar with different concepts of bureaucracy long before the juncture with Weberian sociology.

THE IDEA OF BUREAUCRACY

The first evidence of this surrender is that the widely used term *bureaucracy* has almost no focused meaning, although it has been diffused in common, everyday speech. The word, derived from the French *bureau*, seems to have crossed from France to Great Britain early in the nineteenth century. The *OED* quotes an example from 1818: "Mr. Commissioner . . . represented the *Bureaucratie*, or office tyranny, by which Ireland so long had been governed." In 1837 John Stuart Mill wrote of "that vast network of administrative tyranny . . . that system of *bureaucracy*, which leaves no free agent in all France, except the man in Paris who pulls the wires." The 1853 *American Dictionary of the English Language* (later called *Webster's*) contained this definition: "A system in which the business of government is carried on in departments, each under the control of a chief, in contradistinction from a system in which the officers of government have a co-ordinate authority."

A common denominator may have been captured in Webster's 1888 edition: "Government officials collectively," a definition nearly contemporaneous with Wilson's preparations for his 1887 Cornell lecture. But the definition is too simple and general to be of much use. That definition refers to the organizational structure, and makes no qualitative judgment about the character of the organization or decision making therein.

The general public view of bureaucracy is negative, although Goodsell argues that bureaucracy has a socially constructive function,[43] and there is also little patience for Norton Long's argument that bureaucracy in the United States, through the system of civil service recruitment, may be more representative of the backgrounds, values, and interests of the populace than is Congress itself.[44] Rough is the road and narrow is the way for those who make that unpopular case.

On the other hand, Wilson implied that there was something unacceptable about the behavior of a bureaucracy when he said it could "exist only where the whole service of the state is removed from the common political life of the people, its chiefs as well as its rank and file"; in that case, its "motives, its objects, its policy, its standards, must be bureaucratic."[45] A more extreme, explicit formulation appeared in the 1890 *Cyclopedia of Political Science*: bureaucracy does not depend on any particular constitutional form, but is a system of centralized overgovernment characterized by formalism and a sense of caste separation from the rest of society.

That idea was also current in England in the 1890s. Sir Stafford Northcote forecast "bureaucratic despotism" as the consequence of the Reform Bill of

1884: "The permanent officials will take the management of affairs into their own hands, and Parliament will have little to do."[46] (In the preceding sentence, of course, he uses the term *officials* to mean administrative officials and does not include judges, legislators, or even ministers, as in the United States.)

Over the next half century, the terminology was sharpened to emphasize behavioral qualities. Webster's dictionary offers three choices in the 1936 edition.

> A system of carrying on the business of government by means of departments or bureaus, each controlled by a chief who is apt to place special emphasis upon routine and conservative action; officialism; also, government conducted on this system. Hence, in general, such a system which has become narrow, rigid, and formal, depends on precedent, and lacks initiative and resourcefulness.

This attitude is also found in the definition offered by the celebrated English political scientist Harold J. Laski in 1930: "The characteristics of such a regime are a passion for routine in administration, the sacrifice of flexibility to rule, delay in the making of decisions and a refusal to embark upon experiment."[47]

Webster's offers a second usage: "A system of government by bureau heads, responsible only to administrative officers above them, having complete power over subordinates and, in official duties generally, not subject to the common law of the land."

There are some inherent contradictions here. Laski's discussion led with a key element: "Bureaucracy is the term usually applied to a system of government the control of which is so completely in the hands of officials that their power jeopardizes the liberties of ordinary citizens."[48] It seems almost impossible that any group that is so restricted by rule and practice, as the earlier definition implies, could act freely and arbitrarily. Clearly, professionals dealing with the subject had opposite conceptions of bureaucracy, and a definition had to recognize both. Laski goes on, "In extreme cases the members of a bureaucracy may become a hereditary caste manipulating government to their own advantage."

The idea of bureaucracy as implying a special form of action is implicit in Laski's treatment:

> It should be pointed out that these undesirable characteristics of bureaucracy are not in the least confined to the service of the state; they operate wherever there is large scale organization. Trade unions,

churches, institutions for social work, great industrial corporations, all these are compelled by the very size of the interests they represent to take on the same habits of bureaucracy.

Three usages may be more distinctive: bureaucracy as rationality, pathology, and despotism.

WEBERIAN RATIONALITY

In political science, the concept of bureaucracy as involving a special form of action or a special means of acting, hence requiring particular study, has sometimes taken on an overlay of sociological thinking as influenced by Max Weber.[49] Weber was a German economist-historian with a strong interest in legal institutions. A late nineteenth-century liberal, both in the economic and the political sense, he was profoundly pessimistic about the future of German politics and society and was rather active in politics at the end of World War I.[50] Weber's importance in social science is less a function of his prodigious scholarship than of his political value as a source of encouragement to social scientists as to what they wanted to believe rather than what they wanted to know. Weber has been a figure of great controversy in Europe since World War II. For some, Weber appears to have offered tough-minded thought about democracy and its prospects. Wolfgang J. Mommsen portrays a more equivocal view of Weber, stressing his German nationalism, his power-mindedness, and his assertion of a concept of plebiscitary democratic leadership in which the one chosen leader would be responsible only to his conscience. This view obviously excited much controversy in Europe because plebiscitary leadership could potentially be a species of fascism.[51]

Weber's ideas about government are saturated with his worries about his own society. At Munich University, four years before the Beer Hall Putsch, Weber gave one of his most famous lectures about the revolutionary ferment then bubbling in Germany.[52] In the peroration, he said:

> Now then, ladies and gentlemen, let us debate this matter once more ten years from now. Unfortunately, for a whole series of reasons, I fear that by then the period of reaction will long since have broken over us. . . . Then, I wish that I could see what has become of those of you who now feel yourselves to be genuinely 'principled' politicians and who share in the intoxication signified by this revolution.

In a tone of an elder who expects not to be believed, he continued, "Not summer's bloom lies ahead of us, but rather a polar night of icy darkness and hardness, no matter which group may triumph externally now." In this lecture Weber said that politics was the strong and slow boring of hard boards, that to attain the possible one must reach for the impossible, "with that steadfastness of heart that can brave the crumbling of all hopes. Only he has the calling for politics who is sure that he shall not crumble when the world from his point of view is too stupid or too base for what he wants to offer."

American scholars who encountered Weber in translation after the war also found that his work met a vital need. He was their alternative to Marx just when they required it. At that time, laissez-faire capitalism was in lower esteem among intellectuals than in more recent times.[53] Friedrich von Hayek, whose work has recently experienced a resurgence of interest, was countered by Herman Finer, who is hardly remembered at all.[54] Even Joseph A. Schumpeter, no friend of socialism, was pessimistic about the natural consequences of capitalism.[55] At the same time, U.S. intellectuals were strong believers in the New Deal and hoped for a social democratic future. But they were democrats, American patriots, and wanted to reject the Communist left. They needed an intellectually convincing basis from which to reject Marxism. Weber's *The Protestant Ethic and the Spirit of Capitalism* met their need without requiring them to join the political right.

The compelling power of Weber's ideas drew attention to Weber's incredibly wide intellectual range, one expression of which were his reflections on bureaucracy.[56] Weber's work had begun to be cited by scholars who read German. Laski's 1930 article, for example, refers to the same portion of Weber's work that was later translated as the famous article on bureaucracy.

Weber's conception of bureaucracy is expressed as part of his broader inquiry into authority relations. It makes little sense to read Weber on bureaucracy separately from his lecture on politics as a vocation. Weber distinguishes between power *(Macht)* and imperative control *(Herrschat)*, or "the probability that a command with a specific content will be obeyed by a given group of persons." Part of this idea, often remarked on, is the common-sense affirmation that some division of labor and delegation, a vertical division of labor, are inevitable. "Normally [though not always] the imperative coordination of the action of a considerable number of persons requires control of a staff of persons." Moreover, "It is necessary . . . that there should be a high probability that the action of a definite, supposedly reliable group of persons will be oriented primarily to the execution of the supreme authority's general policy and specific commands." While there is some debate among translators as to Weber's exact meaning, he defines bureaucracy in terms of how the administrative staff functions under a system of "rational-legal authority." If commentators sometimes miss the point, Weber's work is predicated on the awareness of other authority structures and other forms of administration.

In Weber's formulation, some authority structures are based essentially on inherited tradition, where obedience and deference are grounded in some form of calculation and where rules of legality in some strict sense govern decision making. This is also what is sometimes called patrimonial authority. Then there are authority structures based essentially on charisma, of the ability of a ruler to get followers to invest themselves, their beliefs, hopes, and aspirations in their sense of the ruler's legitimacy. Finally, there are structures of law and calculation (rational-legal authority structures). Bureaucracy is a rational form of action, within this context. But it is important not to fall backward from Weber's model to the proposition that, as bureaucracy is rational, whatever is called bureaucracy must also act according to rational criteria. Since there is a tendency to use analytical categories as if they were praise words—so that *rational* means inherently desirable, and its opposite means deranged, or crazy—one must be careful about usage.

Rationalization can have many meanings. Stanislav Andreski sometimes interprets Weber as using the term much as business consultants do, meaning streamlining to remove all impediments to a specific goal, such as increasing the rate of return on investment within a certain time.[57] Rationalization can also mean engaging in reflective thought, particularly thought based on scientific reasoning rather than social tradition.

Moreover, some political scientists found Weber liberating. On the whole, however, political scientists writing about public administration have largely dealt with snippets in translation that present Weber's formal definition of the characteristics of bureaucracy. If one seeks to locate Weber's work amid the "accumulated wealth of concepts, questions, and generalizations" that we seek, the net effect of its reception has been anywhere from bad (because distracting) to merely modest. While Weber is given almost the status of a social science idol, after closer examination one may agree with the cool judgment expressed by Dahl and Lindblom.[58] They paid tribute to the scope of Weber's working model, but described it as a melange lacking specific explanations of when relationships changed or why. As great as Weber's scholarship may be, and as fruitful as many have found it, Weber's essay on bureaucracy was, as they saw it, a remarkable mixture of brilliant observations and shrewd insights mixed with unexplained non sequiturs, inconsistencies, and overt errors.[59]

Weber's opening discussion of the characteristics of bureaucracy is coherent, if abstract, and somewhat definitional; it identifies real-world patterns that exist today. Bureaucracy rests, first, on the principle that officials have fixed and official jurisdictional roles. They do not operate, chiefly or mainly, on the sanction of some superior who may vaguely assign ill-defined responsibilities. Other essential characteristics of bureaucracy are: office hierarchy and graded levels of authority; management based upon a system of files containing official transactions, rules, and policies; expert training for capable performance of the functions of the office; full-time service, rather than amateurism; and decision making based on educated knowledge rather than tradition or other such factors.

The staff of persons (bureaucracy), writes Weber, is composed of those who have special training and skills, operate within a formal hierarchy, are paid salaries, and follow administrative careers. They have no other claim on their positions and no authority except what pertains to their specific jobs. It is virtually axiomatic that officials in this kind of bureaucracy are not appointed by partisan or other patronage, but follow a vocation. They do not fight for their offices, like elected politicians, but are appointed for an indefinite tenure, derive a certain social esteem from their position, are paid a fixed salary (in contrast to the fees paid to some officials, including some local U.S. government officials), and are attached to the offices as a career.

Weber is also clear in his discussion of the permanent character of the bureaucratic machine and of the power of bureaucracy. Yet the remainder of the essay, while it is an interesting discussion, leaves many questions unanswered, makes many unfounded assertions, and contains some propositions that seem wrong on their face, even inconsistent with Weber's own basic terms. Without undertaking a full critique of the essay here, I will provide two or three illustrations to show why this model poses many challenges in relation to other writing on the subject.

Weber treats the money economy as necessary to provide the tax revenues with which to support a full-time bureaucracy that exists on salary. While this may sound unexceptionable, when Weber wrote, it had not been long since bureaucrats purchased their offices and profited (legally or extralegally) from their offices; the money economy had been in existence for a very short time indeed, and in very few places. As late as the mid-nineteenth century—Weber's time of birth—in most countries, including France and Great Britain, many officials still received fees and there was a good deal of corruption. Decisions that should, by some criterion, have been made on some objective basis were, in fact, designed to enrich the official.

Weber's observations about the qualitative changes in administrative tasks are of particular interest because they can easily be turned into a set of testable hypotheses. Yet I have never seen a relevant research study. Weber writes, for example, "Bureaucratization is occasioned more by intensive and qualitative enlargements and internal deployment of the scope of administrative tasks than by their external and quantitative increase." What this is based on (and what it means) is not obvious. Will a definition of what is essential be more likely to result from some internal need than from external challenges? Why should that be so? Why would not there be more rigorous rules and more effective methods for defense contracting if there have been losses caused by defective weapons?

These questions indicate some areas of interest, rather than any dogmatic conclusions. This ideal type, or model, of bureaucracy is not precisely to be found anywhere, and historical circumstances differ from one situation to another. Weber's characterization of bureaucracy answers the questions: What kind of society is this? What is its dominant feature? At one level, Weber's concept of bureaucracy is quite similar to Wilson's sense of the science of administration.

Sometimes, the answer that Weber gives is decisively wrong. The United States was not, he said, yet fully bureaucratic. It would, in due course, be bureaucratized by the effect of "zones of friction with the outside" and "needs for administrative unity at home." Such an interesting hypothesis invites testing. On the basis of an unsystematic but somewhat informed understanding of American political parties, Weber led himself astray. The United States did not have a bureaucratic state structure, he wrote, but it had a "more strictly bureaucratic party structure." This might be a natural inference for a man who had been denied nomination in a party in his own country. Political bosses still operated in the United States and, if Weber had good informants, they might have given him much information. But American political parties in no way fit the bureaucratic format that Weber presented.

The most striking fact about Weber's acceptance by American political scientists, says Edward C. Page, is that it has produced so little new research, so little integration with or purposeful and tested rejection of previous expectations.[60] The formal definition of bureaucracy, a model necessarily abstract and not a literal picture of the real world, may be less important than the substantive content of that famous chapter. Four points merit closer examination.

1. If bureaucracy is powerful, what makes it so? Weber's answer seems to be its efficiency. Is it efficient in effectively acquiring social goods for its members, or in producing desirable benefits for the society? The role of the police and the military provide a crucial test. Is the bureaucracy powerful because it produces benefits to the people and is thus rewarded by popular

support? Are there no institutions other than bureaucracy that function in this manner?

The question is particularly compelling because Weber denies that a bureaucracy is powerful because it is indispensable. "If 'indispensability' were decisive, then where slave labor prevailed and where freemen usually abhor work as a dishonor, the 'indispensable' slaves ought to have held the positions of power, for they were at least as indispensable as officials and proletarians today."[61]

2. The proposition that the bureaucracy has a monopoly on expertise deserves to be examined more closely by political scientists who repeat it, with or without deference to Weber. This may have been true when literacy was rare and when persons of high status scorned to cultivate book knowledge or refused to do the work of clerks. However, the image of the inexpert king versus the expert subordinates has always had its limits. The Roman emperor was expected to have the skills of a lawyer (and often did), and to sit in judgment (and often did). Philip II of Spain was notorious for his long work days, and he effectively ruled a worldwide domain without leaving the Escorial.

If the problem is the inevitable necessity to ration time and energy, that is one matter. That is not expertise. Moreover, when specialized knowledge (of finance, of agriculture, of weapons and tactics, of foreign languages) is diffused beyond the bureaucracy, the administrative staff differs from the rest of the world only in having more current information, it cannot truly have better criteria for judgment. Many citizens, for example, may not know all the details in a secretly negotiated government deal but are ready to evaluate the whys and wherefores of such a deal. If their judgments are adverse, that will quickly become part of the judgment process that affects the next deal.

3. There is a persistent contradiction, in what Weber wrote, as to whether the bureaucrat is a cog in a machine or an actor with power. If the bureaucrat is pure cog, then secrecy is part of the mechanism and the bureaucrat can no more influence it than a fish can influence the oxygen content of water. However, Weber repeatedly refers to bureaucrats as if they made active choices based on strategy. "Every bureaucracy seeks to increase the superiority of the professionally informed by keeping their knowledge and intentions secret." Weber continues, "The pure interest of the bureaucracy in power . . . is efficacious far beyond those areas where purely functional areas make for secrecy."[62]

4. Finally, Weber was fully aware of the importance of public opinion, as can be seen throughout the lecture "Politics as a Vocation." It is at this level that we can see that Weber never resolved the problem of how the bureaucracy

should stand in relation to the common political life. These issues are not so much unresolved as nearly untouched by students of political science. This is an indication of how a systematic study of organization theory has been neglected in political science.

PATHOLOGY

An empirical political theory of administration should take into account another connotation of bureaucratic, namely, characterized by *pathological* administrative behavior. The negative image attached to bureaucracy is very powerful.[63]

There is a ready audience for the idea that bureaucracy is essentially a pathological phenomenon. This is a crucial element in the conception of bureaucracy that Michel Crozier develops.[64] To call a predicament "Kafkaesque" or a "Catch-22" situation is to invoke literary terms to convey this attitude. There are two simple illustrations. One concerns searching for information by telephone. Seeking a simple datum about United States judges, I dialed the number listed in the telephone book for the Administrative Director of the U.S. Courts. An electronically recorded message informed me that the number had been changed and that I should consult the directory or call the operator. The directory having been consulted, I called the operator who repeated the incorrect number listed in the directory. When asked what other source of information might be available, the operator expressed some irritation and recommended the course of action that had been followed already.

Only after a certain definite, but diplomatic, persistence did I hear the operator say, "I'll give you my supervisor." The supervisor proved more understanding and provided a number for the director's office, which led ultimately to the desired information. The telephone problem shows, in miniature, how one can become engaged in administrative steps that yield the same futile answers each time. There is a high level of bureaucratic pathology in police organizations, where the terms of recruitment, the psychological needs of personnel, and the realistic sense of threat all combine to produce an atmosphere in which the officer's first need is to intimidate and to abuse anyone the officer cannot verify, by immediate criteria, as "all right," and particularly as "too important" to treat in the ordinary way. To describe bureaucracy as pathological implies that it is "an organization that cannot correct its behavior by learning from its errors."[65] This may be regarded as a means of coping with conflict, but an unintelligent handling of conflict. There are no perfect organizations in perfectly conflict-free situations. Rigidity comes not only from pressure from above, but also from below. To quote Crozier, a "study of the way power is allocated and an analysis of the bargaining strategies between individuals and groups within an organization are unusual starting points from which to try to reach an understanding of the function of an organization."[66]

This may be what Wilson contemplated when he discussed how a professional approach to administration might be adopted with "safety and profit." If we ask what happens when professional administration has been adopted without the necessary constraints, the answer may be bureaucratic pathology. The organization that cannot correct its own errors may also be one saturated by formalistic impersonality.

Crozier is right in saying that a study of how power *is* allocated, not how it *should be* allocated, is an unusual starting point from which to understand how an organization functions. Sociologists, in particular, pay attention to what goes wrong, or the dysfunctions of bureaucracy. A political assumption is that those in whom power is vested will serve themselves. But a large and ordered body of data has yet to be produced on a pathological bureaucracy, whether highly quantified or impressionistic. Frank Goodnow was aware that party officials, whom he linked to administration, might act in their own self-interest. Why should not self-interest be found in others in administrative roles? If political scientists followed the logic of Follett, Gaus, or Gulick, Crozier's proposition would appear as a natural derivation. We can put it in very simple terms. Public employees have to eat and do not wish to be fired. Public employees have values and will defend those values. It makes little difference if they are social workers or police officers. Public employees have egos and will assert them, even to the extent of indulging in petty authority. Finally, public employees want to get off easy and will be lazy. There is much escape from reality, though feedback is corrective.

Weber and Crozier cross paths here. Weber is right to point out the potential for formalistic impersonality. Crozier notes that the organization may become incapable of self-correction. This is most extreme when it takes the character of formalistic impersonality. "Dehumanization" of an individual via bureaucracy is not simply bad treatment; it is bad treatment that applicants cannot get anyone to remedy or to consider how it relates to them as human beings. In contemporary society, it is the "computer letter" that leads to unpleasant consequences, such as a poorer credit rating, a repossession, and so on—all of which are consequences of the capability for programming administration. Bureaucracy exists there in its purest sense.

BUREAUCRATIC DESPOTISM

A third subcurrent is the notion that bureaucratic power is the power of a body of officials to rule against the will of the rest of society. If bureaucrats really could get what they wanted and do what they wanted, this would amount to bureaucratic despotism. Hannah Arendt merges this with the concept of expertise. Whereas she defines bureaucracy as government by experts, she regards it—in tones reminiscent of Rousseau—as a virtual moral disaster. She relies, for illustration, on an English writer with the pseudonym A. Carthill who described the administration of India during the years of British control as government by reports. Despite this neutral phrase, Indian governance was as nearly bureaucratic as anything could be. "Bureaucracy was the result of a responsibility that no man can bear for his fellows and no people for another people," writes Arendt. It is "always a government of experts, of an 'experienced minority,' which has to resist as well as it knows how the constant pressure from an 'inexperienced majority.' "[67]

Whatever the reasons, agencies go to ridiculous lengths to deny claims they find uncomfortable. Bureaucracy is often conceived of as governance by precise and rigid rules. But this is only one pole of administrative government. Speaking statistically, administrative government might be said to have a bimodal distribution. Government is pure administration not when decisions makers have no choice due to rigid rules or routines, but when decisions are entirely at the discretion of the decision maker.[68] Arendt's point is tested by much ordinary experience.

Administrative professionals—bureaucrats—are likely to regard themselves as virtuous in their purposes and knowledgeable about the problems at hand. Those who disagree may be regarded as ignorant, perverse, even corrupt. As Gulick notes, experts themselves will often be both dogmatic in believing that their "particular technology [is] the road to salvation" and inclined to "step without embarrassment into other areas." Here there is no concept of administration at the service of politics. It is not surprising that sociological studies of bureaucracy are so often studies in pathology. The question is: is any attempt made to overcome the pathology?

The New Management Science

The third area in which political scientists surrendered the intellectual initiative is reflected in the idea of management. Political science and to some extent sociology have tended to take a Murphy's Law approach, if in more sophisticated terms. Merely analyzing patterns of action, however, without some concept of improvement is incompatible with good management.

Plato was aware of the problems of moving from a concept or policy through all the aspects of execution. That recognition is central to the work of Wilson and Goodnow, and to many who commented on public administration in the years before World War II. Nor has it disappeared from much other work, including some of the recent interest in development administration. Nonetheless, research often stays at such a general level, with such a defined focus, that the question of how to give direction, overcome problems, and achieve results is not often found in the political science literature on administration.

These imperatives are recognized in the writing of others who feel a different need, like policy analysts or students of management science, who systematically study the requirements of managers. Modern approaches to public administration also will borrow from management science, if only because of the compelling advantage enjoyed by quantitative management science in the world of practice beyond the social sciences.

On the other hand, management science has yet to overcome its roots in the Taylor tradition, and still tries to treat administrators as if they were interchangeable units. The most advanced concepts, methodologically, are importantly connected to present-day activity in operations research, which also is the link to modern systems analysis. Operations research began for military purposes during World War I, and during World War II, it became more practical.[69] Operations research was used, for instance, to help anti-aircraft guns aim more accurately and quickly at invading bombers. It was extended after the war into defense systems analysis[70] and quantitative management science, to serve decision making for private firms.[71]

The Critical Path Method (CPM), Program Evaluation Review and Technique (PERT), and Planning-Programming-Budgeting Systems (PPBS) are by-products of this approach to decision making.[72] CPM and PERT are related. Both are highly structured, logical systems that rely on network analysis. The network is made up of events (specified program accomplishments to be achieved in a specific time) and activities (time and resources necessary to move from one event to the next). The critical path, in either case, is the event that will take the longest time and greatest resources to achieve. Obviously, each methodology is oriented toward fulfilling a goal.

In the 1990s, the expert systems concept is emerging as a potential management method. Administration as the actual use of information would, to some degree, be turned over to expert systems. This is occurring through computerized, highly structured data bases containing rules of thumb on a given subject.[73] In that respect, such systems embody Taylor's concept of capturing experience and placing it in the heads of management. Such systems have been applied commercially in drilling oil and gas wells; monitoring the performance of electric utility turbines; authorizing American Express credit accounts; reviewing tax accruals and tax planning; interpreting data from chemists' instruments and giving advice on the structure of unknown compounds; manipulating complex symbols in calculus and higher math; and prescribing treatments for meningitis and infections of the blood.[74] Expert systems, now being tried in industry and taught in engineering schools, are also being discussed, at least conceptually, for government decision making in regulating nuclear power and defense management.[75]

New management science also turns toward human—thus political—applications. These are issues that political science has neglected by carrying its analytical structure to industry where, in principle, it is highly relevant. The study of management offers answers that come directly or indirectly from political science—including the motivational concept of ownership. Employees, it is said, perform better if they feel that they "own" an idea. This concept is substantially like the consent of the governed idea translated to governing the workplace. The principle was long ago expressed by John Gaus, when he remarked that "the best effort of the individual is not put forth unless he feels that he has some share in the creating of that purpose or some participation in determining how that purpose shall be made effective by the organization of which he is a member."[76]

The experience of industry creates a demand (in the economic sense) for people who can think "politically." In contemporary industrial management, for instance, project management is a big item.[77] Whatever the graduate schools of business (in whose curricula project management courses appear) may now think, the experience of industry leads to demand (in the economic sense) for people who can think politically.

Project management entails winning the cooperation of persons with varied interests and needs, and thus involves a departure from the more simplified concepts of management that start from models of rationality in which there is one overriding value. Contemporary operations research–management science is now beginning to incorporate the concept of *stakeholders*. This concept was originally used in the management literature as an alternative to *stockholder*. Stakeholders were "defined as 'those groups without whose support the organization would cease to exist.'"[78] R. Edward Freeman, an advocate of stakeholder analysis, depicts this graphically: the firm is at the center, surrounded by interests labeled *political groups, financial community, owners, activist groups, customers, customer advocate groups, suppliers, competitors, employees, trade associations, unions,* and *government.*[79] This figure is a wonderful example of independent invention, being virtually identical to a graph designed by Wallace S. Sayre showing the relationship of bureau leaders to presidents, Congress, other agencies, courts, and the mass communications media, the specialized trade media, and both friendly and unfriendly interest groups.[80] The stakeholder model is apparently derived from some other source, but its intellectual connections to Sayre's work are completely unrecognized.

Summary and Conclusion

The theme of this chapter is to suggest how to go forward in the study of public administration. It is critical to recover lost knowledge and to negate an earlier intellectual surrender. Regarding the politics of administration, for instance, Gaus spoke in 1947 of the importance of administrative discretion. He wrote that administrators "must, of necessity, determine some part of the purpose [in public action] and a large part of the means whereby it will be achieved in the modern state."[81] By the time of Norton Long (1960), more people recognzed the importance of power. Long's theme is that the lifeblood of administration is power, and its "attainment, maintenance, increase, dissipation, and loss are subjects the student and practitioner can ill afford to neglect."[82] Despite the many reprintings of Long's paper in various anthologies, the conceptual structure behind the study of public administration falls far short of giving systematic attention to the attainment of power, the maintenance of power, the increase of power, the dissipation of power, and the loss of power in administrative situations.

The value of recovering the intellectual work of the past if clear when we realize that from Follett, Gaus, and Gulick, a line of continuity runs to contemporary researchers. What accounts for the "decision to produce"? This question, explicitly raised by Gulick, becomes central to March and Simon's formulation in 1958.

As we have noted, for example, the much criticized POSDCORB could validly be regarded as an analytic construct to organize inquiry into how the chief executive functions at the nation-state level. That is a correct restatement of what Simon says. The concern with the "foundation for action and self-coordination" is a linkage to Follett, to Gaus, and anticipates Chester Barnard. It also anticipates by twenty-five years Richard Neustadt's famous *Presidential Power: The Politics of Leadership* (1960), which argues that the power of the president is the "power to persuade."[83] The study of American politics still needs a good examination—to paraphrase Wilson—of what presidents do and how they do it.

James Clay Thompson and Richard F. Vidmer, in comparing administrative science and politics in the USSR and the United States, offer a common response to POSDCORB. "As Herbert Simon noted thirty years ago, the principles that Gulick developed are not principles but proverbs."[84] Simon's contribution to organization theory, of course, was decisive. No one doubts that. However, I do not agree with the received doctrine that Simon demolished principles in discovering that they were "proverbs." What that remarkable scholar might have accomplished in organization theory, had he sustained his interest, is impossible to guess. No superior criteria of action are contained in the Simon foundation. Nor is there better empirical theory of politics. From the point of view of politics, however, it may have been a diversion. Simon ultimately turned away from decision making as politics to decision making as reflecting the internal competence of the administrative person.

Weber's concept of bureaucracy may show the most unalloyed borrowing, having little firm connection to the main corpus of political science, despite his use of the word *bureaucracy*. His very concept reflects various kinds of dissatisfaction with the ordering of society. In one sense, *bureaucracy* came to be used in political science as a defense for administrative latitude at a time when political scientists saw such latitude as a means of sustaining values they believed should be sustained. Such, indeed, is the concept of representative bureaucracy, carried to its fullest perhaps by Long, though challenged on the empirical ground that later studies did not validate this idea. The alternative concept reflects the doctrine that legitimate power depends upon election, and that the exercise of discretionary authority by others is not legitimate.

Bureaucratic theories, insofar as *bureaucracy* is not merely another word for large-scale administration, seem to deal with three distinguishable phenomena. Three questions recur. Is bureaucracy rational, and of what sort of rationality? Does bureaucracy tend toward elephantine complexity and lethargy or rigidity, so that its members are incapable of intelligent action? Does bureaucracy tend toward despotism, so that it is inevitably in conflict with law and/or democracy?

Finally, the newer management science is a return, conceptually, to something akin to Willoughby's earlier work. Its modern version takes the form of expert systems. In the 1990s we are seeing a new Taylorism, based upon the more sophisticated handling of information, including expert interpretation, and the alternative attempts to incorporate the human and the political into mathematical management science.

When Lindblom asked, in effect, "Why do not political scientists work out the consequences of their own models?" his question was most penetrating for public administration. The question demonstrates, when applied to the field of public administration, the degree to which political science surrendered that domain to other forms of inquiry. Redressing the imbalance means staying with each main theme, working out the implications of the theme to determine what hypotheses it dictates we accept, comparing hypotheses to each other, and comparing their consistency with empirical studies over a long time. If we are able to integrate the several themes, then we approach more clearly an empirical political theory of administration.

Philip Converse writes, "When findings that appear robust in one world fail to replicate in some other world, it should be the beginning of a new round of inquiry, not a point of abandonment."[85] Converse's interpretation is particularly relevant to the intellectual future of political science and the study of public administration.

There is, however, a recurrent difficulty. A powerful tension exists between an empirical political theory of administration, in which one is willing to subject one's thought to some form of discipline of disproof, and the necessity of administrative theory as a form of dogma. We turn to this problem next in discussing the concept of executive leadership—the principles enunuciated by the Brownlow Report, the incorporation of these principles into the doctrines of separation of powers and presidential primacy; and the conflict between those ideas and the operational reality whereby enormous numbers of decisions are made at lower levels, so that the notion of presidential responsibility is often mythic.

People in government may not be willing to hear, accept, or treat seriously scholarly interpretations of administration. If scholars wish to have any influence, they must find the audiences that will listen to them or need them. Alternatively, they must be able to assimilate their own modes of analysis to preexisting patterns of interest.

We can, of course, avoid discussing such matters. But no one can avoid discussing them who takes seriously a concern with intellectual health. Political science, both in its study of administration and elsewhere, is often characterized by internal contradictions, paradoxes, and anomalies. These should be neither denied nor obscured. Internal contradictions (or paradoxes) alert us to projects that should be studied.[86] If scholars can do this for public administration, it will mean recovering many fruitful ideas from premature abandonment and turning away from a debilitating surrender of intellectual initiative in a most vital area of politics, and thus of political science as well.

II
Dogma and Controversy

3

THE DOGMA AND THEORY
OF EXECUTIVE LEADERSHIP

BROWNLOW, THE JUDGES, AND
OPERATING ADMINISTRATION

Dogma as Control over Uncertainty

In the two preceding chapters, we focus on conflict and disruption—hence, turbulence—in the intellectual history of public administration. In chapters 3, 4, and 5, we turn to conflict and disruption in thinking about the practicalities of administrative government. Thus, we deal with the problem of dogma as applied to theories of executive leadership and as applied to an understanding of the administrative law process.

The central importance of administration to politics also leads us to recognize that relationships concerning administration should never be neglected in the study of presidential government. I do not here examine the deepest issues of the presidential system, though that is a most urgent enterprise. I limit my attention to the conflict between empirical theory and dogma as it is manifested in debates about American government. The function of empirical theory is to explain what can be observed and to estimate or predict systematically what is to come. A truly sound theory must also be susceptible to empirical tests.

Dogma stands as an alternative to empirical theory. I do not use the term *dogma* here in the common sense, meaning merely some unreflective prejudice. The dictionary definition is "something held as an established opinion; *esp*: one or more definite and authoritative tenets." Dogmatic, or doctrinal, theology "seeks to present the intellectual content of a religious faith and to explicate its meaning from the base of authoritative opinions generally regarded as derived from revelation." Dogma means a belief that one is prepared to take responsibility for deciding not to examine. Dogma can conflict with the function of empirical theory, estimates, or systematic predictions of the future. Executive leadership is a concept that many are prepared not to examine, even at the price of inviting profound and serious dilemmas in governance.

One must choose among competing theories of administration before undertaking any action or research, as no one can accept all theories simultaneously. What usually happens is that an administrative theory is adapted to facilitate some administrative practice that is made necessary by some political dogma. One could study executive leadership either in light of an empirical theory or as a means of deriving an empirical theory.

There is an inevitable tension between dogma, or the powerful continuity of belief, and empirical theory open to new tests and possible rejection. The tension between dogma and theory is a recurrent source of turbulence or disruption in any field, and it is prominent in the study of public administration. There is also turbulence—a result of the tussle between the forces of continuity and those of disruption—in the practical world of administering the law.

Some of the relevant issues are seen in the ideas about executive leadership expressed in the Brownlow Report of 1937. They have been transformed into virtual dogma in U.S. political language, and they have been absorbed into recent judicial-political theory expressed in separation-of-powers litigation and in the complex issues thus evoked regarding how the administrative system should be controlled.

Nowhere is this more dramatic than in the struggle between various institutional or power centers for control over administrative operations. In the United States, the assertion of executive leadership at the chief executive level—the presidency—has long been a source of such turbulence. Leonard D. White traces this as struggle between the president and Congress in his four-part administrative history from the Federalist era down to the Wilson administration.[1]

The Idea of Executive Leadership

A virtual dogma of belief regarding executive leadership now dominates American political thought. It is the main theme of current scholarship in political science and history. It is asserted by political journalists and is especially powerful in the political theory taught by recent judicial decisions. The dogma of executive leadership, characterized by Goodnow as "the one-man idea," is particularly powerful in the private sector. But it also is asserted in the public sector. It is a creation of the last part of the last century. The concept of the president as the natural and dominant center of government was evidently *not* what the Constitutional Convention of 1787 thought it had created. Otherwise, there would have been much less concern that the president would be overawed by Congress. The Whig opponents of Jackson, and others such as Daniel Webster, still had the opportunity to put forth claims that would have made the president much more a ministerial officer.[2] Andrew Jackson made large claims for himself, but they did not establish themselves as common doctrine. Abraham Lincoln acted on very broad terms in the context of the Civil War. Yet the almost monarchic quality that came to characterize the presidency did not take firm root until long after that time.

When he was writing *Congressional Government* (1887), Wilson expressed a far less definitive view of the president's power than that expressed in current scholarship and commentary. Indeed, he said that the business of the president, occasionally great, was usually not much above routine; and that most of it, most of the time, was mere administration. It was mere obedience of directions issued by the masters of policy, the Standing Committees. Wilson evidently did not think it absurd to imagine a president in a far more restrained role from that to which he as president actually attained. "Except in so far as his power of veto constitutes him a part of the legislature," Wilson wrote, "the president might, not inconveniently, be a permanent officer; the first officer of a carefully-graded and impartially regulated civil service system, through whose sure series of merit-promotions the youngest clerk might rise even to the chief magistracy."[3] In fact, a footnote reads, "Something like this has actually been proposed by Mr. Albert Stickney, in his interesting and incisive essay, *A True Republic*." Such a proposal by a doctoral candidate in 1995 or 1996 would be so idiosyncratic and would deviate so violently from today's professional norms as virtually to guarantee career oblivion.

The facts of life have carried us far from Wilson's empirical assessment of 1887. He himself must have changed his mind. By the time Woodrow Wilson delivered the lectures that were published as *Constitutional Government*, he had come to have a strong appreciation of executive leadership. Wilson was not alone in advancing the image of the president as a strong leader, however. The real intellectual herald of this position—according to Edward S. Corwin, "its John the Baptist"—was Henry Jones Ford, a newspaperman hired by Woodrow Wilson (then president of Princeton) as professor of politics. As we know, Theodore Roosevelt became the archetype of the strong president.

Corwin writes, "Theodore Roosevelt was the first Presidential exponent of the modern Presidency," the first overtly to claim the role. Corwin adds wryly: "Wilson openly admired Ford, [but] 'his indebtedness to Roosevelt he was less prompt to acknowledge.'" He mentioned Roosevelt once in the index to *Constitutional Government*, in a reference of no significance.[4]

The Brownlow Criteria as Support for a Dogma

The idea that presidential election was a sort of expression of the general will became common academic doctrine during the New Deal years. Nowhere is this doctrine more strongly articulated than in public administration. There was a time when a different intellectual result might have been obtained. However, intellectual conversion to the dogma of executive leadership may be focused upon the Brownlow Report.

Franklin Delano Roosevelt's style was ever to concentrate power in himself. He appointed Louis Brownlow, Luther Gulick, and Charles Merriam to help devise an administrative structure suited to his purposes. All three were well connected to the academic world and experienced in the public arena. Louis Brownlow was a Tennessean who had made a career as a newspaper writer, then as a member of the District of Columbia Commission (as memorialized on Washington's Q Street bridge leading to Georgetown), and in other capacities.[5] Luther H. Gulick was head of the Institute of Public Administration in New York, from which he made many forays in the service of improving public administration as he saw the need.[6] Charles E. Merriam, who built the University of Chicago's Political Science Department and founded "behavioral" political science, was an entrepreneur on the Social Science Research Council and a sometime candidate for mayor of Chicago.[7]

This trio was ready to help the president get what he wanted. Their young staff consisted of persons who would later constitute a "who's who" of important figures in academic public administration, including James W. Fesler and Wallace S. Sayre. The Brownlow Committee, officially the President's Committee on Administrative Management, yielded a creative product. In two pages, the committee set forth the scripture for a secular religion of executive leadership.

> Our Presidency unites at least three important functions. . . . In many types of government these duties are divided or only in part combined, but in the United States they have always been united in one and the same person whose duty it is to perform all of these tasks.[8]

The above statements open and close a paragraph. The intermediate sentences set forth three distinct propositions about the president's leadership.

The first Brownlow proposition is: the president is the ceremonial head of the nation, the symbol of national solidarity. We need not examine this concept further here, although it is so often cited that it deserves deeper thought and some empirical study. Few recognize the consequences of the fact that all presidents face the opposition of at least a third of the population *ab initio*. On its face, the doctrine appears akin to the dictum, attributed to Theodore Roosevelt, that the White House is a "bully pulpit." Political scientists who speak of the president's symbolic leadership might notice how few sermons are preached until the public audience appears already converted.[9]

The second Brownlow proposition on presidential leadership is: from one point of view the president is a political leader—leader of a party, of the Congress, of a people. If the president is now understood to be leader of the Congress, not all perceptive observers have agreed. Almost a century ago, Paul S. Reinsch collected a reader for his students that includes the following introductory passage to one section:

> The relations of the Executive to Congress has been subject to special discussion of late. The strict separation of the three departments in matters of government being impossible, there has in general been a feeling that it is entirely proper for executive officials and the President to interest themselves in legislative measures affecting their particular work. This opinion has, however, not passed without opposition as other men have held that while it is allowable for the executive to suggest legislation, a direct interference in the process of legislative work would lie beyond the proper sphere of executive duty.[10]

This proposition adopts an idea about party leadership that entered avant-garde political science in the early twentieth century. Jesse Macy, a pioneer in the study of parties, saw the distinction between U.S. and British politics as *executive* versus *collegial* leadership. In national affairs, he said, Americans "have acquired habits of dependence upon a chief person, to whom they looked for fulfillment of party pledges."[11] Other than this general reference, the Brownlow Report seems to give slight attention to executive-legislative relations. The report says, as part of a brief discussion, "Preservation of the full accountability of the Executive to the Congress is an essential part of our republican system."[12] This has the same quality as Ronald Reagan's citations of Franklin Delano Roosevelt and John Fitzgerald Kennedy. It does not take much imagination to see people struggling over a rhetorical formula that would make it difficult for members of Congress to object to the report. Nor is it hard to see that the report implies, in principle, significant reductions in characteristic forms of congressional leverage.

The Congress of the United States is the most powerful legislative body in any major democratic country. It is not mainly designed to sanction or sanctify the executive. Congress is not powerful just because it is elected, or even because it controls appropriations. Rather, its power resides in its deep engagement in the actualities of the administrative process. Thus, the report says that "there is too little appreciation among the people of the country of the day-to-day work of the Congress" and genuflects before the investigative process. But, says the committee, the problem with accountability is that Congress is also ill-structured to achieve it. There should not be "mandatory and detailed requirements" (about government organization and machinery), either in "general law or in a rider on an appropriations bill." Moreover, once appropriations have been made, Congress should have nothing to do with them until an independent audit has been presented. If something is wrong, the Congress could either take corrective action or discipline an executive officer found guilty of illegality or impropriety. Still further, the report said (no doubt accurately), Congress was not adequately organized to receive and use good information. The organization of Congress also complicated the extent of committee jurisdiction and power, as the Brownlow Committee knew very well.

The concept of the president as leader of Congress, put forth by the Brownlow Committee, is well established in the scholarly literature. It was long associated with a deep-rooted distaste for the congressional process.[13] In *Congress on Trial* (1949), James MacGregor Burns emphasized the power of minorities to resist decisions made by Congress, the power of highly cohesive or financially powerful private interests to dominate legislation, and the risk that Congress as then organized would be inadequate to meet anticipated crises.[14] In his review, E. E. Schattschneider interprets Burns as "profoundly disturbed by conditions on Capitol Hill . . . that seem *too dangerous to ignore*." For Burns, Congress is "an assembly of agents of special interests" and "something of a *menace to the survival of the country*."[15] A deadlock arises from the fact that "individual Congressmen, forced to fight for their lives in restricted constituencies, are vulnerable to the pressures of organized minorities, while the president rallies popular majorities composed largely of people who belong to no pressure groups at all." One may wonder whether Schattschneider's review reflects his own ideas more than Burns's. Clearly, both intelligent observers were deeply concerned by what they saw.

What Burns wanted, essentially, was a mechanism for effective party government, to allow and enforce joint action by president and Congress. James M. Burns has tirelessly advocated his views in proceedings of the Committee on the Constitutional System[16] and other groups and has maintained a remarkable consistency in his underlying views. He is still as concerned with the nation's potential incapacity to respond to a crisis as he was in 1949. Whereas the threat of crisis is very real, I disagree with Burns's analysis of the U.S. institutional structure.

The executive leadership concept at first meant presidential leadership in the legislative process. The question evidently concerns the extent to which members of Congress should accept the president's recommendations. It is not clear whether the later nineteenth-century presidents had less actual control over what Congress did than their twentieth-century successors. However, even the fact of argument against "direct interference" suggests that the norm of powerful presidential leadership had not yet become a part of the political culture. Judging from what now appears in the curricula of public administration programs, the argument that the president has no right to interfere in Congress sounds bizarre.

This concept of the primacy of presidential leadership was a moral defeat for the legitimacy of the Congress. The presumption seemed to be that, in any disputed situation, the president represented the American people better than Congress. It meant that groups, especially numerical minorities, should not prevent the adoption of proposals put forth in the name of the president. Exactly when Congress began to be seen as morally less legitimate than the president is a fascinating question. Before the Civil War, Congress and the president were never presumed to be differentiated in this way. Nor were they after the Civil War, except for the early years of Reconstruction, when this distinction was made.

In this century, the case is different. Intellectuals writing American history and politics have increasingly assumed that extolling the president is consistent with the norms of democracy, with the preferences of the public. Thus it was with Theodore Roosevelt's trust busting and Woodrow Wilson's New Freedom. (Curiously, Wilson also gets the benefit of having advocated— and the Senate the burden of having rejected—the League of Nations, although the 1920 election demonstrated the public unacceptability of Wilson's posture.)

The specific features of the two Roosevelt administrations and of the Wilson administration also suggest that the presidency would be progressive or liberal, and that the Congress would be conservative—with the further presumption that the real public was progressive or liberal. This seems very doubtful. At any given moment, a serious difference of approach could exist between the president (or the coalition organized around the president) and the Congress (or the coalition dominant in the Congress). However, it is not correct—over any extended time—to regard the Congress as either notably more conservative or more liberal than the president.

The reputation of the Congress also suffered in the years of Franklin Delano Roosevelt and Truman, and only began to experience some change during the time of Richard M. Nixon, as his popularity fell. Once the Supreme Court ceased to be a dramatic impediment to Roosevelt's policies, the people who opposed Roosevelt were forced to turn relatively more of their effort to the Congress. They were already making a serious congressional effort, as will be discussed in the next chapter. The 1938 elections forged the "conservative coalition" of Republicans and Southern Democrats that became a fixture of congressional politics until the civil rights movement became the occasion for a break within the Democratic party. In particular, the reputation of Congress was tarnished when southern Democrats used it as a forum to defend the regime of racial apartheid that existed across the South.

It is hard to say what the dominant conception of the presidential leadership role is now. The president does play a significant, at times dominating, role in setting the congressional agenda. The president's ability to get the legislative results desired, however, is another matter. Moreover, the process is necessarily influenced by idiosyncratic swings from one president to another, and with the swings in the disposition of recent presidents to adopt the role of either partnership with Congress or independence from Congress.[17]

Contemporary scholarship, in step with contemporary practical assumptions, discusses the president as if he were entitled to the special treatment of a king.[18] An important factor underlying this attitude is psychological and deep-rooted. Political scientists, above all others, have seen the touchstone of the president's power in his role as representative of all the people. There is a deep popular desire for strong leadership. Richard Neustadt's *Presidential Power* (1960) starts with the assumption that the president is the natural leader, though deprived of resources, and his task is to aggregate those resources and translate them into effective personal power.[19] Barbara Kellerman's thoughtful study of recent presidents, *The Political Presidency* (1984), is predicated on this idea and examines how they have done it.[20] Bert Rockman is unusual in that he largely departs from this theme in *The Leadership Question* (1984), with a deeper scrutiny of the constraints on presidential leadership and the inevitable uncertainty of such leadership.[21] Such an inquiry is dictated by a concern with the administrative system, since the executive leadership concept has been extended to administration.

The third Brownlow proposition says: from still another point of view, the president is the chief executive and administrator within the federal system and federal service. The Brownlow criteria have had a profound influence on administrative thought; much contemporary administrative theory, derived from Brownlow, takes as its prime reference point the unique, indivisible, just authority of the president. Executive leadership has been translated into the president's leadership and direction of the administrative process in government.

Yet the Brownlow criteria predicted results that did not occur. Observe the committee's description of the kinds of staff assistants it proposed for the president's office. For the sake of clarity, I separate the description into a series of subpropositions, with no other change of language.

1. [The president's] aides would have no power to make decisions or issue instructions in their own right.
2. They would not be interposed between the president and the heads of his departments.
3. They would not be assistant presidents in any sense.
4. Their function would be, when any matter was presented to the president for action affecting any part of the administrative work of the Government, to assist him in obtaining quickly and without delay all pertinent information possessed by any of the executive departments so as to guide him in making his responsible decisions; and then when decisions have been made to assist him in seeing to it that every administrative department and agency affected is promptly informed.
5. Their effectiveness in assisting the president will, we think, be directly proportional to their ability to discharge their functions with restraint.
6. They would remain in the background, issue no orders, make no decisions, emit no public statements.[22]

These statements, made in 1937, might be regarded as the committee's predictions for the future. The basis for these judgments can only be speculated on. Neither the report nor the staff studies published with it explains the reasons for these propositions. Perhaps the committee took its cues from the broad discussions of line-staff relationships then in circulation. However, anyone who knew court politics might have predicted that aides without formal power to make decisions or to issue instructions in their own right would soon tend to act *as if* they had such power.

The Brownlow Committee could assert such propositions, but in so doing they defied insights about the behavior of administrative staff dating back at least to Benedict and Machiavelli. Indeed, if one asserted the opposite of these propositions, they would have turned out to be closer to actual experience. The staff—or, as I would prefer—*entourage*, of the president has achieved high visibility and substantial operational engagement. As a result, they are necessarily obliged to act in their own best interest unless they are either self-destructive or extraordinarily self-sacrificing toward the incumbent. They hardly play a "background" role, although their lack of anonymity may be exaggerated by the electronic rapidity of our lives. The notion that such assistants would not have operational responsibilities flies in the face of fact. Furthermore, one can argue that a categorical exclusion from accountability is unsound. The responsibility that Hamilton Jordan claimed to have had in the 1978 Panama Canal Treaty negotiations was crucial. So was his interest in the hostages in Iran during 1979–1980. Bradley Patterson, who worked in the Ford White House, once pointed out to a group of assistant secretaries how much White House staff assistants feel obliged to go deeply into details. So important is the president's legislative program that it may be impossible to disengage operational decision making from the commitments required to sustain a legislative majority.

The Dogma of "Separation of Powers":
Adoption of Executive Leadership by the Reagan Judges

The 1980s brought a new phenomenon to the United States—a new wave of court judges that constituted a new wave of political and organizational theorists by virtue of their decision-making authority. The judicio-political theory has two elements. It combines a political theory of rigid separation of powers and the executive leadership concept. Something very similar to the natural consequence of the Brownlow propositions now reappears in the form of judicial decisions.

The dogma that the courts now appear to adopt is that the power of the Congress should be reduced through the separation of powers doctrine. Many political science functionalists, such as Frank Goodnow, maintain that the separation of powers is a fundamentally misleading concept and that institutional functions cannot be hermetically isolated. That is why *politics* is conceived as one function and *administration* another.[23]

This new formulation of the dogma of executive leadership was manifested in two court cases based on the separation of powers issue.

BOWSHER V. SYNAR

The case of *Bowsher v. Synar* (1986) has come and gone, as has the case of *Synar v. United States* (1986), which was the same litigation in the lower court.[24] But the treatment of that case in the courts brings to the surface some extremely important issues that involve both administrative organization and dogmas about the separation of powers. The Gramm-Rudman-Hollings legislation of 1985 established certain dollar amounts as the maximum federal budget deficit in each of five succeeding years. Under that legislation, the Office of Management and Budget (OMB) would submit data to the General Accounting Office (GAO). The comptroller general, head of the GAO, would identify the amounts to be cut, on the basis of those calculations, to bring the deficit in any given year to the allowed maximum. The president would then be obliged to make those cuts in accordance with the comptroller general's finding.

Upon appeal, in *Bowsher v. Synar,* the Supreme Court agreed that assigning this authority to the comptroller general constituted an impermissible breach of the separation of powers. My comment here is not based on the Supreme Court's decision but on a decision from the lower court, the U.S. district court in the District of Columbia. The case, *Synar v. United States,* was tried before a three-judge panel in district court. Two were judges of the district and the third, sitting in district court for this purpose, was Justice Antonin Scalia, then on the U.S. Court of Appeals for the District of Columbia.

As in many important cases, the court could have based its decision on various grounds or theories. The grounds it expressly chose entailed a crucial adoption of the dogma of executive leadership. In order to reach its decision, the three-judge panel included a discussion of the president's power to remove executive officers, and the issue involved statistical tests of discrimination and whether jury selection had been unfairly biased against Mr. Moultrie.

The panel virtually invited the conclusion that *Humphrey's Executor v. U.S.*, which held the president unable to remove a Federal Trade Commissioner, was wrongly decided, or in any event that it no longer provides a basis for congressional restrictions on the president's power to remove officials.

> It is not as obvious today as it seemed in the 1930s that there could be genuinely independent regulatory agencies, bodies of impartial experts whose independence from the president does not entail correspondingly

greater dependence upon the committees of Congress to which they are accountable; nor, indeed, is it assumed that the decisions of such agencies so clearly involve scientific judgment rather than political choice that it is desirable to insulate them from the democratic process.[25]

The Humphrey case should be seen in a fuller perspective. Macroeconomic policy was not yet so strongly emphasized in the 1930s. People still thought of the economic regulatory agencies as the main instruments for asserting government control over the economy.

FDR tried, as a matter of policy, to get the commissions to agree that they should coordinate their actions with his policies. Very early in his first term, he convened chairmen of several agencies and asked them to report directly to him. One commissioner, Joseph B. Eastman, the highly respected and long-term head of the Interstate Commerce Commission, refused. Other heads bobbed in agreement, but Eastman cited the independence of the ICC. There was apparently some respect between Roosevelt and Eastman, but on various occasions Eastman was reluctant to accept the limitations the president had in mind. Eastman was, however, too much a respected New England establishmentarian to be attacked with impunity.

Very early in his administration, Roosevelt dropped William E. Humphrey—a former Republican congressman from Washington and former lobbyist—from the Federal Trade Commission. There is some mystery as to why FDR took this step; as William E. Leuchtenburg notes, soon Roosevelt would have been able to appoint a working majority of his own appointees. The most plausible explanation is that Roosevelt thought the FTC was too important to be left in limbo. Arguably, he might have thought this insufficient. He might have been conscious of President Theodore Roosevelt—"Uncle Ted's"—experience on the *Northern Securities* case.[26] (TR attached importance to the case, pending the Supreme Court, and appointed Oliver Wendell Holmes, confident that Holmes would see it his way. Holmes did not.) FDR might well have thought this to show that appointees who are beyond control cannot be counted on to do what the appointing office desires. FDR may also have misread the legal signs and believed that the Supreme Court would now sustain a broad removal power. The Court had seemed to recognize extremely wide presidential removal powers in the case of *Myers v. United States*.[27] The architect of that decision was the conservative former president, Chief Justice Taft.

In any case, Humphrey was vulnerable. He was more like the James Watt of his time. He had been appointed to the Federal Trade Commission to bring it under control and make it more friendly to business. A notable bloc of senators fought his renomination, and some twenty or so voted against it. He was the kind of man who responded to provocation. Once he sent a critic an answer that began "yours of unregurgitated filth received."

When Roosevelt summarily pushed Commissioner Humphrey out and appointed someone else to the FTC, the ousted commissioner retained William J. Donovan as his counsel. The narrowest justiciable issue was Humphrey's pay claims. Although Humphrey died between the filing of the lawsuit in October 1933 and the Court's decision in May 1935 (*Humphrey's Executor v. U.S.*), in a unanimous decision, with the opinion written by Justice Sutherland, the Supreme Court held that the removal of Humphrey was invalid. The Court drew distinctions that relied on what Congress had intended in framing the statute and on a conception of the agency's duties as quasi-judicial and quasi-legislative, rather than purely executive. There is a claim (not particularly well supported) that President Roosevelt regarded this decision as an attack on himself. "The *Humphrey* decision," says William E. Leuchtenburg, "may have been as influential as the better known *Schechter* ruling in motivating Roosevelt to seek a showdown with the Court." Whatever the merits of this claim, *Humphrey's Executor v. U.S.* became the foundation on which an elaborate superstructure has been erected to advance the theory that such agencies are "arms of Congress."

Indeed, the panel could well have argued that the commissions had long been under challenge. Indeed, two years after the Humphrey decision came the Brownlow Report, which the district court cited. In 1937, the President's Committee on Administrative Management (the Brownlow Committee) offered a scathing denunciation of the regulatory agencies. The repercussions of the Brownlow Committee's arguments still run through the intellectual community. In one of the most famous statements in the literature of public administration, the committee said the commissions constituted a "headless 'fourth branch' of the Government, a haphazard deposit of irresponsible agencies and uncoordinated powers. They do violence to the basic theory of the American Constitution that there should be three major branches of the Government and only three."

> These independent commissions have been given broad powers to explore, formulate, and administer policies of regulation; they have been given the task of investigating and prosecuting business misconduct; they have been given powers, similar to those exercised by courts of law, to pass in concrete cases upon the rights and liabilities of individuals under the statutes. They are in reality miniature independent governments set up to

deal with the railroad problem, the banking problem, or the radio problem.[28]

Presumably, anything with such formidable powers should be controlled. But by whom? Congress had found no effective way of supervising them, they could not be controlled by the president, and they were answerable to the courts only with respect to the legality of their actions. There was some connection, no doubt, between the president's ideas about administrative reorganization, the controversy over reorganization, and the controversy over the decisional latitude of the administrative agencies. The Brownlow doctrine was that the Congress had engaged in "legislative groping rather than the pursuit of a consistent policy," as shown by "the wide variety in [these agencies'] structure and functions and also by the fact that just as frequently Congress had given regulatory functions of the same kind to the regular executive departments."

Clearly, FDR wanted control of the agencies to be in the president's hands. The commissions should be on a par with the National Recovery Administration and other line agencies. In his retrospective about the New Deal years, Rexford G. Tugwell offers a different interpretation.[29] The commissions were, he said, another sign of "legislative aggressiveness." They were "supposed to be regulatory, but by their elaboration of administrative law and their interferences in economic affairs, they tended to invade more and more deeply the executive territory."

The point is particularly important. The real reason for constraining the claimed removal power—as for attempting to constrain OMB regulatory action—is to maintain Congress's ability to engage in the actualities of the administrative process. The removability of officials is not a question by itself.

The panel's decision goes on to say that the *Humphrey's* decision was "stamped as well, *as President Roosevelt thought*, with hostility toward the architect of the New Deal."[30] The question is whether there was a valid basis for the decision, and whether other valid decisional criteria would have led to a different result. The logical merit does not depend on what President Roosevelt thought. William E. Leuchtenburg, on whose work the court relied, believes that the case "may have been" particularly important in Roosevelt's mind and that Justice Jackson thought "the decision that made Roosevelt madder at the Court than any other decision was that damn little case of *Humphrey's Executor v. U.S.*"[31] Indeed, Leuchtenburg states his argument so carefully that it is clear that he is stating his own belief. It is less clear what Justice Jackson *said*. Moreover, Jackson said he *thought* that *Roosevelt thought* the Supreme Court was merely trying to get at him personally, which would be highly suspect evidence in a trial. The chain of reasoning is hardly definitive. The question at stake is the degree of White House control over agency decision making, on the one hand, and how much control Congress could retain, on the other.

Further, the opinion substantially misconstrues the relationship of regulatory agencies to both the White House and the Congress. The three-judge panel said quite casually that the regulatory agencies are "immediately accountable" to congressional committees. Does immediately accountable mean that the committees should ordinarily direct the agencies on specific matters? Theoretically, one might suppose that the president specifically directs executive appointees. But this is very limited, and a parallel process does not exist between agencies and Congress. The three-judge panel is wrong. As powerful as the committees are, descriptions of their role should be consist with the facts. The need for clarification is indicated in the court's own language. The opinion speaks of independence from the president as involving "a correspondingly greater dependence" on the congressional committees.

Curiously, the Brownlow Committee complained that Congress could not control the agencies, and the judicial panel complained that Congress controlled them too tightly. In *Moultrie v. Martin*,[32] the Court of Appeals for the Fourth Circuit said, in effect, that if the concepts and data of another discipline were used in reaching a decision, they should be used consistently according to the principles of that discipline. The particular case was a lesson on how to use statistical evidence.

If the *Moultrie* standard were applied, the panel would have to practice political science as political scientists practice it—thus yielding a substantially different opinion. The *Synar* panel referred to *Humphrey's Executor v. U.S.* (1935) as "stamped with some of the political science preconceptions of its era and not of the present day."[33] Presumably the court thought that this comment added analytical strength to their decision. (I doubt the court referred to political science as an artistic gesture, as judges sometimes use Shakespearean quotations.) The court can only have meant that in 1935 political scientists—a group competent to offer expert opinion on government organization—believed in independent regulatory commissions, but they do not now.

The court would have been right to say that in 1935 many political scientists had as strong opinions against the independence of commissions as for it. Much of the political science thinking in 1935 was antagonistic to the court's conclusion. Of course, one should ask why if, after argument, the Supreme Court found one view more compelling than the other. The panel would have

to change its view. One might also point out that the "political science preconceptions . . . of the present day" are *not* strikingly well formulated against the
old view. They are simply fluid. Moreover, the language of the district court's
opinion, if sustained, would imply a fundamental change in the whole regulatory structure.

If political scientists were to assess agency dependence on Congress, they
would logically be required to evaluate regulatory decision making. Among
other things, they would have to evaluate not only Congress's connection, but
also the White House's possible connection to regulatory decision making. An
illustration arose when Chairman Mark Fowler of the Federal Communications Commission proposed that the FCC change certain syndication rules
regarding broadcasting movies on television. These rules were the object of a
fight between the broadcast networks and the motion picture industry over
ownership rights. Chairman Fowler, sensing that President Reagan might be
interested, visited the Oval Office to explain the FCC's proposed revision of
the rules to the president and to senior members of the White House staff.
Fowler's visit caused controversy; many experienced and sophisticated people
thought it unusual; some thought it unacceptable. When I asked several commissioners (one of whom had been on the FCC) if this were normal practice,
they said no. If regulatory agencies were "correspondingly" more dependent
on Congress, the Fowler visit should not have occurred. Nor should the
recurrent public struggles in which committee chairs or subcommittee chairs
seek to pressure an agency into doing what it does not want to do.

The court is equally casual in its treatment of the functions of independent regulatory agencies. Recall the language quoted above: "It is not as obvious today as it seemed in the 1930's that . . . *the decisions of such agencies so
clearly involve scientific judgment rather than political choice that it is even
theoretically desirable to insulate them from the democratic process.*"[34] It is not
apparent why summary removal power, lodged in the president, is necessary
or why constraint of this power automatically violates the democratic process.
It is even less clear why the panel chose "scientific judgment" as the criterion
by which to constrain the power of removal. This is a new creation; the
interest in substantive expertise and the ability to view a problem comprehen-
sively were vastly more important in the decisions on the Interstate Commerce Commission (1887), the Federal Trade Commission (1914), the Federal
Radio Commission (1927), the U.S. Tariff Commission (1916), the Federal
Power Commission as reorganized in 1929, and the Securities and Exchange
Commission (1934), which had been created by the time of the *Humphrey*

decision. As the restrictions had been grounded on points other than scientific judgment over a very long period, by what rationale could the three-judge panel suddenly swing to the scientific judgment criterion as the one apparently legitimate departure in 1986? (Incidentally, one wonders what the court would have done with such an agency as the Nuclear Regulatory Commission, which clearly does involve scientific judgment.)

The problem concerns not merely what the *Synar* decision may have done to the regulatory process, but also to future administrative issues. Congress may be strongly disposed to control the OMB's exercise of regulatory jurisdiction, particularly as it is claimed and exercised on the basis of various executive orders. If the language of the district court's opinion in *Synar v. United States* had been sustained by the Supreme Court, it might well have blocked such congressional efforts. The implication of the three-judge opinion seems to be that the removal power cannot be constrained. One should also study the ramifications of note 23 in the panel's opinion. In principle, above what level is the power of removal unconstrained? *Or is there no limit?* This raises profound questions. If it were held that there is no limit on the removal power, theoretically the federal personnel system would be solely under presidential control.[35] Chapter 4 will show the strong interest on the part of financial and industrial leaders in protecting management discretion. What would follow if members of the Securities and Exchange Commission, or the Federal Reserve Board, were subject to summary removal?

It was quite possible to reach a decision on the powers of the comptroller general without going into matters that the three-judge panel chose to discuss in the *Synar* decision. While no one knows how the panel reached its decision, we may infer that the other members of the panel deferred on this question to the intellectual and policy leadership of the one member of the panel with a vast public reputation for knowledge of and interest in administrative law. That was Judge Scalia. The result is fully consistent with opinions that he had written as a law professor. One could hypothesize that the opinion writer was determined to make one more brick for the wall of executive leadership. The court adopted as its inviolable predicate that effective congressional power should be undermined and controlled. Further, the opinion writer faced the task of making bricks without straw.

MORRISON V. OLSON

The dogma of executive leadership also entered into the dispute concerning the independent counsels authorized by the Ethics in Government Act of 1978.

The case is commonly called *Morrison v. Olson*, its designation before the U.S. Supreme Court. However, we here use the term *In Re Sealed Case*, as discussed by the majority in the Court of Appeals for the D.C. Circuit.[36]

Morrison v. Olson arose from a challenge by certain former officials at the second and third levels of the Department of Justice—one deputy attorney general and two former assistant attorneys general. An independent counsel had been appointed. Part of the legal defense in the *Morrison* case was that the independent counsel lacked power because the statute was invalid. The statute, they claimed, had violated the president's power under Article II of the Constitution by placing the appointing power in courts.

The function of such independent counsel, appointed by the federal courts at the behest of the attorney general, is to conduct investigations, seek indictments, and conduct prosecutions, if that should be the determination. Under the statute in question, at a certain point the attorney general conducts a preliminary investigation to determine whether to ask the court to appoint independent counsel (a special prosecutor). The decision to request to appoint an independent counsel (special prosecutor) is at the discretion of the attorney general. The decision is not judicially reviewable. In other words, no other person can ask the court to compel the attorney general to request an independent counsel. Lay scholars in the social sciences may not appreciate the vast reach of the term *prosecutorial discretion*. In all likelihood, the court will decide that such a matter lies within the broad realm of prosecutorial discretion.[37]

Moreover, the attorney general has the discretion to remove the independent counsel for cause. Judge Silberman's opinion states it in the negative. The Ethics in Government Act, he states, provides that an independent counsel "may be removed from office, other than by impeachment and conviction, only by the personal action of the attorney general and only for good cause, physical disability, mental incapacity, or other condition that substantially impairs the performance of such counsel's duties."[38] An attorney general would likely find considerable leeway in the language describing each basis for removal. Obviously, such an attempt by an attorney general would lead to litigation, unless the independent counsel were in a very untenable situation. Finally, in applying for independent counsel, the attorney general has the right to set boundaries for the investigation.

Chief Judge Silberman's opinion is almost a pure exercise in political and organizational theory. The available precedents, and the history of American government, provide far too much material that would lead to a different result, unless one is already governed by a dogma that dictates a given outcome.

The majority opinion (by Judge Silberman) glosses over the constitutional language that allows the Congress to provide for the appointment of "inferior" officers by courts. Judge Silberman relies on a previous decision in the D.C. circuit in which the question had turned upon the test of inferiority; and, in effect, decided that the inferior officer was in a reporting line to the attorney general. It is absurd not to admit other conceptions of inferior officer. That could be anyone of lower rank than a presidential appointee, subject to Senate confirmation, at the cabinet level. It must be, given the constitutional language, within the discretion of Congress to determine what inferior officers are to be appointed by courts. That could be blocked only by some other constitutional language not open to question. The appointment of officers within the executive *branch*—a term unknown to the Constitution—was obviously not so patent or blocked, as manifested by the continuing controversy, from 1787 until the failure to impeach Andrew Johnson, over how to handle executive appointments and removals.

The argument that the independent counsel (special prosecutor) interferes with the constitutional obligation of the president to "take care that the laws be faithfully executed" makes no sense. Insofar as laws are executed by presidential agents, they must be executed by the attorney general or by someone else. If the president is unwilling to see the laws executed, or is intellectually or technically incapable of ensuring their execution, the president must have the choice to place that responsibility elsewhere than in the attorney general. If, in a most unusual situation, the attorney general or the Justice Department itself is compromised or under suspicion, the constitutional structure is jeopardized if there is no alternative except impeachment.

Moreover, the judge sought to define the case as preeminently one of threats to individual liberty—that is, the liberty of high officials who have come under suspicion. Criminal prosecution obviously is a very severe sanction. But its severity is not reduced by the fact that it is exercised by a United States attorney, an attorney general, or a prosecutor chosen in another way.

It is also irrelevant to the issue.

"The constitutional scheme," says Judge Silberman, "is as simple as it is complete—Congress passes the criminal law in the first instance, the president enforces the law, and individual cases are tried before a neutral judiciary involved in neither the creation nor the execution of the law."[39] This scheme, stated so simply, is not so simple. The present arrangements took a long time to work out, not only for Justice but for the whole government. They are not "simple" or "obvious" in the language of the Constitution, which is why the idea of executive leadership discussed above developed so haltingly.

There is no warrant for the belief that the particular arrangements existing in our time are mandated by Article II. They are definitively not obvious in history. At one point in the past, there was strong support for the idea of devolving administrative activity to the states. Democrats consistently supported this approach, and Whigs apparently felt obliged to go along whether they agreed or not. According to Leonard White, Senator Mason of Virginia asserted, when the bill to create the Interior Department was debated in 1849, that the new agency would "absorb hereafter as much power as those who hold the reins of Government shall see fit to place in their hands." Senator John Calhoun declared, "there is something ominous in the expression, 'The Secretary of the Interior.' . . . Everything upon the face of God's earth will go into the Home-Department."[40]

Other critics spoke to the same theme, and President Polk "signed the bill with reluctance, suspecting its centralizing tendency." The general case for devolving administrative functions to the states was, as we can tell from the present structure, increasingly rejected. The fact that it was even considered does not reveal what someone's intentions were in 1787; but it is at least clear evidence that over the next fifty to sixty years the regiocentric concept of government now found in administrative argumentation was not deemed self-evident.

Administrative arrangements for federal criminal jurisdiction were very weakly structured until after the Civil War. There was the U.S. attorney general in the nation's capital. The first legislation setting up federal trial courts, the Judiciary Act of 1789, authorized a United States attorney for each state. But they were not under the control of the attorney general, and it was not until June 22, 1870, that the Department of Justice was created.

The opinion by Judge Silberman in the Court of Appeals version of the *Morrison* case also ignores the critical fact that federal courts have, at times, been authorized by statute to appoint other administrative officers. When steamboating was the bold new transportation technology, the Congress had to decide how to oversee the safety of steamboats and their passengers. (So-called new social regulation is not so new.) How were the first steamboat inspectors appointed? By federal judges. Under legislation adopted in 1838, White tells us, "authority was vested in the hands of the several district judges, each of whom was to appoint one or more persons to be inspectors of hulls, and inspectors of boilers and machinery."

These inspectors, with no legislative criteria to guide them, had the sole authority to certify if vessels were seaworthy or not. Later, Congress changed the system. For a time, it provided for nine supervising inspectors, who were presidential appointees with the advice and consent of the Senate. But the judges were not altogether excluded. Inspection districts were organized around the major ports; and in each district the collector of the port, the supervising inspector, and the judge sat as a board to appoint the inspectors. In this new arrangement, as in the old one, the mixing of activities of officials chosen under Article II and those under Article III went much farther than the contemporary court would allow today. The court also ignores contemporary legislation and facts, such as present statutes allowing temporary appointments of United States attorneys, under certain circumstances, by the judges in their districts.[41] The court further ignores the long struggle over the meaning of "take care that the laws be faithfully executed"—including a claim that this merely meant that the president should seek criminal prosecution for officials who did not carry out the law.

The court in the *Morrison* case substitutes for history an exercise in intentionality —the intention of the Framers. Evidently, history is not taken seriously in Judge Silberman's jurisprudential venture in political theory. The court asserts that "the president's ability to execute the law [is] a duty the president can practically carry out only through appointed officials," and on this point cites Alexander Hamilton in nos. 70, 76, and 77 of the *Federalist Papers*.[42]

Judges can cite anything they wish. What judges say becomes true unless overruled by some higher judge. A judge who cites someone else is effectively saying: (1) the cited source has thought about this issue more than I have and has better facts or logic than I could have alone; or (2) the cited source simply has nicer words than mine; or (3) the cited source has greater precedential authority than I have; or (4) it makes a nice flourish, as when one cites Gilbert and Sullivan, or Shakespeare, or Irvin S. Cobb.

The exact basis of the judge's reasoning in this case is unclear. Surely, Hamilton is not needed to show that the president acts through others. Everybody acts through others except the last person in any chain of actions, the last clerk or foot soldier. No one doubts that the president largely acts through others. What is more curious is that Hamilton does not even remotely suggest that the president's duty can be carried out only through *appointed* officials. In *Federalist* no. 70 Hamilton lays out his famous dictum: "Energy in the Executive is a leading character in the definition of good government." But energy might well be taken to mean rapid and expeditious implementation of settled legislative policy, which is not the subject the court is discussing. Hamilton further discusses the "ingredients which constitute energy," to wit: unity, duration, provision for support, and competent powers. Unity merely means that effective leadership is more likely to come from decisions made by a single person and not a collective decision-making body. It is not relevant to the case.

Federalist no. 76 does deal with nominations, but it is chiefly relevant here as a statement about why the president should not have unqualified right to appoint subordinates. No. 77 further discusses the role of the Senate and includes the famous sentence, "The consent of that body would be necessary to displace as well as to appoint." Whether it would be a good idea to have the Senate concur in firings as well as appointments may be debated; but it has not become historical practice, nor has it even been much advocated since Andrew Johnson escaped impeachment for violating one of the Tenure of Office Acts. (One might wonder if the opinion writer were victimized by his word processor, since the standard of work required for clerkship at the Court of Appeals must be rather high.)

If Silberman's citation of Hamilton is partly superfluous and partly irrelevant, one might suppose that he invoked Hamilton's name as a form of argument by intimidation, like the medieval use of Aristotle. It coerces the average lawyer, who studied very little constitutional law. It is, of course, common for judges to call upon the writers of the *Federalist Papers*, contemporaries of the Framers who knew something about the making of the Constitution.

The citation is the equivalent of going to legislative history to find an acceptable meaning for a statute. But what is said after the fact has very little authority. Every Washington insider hears about "misleading legislative history inserted on a Saturday morning by one senator." After signing the Hobbs antiracketeering bill, President Truman attached a message to it purporting to interpret certain of its provisions. Arthur Krock wrote in the *New York Times* that this message should be given great weight by the courts when they came to interpret the law.

Not so! said Corwin:

> There is a vast difference between the assumption that Congress's purpose in passing a bill can be gleaned from a study of its reports, etc., that Congress had before it while the measure was under consideration and, on the other hand, the assumption that similar light can be obtained from the study of a presidential message that followed the measure's passage by the houses. Equally obvious is that an act of Congress gets its intention from the houses in which the Constitution specifically vests "all legislative power herein granted." For a court to vary its interpretation of an act of Congress in deference to something said by the president at the time of

signing it would be to attribute to the latter the power to foist upon the houses intentions that they never entertained, and thereby to endow him with a legislative power not shared by Congress.[43]

A judge should know that eighteenth-century political practices were no more fastidious than those of today. There is no reason why the same interpretive principle should not apply to a set of after-the-Convention newspaper articles, no matter how well reasoned. Madison and Hamilton had been at the Convention. Jay had not. Hamilton, turn, had been so alienated from the main flow of Convention debate and politics that he left to attend to other matters. John Roche describes his role in the debates on the Virginia and New Jersey Plans:

> Hamilton, previously mute, arose and delivered a six-hour oration; . . . in essence, the Hamilton Plan contemplated an elected life monarch, virtually free of public control, on the Hobbesian ground that only in this fashion could strength and stability be achieved. . . . From all accounts, this was a masterful and compelling speech, but . . . it had little impact. Hamilton was simply transmitting on a different wave-length from the rest of the delegates; the latter adjourned after his great effort, admired his rhetoric, and then returned to business.[44]

Silberman might also be presumed to know that Hamilton's coauthor, Madison, later held a different view about what Hamilton had said at the Convention. When, in later years, Hamilton denied having advocated a life monarch, Madison said that this must have been due to "want of recollection."

Such an after-the-Convention public relations document cannot reliably be treated as an indication of what the drafters intended. It is illogical to derive meaning for the Constitution on the basis of the *Federalist*. The fact that Madison and Hamilton voted for something and later stated reasons does not mean that the reasons were correctly stated, nor that other delegates voted for the same reasons.

Indeed, in some respects Silberman's reliance on Hamilton—apart from the fact that the point cited is only vaguely related to Hamilton's text—is intellectually pernicious. To cite the *Federalist Papers* on intentions is tantamount to saying that the Constitution is what the judge says the *Federalist* writers—or any writer he happens to choose—said it meant. For William L. Anderson,

> Intentions are the intentions (purposes, choices, acts of will, desires of a certain outcome) of individual human beings. Every man, being a

different and distinct individual, unavoidably has intentions that are somewhat different from those of everyone else. Such a thing as a solid, completely unified intention of all the members in any group would be hard if not impossible to find. Furthermore, intentions are highly subjective and personal things. They are not like badges pinned to a coat lapel. They lie deep in the hearts and minds of men. They are not always clearly stated by those who have them, more even capable of clear and specific formulations. The words used to convey them seldom do so perfectly.[45]

Moreover, James Madison, in his own lifetime, specifically denied the usefulness of the after-the-Convention public relations document as a guide to constitutional interpretation. In 1821, he wrote to Thomas Ritchie:

As a guide in expounding and applying the provisions of the Constitution, the debates and internal decisions of the Convention can have no authoritative character. . . . The legitimate meaning of the Instrument must be derived from the text itself; or if a key is to be sought elsewhere, it must not be in the opinions or intentions of the Body which planned & proposed the Constitution, but in the sense attached to it by the people in their respective state conventions where it rec'd all the authority which it possesses.[46]

It is unlikely, but possible, that the court spoke from historical ignorance.

Decision making on the basis of dogma is uniquely feasible for a judicial forum, as there is no means—except to some degree by appellate argument—to challenge the overall structure of the argument. The problem of the court is not to state a case in a scientifically valid manner, but to state a decision coherently. Judges necessarily have authority over their own arguments—except within the constraints of review. As a result, they have the latitude to assert authoritatively what would otherwise be deemed irrelevant, irrational, or incomplete arguments. That is the character of argument from dogma.

The two cases—*Synar v. United States* and *In Re Sealed Case*—express the judicial acceptance, through law school political theory, of the primacy of executive leadership as dogma. Whether they could do so with equal ease in light of contemporary political practice may be doubtful. However, most law schools now teach, or incorporate, economics but they do not incorporate systematic political science.[47] Contemporary political science could not today sustain the Brownlow propositions as they were stated in 1937. However, judges of a certain persuasion have armed themselves precisely with the

Brownlow propositions and their cognate theory. I accept that judges generally pursue what *they* deem right and just, meaning that they are powerfully armed with a dogma. The dogma of "executive leadership" asserts an extremely strong statement of separation of powers, which has the necessary consequence of reducing the power of Congress vis-à-vis the president.

The hypothesis that I find more plausible is that a bigger intellectual strategy is contemplated. Some judges have recently come to the bench committed to economic laissez-faire as a constitutional mandate, reviving old "substantive due process" as "economic liberties."[48] Others are committed to reversing judicial decisions and curtailing legislative decisions opposed to racial discrimination and the rights of women. Others seem aimed at installing the *Pacificus* doctrine, in which Alexander Hamilton claimed that the president has almost plenary powers over foreign affairs.[49] The consequence, once these judicial dicta are accepted, is to reach outside the Constitution and confer the authority of judicial precedent on the writer—in this case Hamilton. Giving such authority to a selective reading of the role of the presidency as the asserted intention of the Framers is the intervening step, and it brings the campaign within striking distance of its goal. In my opinion, this is what contemporary advocates of the executive leadership dogma, teaching political theory from the bench, seek to do.

The Dogma of Leadership and Operational Reality

The basis for considering the legal argument as dogma is immediately demonstrated by certain other significant relationships that this school of judges refuses to consider. What turbulence should be expected merits the most careful thought. We begin with the hypothesis that delegation is a necessary response to the physical and intellectual limitations of all human beings.

Courts frequently engage in decision by evasion, as in the phrase "We see no reason . . ." So it occurs in the *In Re Sealed Case* opinion, when the court says that *if* the president takes care that the laws be executed, "we see no reason" why he cannot get the attorney general and the Justice Department to do the same. In the independent counsel case, Chief Judge Silberman evades operational realities that, as a former subcabinet officer, he must know very well. He knows that, given the scale of modern government, the president is not likely to have a detailed grasp of most government matters, except when advised by those who know about them in more detail.

This situation is the natural consequence of big government, especially of a more or less twenty-person government. Moreover, presidents often speak of the physical burdens of the office. At least since the administration of William Howard Taft, most presidents have complained of an excessive burden of work. Yet the *Synar v. United States* decision fails to recognize the implications of the president's limitations.

Ralph Huitt notes, "The president has no more hours in a day than any other man," and Luther Gulick defines the span of an executive's control as "partly a matter of limits of knowledge, but even more . . . a matter of limits of time and of energy."[50] Under the principle enunciated by Judge Silberman, we need an honest answer to Gulick's question, "What is the work of the chief executive? What does he do?" The activities entailed, or implied, in the shorthand definitions of the president's duties involve a very complex set of relationships. Gulick continues, "In the large enterprises, particularly where the chief executive is as a matter of fact unable to do the work that is thrown upon him, it may be presumed that one or more [of the president's functions] should be sub-organized" or delegated to some lower level of authority.

The dogma of executive leadership, embodied in judicial political theory, promises an administrative state in which the president has remarkably little capacity, except when he chooses to act at random or arbitrarily, and in which the "ultimate responsibility of the president," under a sharp separation of powers theory, protects subordinates against available forms of oversight.

The Department of Justice illustrates the relationship to the president that characterizes executive agencies in general. The lawyers' insistence that the Department of Justice *should* be independent of the president's political considerations will always be a deterrent to effective presidential control. Several very senior officials, including two former attorneys general and one former solicitor general, have put forth arguments hinting that it would be improper for the president to have much to do with the department's decisions. They seem even more strongly to favor the proposition that, at all odds, the president ought not to decide against the preferences of the attorney general. They insist that the Department of Justice should not be influenced by anyone else, such as presidential staff.[51]

If that is so, then departmental control over the field officials, the United States attorneys, might be fairly strong. The data that would be helpful for this judgment have not been reported in full detail. John G. Heinberg reported on the centralization of federal prosecutions.[52] The Department of Justice exercised fairly tight central departmental control—through standardized manuals, instructions, requirements for advance memoranda of approval for dismissals and *nolle prosequi*, and the appointment of special assistants to the attorney general to work with the local U.S. Attorneys in particularly important cases. Control was not uniform, however, but depended on the particular kind of case, with the most stringent controls applied to internal revenue matters.

James Eisenstein has reexamined these relationships and finds that although cooperation and mutual accommodation normally prevail, "mutual resentment, jealousy, and even overt conflict occur." According to one U.S. attorney, these controls offend their pride: "We all have our sensitivity out here. We're sensitive to anyone coming out from Washington. It's sort of a reflection on our competence—that we aren't competent to do the job."[53] The Department of Justice is sometimes seen as bureaucratic in that it requires an extraordinary amount of red tape, thus causing delays. Moreover, its intervention is said to provoke local problems that the U.S. attorneys would rather avoid. Imagine their response to a visitor who announced, "I'm so-and-so from the antitrust division. We're getting ready to file antitrust suits against the ten top building contractors in the city." The U.S. attorney interviewed by Eisenstein resented this, felt he should have been consulted. At least he could have been prepared for the news reporters when they besieged him.[54]

On occasions the Department of Justice is even suspected of serving the interest of the president alone. The best recent illustration of this attitude is provided in accounts of the Watergate scandal. The central office of the Department of Justice was directly implicated. The attorney general at the time of Watergate, John Mitchell, had a presumed vested interest in a routine investigation leading to a trivial conclusion, for he was executive director of the Committee for the Reelection of the President (CREEP), under whose auspices the famous burglary at Democratic party headquarters was conducted. Attorney General Richard Kleindienst had been Mitchell's principal departmental subordinate, or deputy attorney general, and also had a patent interest in the political success of President Nixon. The assistant attorney general responsible for conducting the investigation, Henry Peterson, was suspected (and this was later proved to be true by the White House transcripts) of supplying the president with detailed accounts of the investigation's status—information the president transmitted to his subordinates under investigation.

The U.S. Attorney's office, under which the investigation then fell, was indeed suspicious of the department. Moreover, the relevant constituency was the press, which applied such intense pressure on the U.S. Attorney's Office that it began to withhold information that might reach the president.[55] In that way, it began to play an independent role in the Watergate affair, despite its theoretical subordination. Lawyers may rightly argue for an independent Department of Justice. But if their preferences were followed, the organizational system would not produce the necessary results for Judge Silberman's argument to have any validity.

The questions about the organizational system extend over the whole government, and are not limited to the unique features of the Justice Department. Structure, policy and program, and money are all very important. The department's formal, prescribed organization is declared by statute and represented on charts with named boxes to represent positions and solid or broken lines to represent channels of authority or advice. Most departments (or comparable agencies of any importance) have at least five rungs of decision-making authority. At the topmost management level, we have the secretary or comparable official. Then there are probably at least four other levels—sometimes more—where officeholders have some degree of authority.

The formal structure also encompasses some form of field organization. If decision makers want their political enterprise to go forward as they contemplated it, they must cope with these problems which—unlike problems in mathematics—have no right answers but can have wrong answers that are painful and destructive.

Field administration has much to do with linking a president's concepts to working results. Getting a *policy* settled means getting a definitive sense of purpose or direction, in the form of law or formal decision: this is what is entailed in the president's legislative leadership. But policies have to be translated into programs. Adam Yarmolinsky emphasized a facet of this when he wrote that getting better ideas may not be the most important thing in government. The difficulty is getting ideas translated into programs.[56] Finally, a program is realized, in practice, only through an unending series of operational details. If a policy is to succeed, there must be some reach in administrative control and success in the field results.

A department head has a great responsibility, even if the agency's functions are quite routine. The problem of expenditures, for example, is always present. An administrator may be held accountable and suffer some pain, penalty, or loss of reputation for debatable or foolish expenditures by the agency. Lower-level decisions create both problems and opportunities for top-level executives, even for the chief executive and entourage. An administrator has to cope with the external environment and may have a hundred employees, persons whose decisions could precipitate major disputes.

A natural tension exists between the preferred policies of the professionals and the preferences of political newcomers. The president's personal role is necessarily constrained. The president can, subject to legal barriers, reach deeply into an issue, but the myriad claims on the chief executive's time make this unfeasible.

The implication of the judicial-political theory is that the president should function as the general manager of the United States. It is not a new idea, a version of it having been advanced by Willoughby and by one of the Brownlow Committee staff papers. Such a proposition should be understood not only in the usual political terms, but also as a simple problem of recognizing the cognitive and physical limits on the human being. The president could not carry the responsibility of general manager unless the government is, as Gulick put it, suborganized. Substantial portions of important decisions must be delegated to others. How do the political forces of the nation represented in Congress adjust? If they can exert some influence on the suborganized part of government, they will make their accommodations.

Conclusion

In the study of the administrative system, the dogma of the primacy of executive leadership implies a serious reconsideration of how political responsibility is established. On the other hand, if one begins with the presuppositions of the Weberian model of bureaucratic theory, assuming that there is any political responsibility in the administrative process is wishful thinking. The administrative process stands on its own, self-contained and beyond external control. Which of these hypotheses is the sounder empirical estimate is exactly the issue to which political science has yet to turn.

Management science, in its various forms, is profoundly attractive to many because it reinforces the dogma of management prerogative. Management science provides what bureaucratic theory cannot provide: namely, a positive program and method for decision making without politics. The human relations movement is an adaptation that serves the management prerogative concept, while it induces more loyalty, provides for more voice, and diminishes unwanted exits—all without the tool of fear.

A natural tension exists between administrative theory and political dogma, as there is always a tension between any two claims to knowledge or bases of action. Everyone has political beliefs and preferences that—despite all our self-conscious rationality—we are prepared not to examine. Thus, to achieve some compatible administrative theory, we may persist in a belief even when experience and empirical analysis so thoroughly discredits it that it can stand only as doctrinal faith.[57] This refusal to scrutinize the foundation of one's ideas, of course, may also occur in conflicts about dogma within a discipline.

The difficulty, however, is that one may persist in advocating a given theory that is based on a normative standard that is increasingly violated in practice. One may adhere stubbornly to the original doctrines in the face of compelling new facts. When adherence to dogma precludes new thought or new interpretation of data from experience old and new, it frustrates the best efforts of empirical analysis. Judicial-political theory that enforces the dogma of the primacy of executive leadership, which the Brownlow propositions helped to seem to be "common sense," cannot fail to create further turbulence in U.S. public administration.

4

DOGMA, INTERESTS, AND ADMINISTRATIVE LAW AS POLITICS, I

Dogma and the Politics of Administrative Law

Kenneth Culp Davis began a powerful article with the observation that "political scientists and lawyers, [though] in quest of better understanding of the same processes of the same administrative agencies carrying out the same programs," [nonetheless] characteristically work quite independently of each other."[1] Much the same statement could now be made. In political science, at any rate, there is a need, both intellectual and practical, for new work leading toward an empirical political theory of administrative law, a theory that places administrative law in relationship to the political environment. This is important as we seek substantial knowledge for the teaching, advising, consulting, and management roles assumed by political scientists.

The first thing to remember, and to take as the foundation stone, is that administration is the exercise of discretion about the actual use of the basic resources of human control: information, money and its surrogates, and force. Continuity is nearly always sought in such a process, and disruption nearly always presents itself. That is the background against which one must comprehend administrative law.

Administrative law, as it works in the United States, contributes to continuity and disruption as simultaneous features of the administrative system. Administrative law, in the simplest and most conventional definition, concerns the procedures that government agencies use in dealing with matters falling under their jurisdiction.[2] That old-fashioned definition is no longer adequate. Administrative law is more broadly defined as the "body of law created by administrative agencies in the form of rules, regulations, orders and decisions to carry out the regulatory power of such agencies."[3] The definition is also too narrow. Government is much more than merely regulatory. Many agencies are engaged in facilitating or serving a variety of human purposes. The biggest civilian program, for instance, is Social Security. To argue more broadly, administrative law is the law and policy that government agencies produce as parties, acting upon those agencies, as they seek, assert, and reject control.[4]

Administrative law is part of a process of social combat, with the "power of [interest] groups involved at every point in the institutions of government."[5] Administrative law provides a means for interest groups to make claims upon other groups "for the establishment, maintenance, or enhancement of forms of behavior" that claimants regard as important.[6] It is a method for group combat, for containing conflicts that cannot be settled, and for achieving settlement. Turbulence is manifested in the transactions within administrative agencies and in their relations, friendly and hostile, to the various constituencies or stakeholders that have dealings with them. Turbulence, both in the operational world of decision making and in the intellectual world of theory, arises when pressures for continuity collide with those for disruption.

Administrative Law and Political Science: Competing Models

If my supposition is accepted, it follows that we seek some supplement to, or even modification of, the dominant model. That model is the aggregate, central tendency, of judicio-political theory, a form of political theory found in law review articles, law treatises, briefs, and judges' opinions.[7] Empirical theory is a set of forecasts and explanations about how society and government work. In principle, such a theory is subject to empirical testing. Normative theory is the set of explanations, prescriptions, and moral justifications about how society and government should work. Judicio-political theory includes both features. Crucially, however, it meets the criterion of dogma, rather than doctrine taken seriously, to the extent that people are prepared to take responsibility for not reexamining it. Dogma is a means of control over the disturbance that comes with having to recognize data and experience that violate other inviolable beliefs and claims.

There is a significant difference between the behavior of a political system that an empirically oriented political scientist expects to see and what is anticipated under judicio-political theory. Judicio-political theory is not merely empirical. It is normative to the extent that it maintains that administrative decision making is not legitimate unless it approximates the procedures and the criteria of American courts. The combination of empirical and normative estimates into dogma is the key to Richard B. Stewart's "traditional model" of administrative law.[8] The crucial concept of the traditional model is that in the end judicial review must always be preserved and given the means to control administrative agency action.

Theoretically, judicial review keeps administrative action within legislative bounds. It "cabins" administrative agencies, to use Stewart's term. All other procedures ultimately give the court the means to exercise review. Those other procedures require agencies to follow decisional procedures promoting the accuracy, rationality, and reviewability of agency decisions. Central principles of this model are that administrative sanctions on private individuals must be authorized by the legislature that controls the agency and that the agency must demonstrate some intelligible principle of delegation. Internal agency procedures must force the agency to comply with the first principle. Agency processes must facilitate judicial review to ascertain whether claimed authority is actually delegated authority, whether sanctions are imposed legally, and whether the agency's actions are authorized by the legislature (the first principle).

There are, indeed, dissenters to the dogma. Jerry L. Mashaw characterizes the court decisions of the 1960s and 1970s in this way: "The process that is due is one that roughly conforms to, or at least borrows its decisional techniques from, judicial process." But, Mashaw goes on, "Why should this be so? Are agencies doing the same thing as courts? Are they operating with similar legal powers, political demands, and fiscal resources?"[9]

Mashaw's questions raise a normative issue in the form of a question about understanding. There is also a question that objective political analysis, subject to empirical testing criteria, could consider. It is not now so considered, for administrative law has not been a major concern for political science. That fact is ironic. In the years when American political science was founded, one might have forecast that administrative law would become a major field of interest. Frank Goodnow, who wrote about municipal government, political parties, constitutional law, and public administration, also wrote about administrative law.[10] His first book on the subject formed part of the syllabus Woodrow Wilson used when teaching at Johns Hopkins. John A. Fairlie wrote on administrative law until at least 1930.[11] Other books on the subject were in circulation as late as the 1950s. Yet to predict a lasting interest in administrative law would been wrong. Goodnow's book went out of use, and when reprinted in 1970 was aimed at a law school market, not political science, although it now shows up in the notes of at least one textbook in each field.][12]

Political scientists and other students of administration have, from the early 1930s until recent years, largely tuned out administrative law.[13] The contrast to constitutional law, where neither lawyers' criticisms nor the behavioral challenge can negate appeal, is notable. Behavioralists and others who thought constitutional law overly formalistic entered the field, rather than withdrawing. The result are new specialties, subfields, and academic courses carrying such titles as Judicial Behavior, Judicial Policy Making, Jurimetrics, and Law and Society.

Three reasons may explain the different treatment of administrative law. The first was a singular article by a singular scholar. Kenneth Culp Davis scared political scientists off the administrative law terrain by publishing in 1953, in the leading political science journal, a withering criticism of political science work on public administration.[14] Davis assailed Leonard D. White's treatment of Albert V. Dicey and "the rule of law," severely criticized both the Brownlow Committee and the political scientists' generally favorable reception of it, and then went on to textbooks.[15]

> To write a reliable summary of the major principles of a complex body of law is a task of considerable difficulty. Such a summary probably can be written only by one who has first developed his own basic understanding of the subject matter. The texts on public administration that include substantial discussions of administrative law show rather clearly that the text writers have developed no such basic understanding. The resulting summaries are in a fundamental sense seriously misleading. The proportion of misinformation is exceedingly high. Even the most elementary ideas are often flagrantly in error.[16]

Davis supported his case by detailed citations and rebuttals of four books he identified by number rather than by name "to minimize possible embarrassment." The fact that he identified the edition, date of publication, and pages containing the cited errors makes it doubtful how much embarrassment was minimized. But that is a side issue. Recognizing some legitimate overlap of political science and administrative law, he nonetheless said, "Some problems should be considered beyond the proper scope of political science instruction, e.g. whether the right remedy is certiorari or mandamus or injunction and whether or not res judicata may prevent a second consideration of the same issues."[17] Such a challenge came when political scientists were already anxious about their own intellectual grounding or respectability in the intellectual community and sometimes saturated by a sense of inferiority. What professor would advise a student to write a dissertation on a topic if both student and professor might be held up to the world as incompetent by one of the country's emerging brightest lights in law?

The second reason that administrative law has been largely left alone goes more deeply into the professional psyche of political scientists that prevailed between the Depression and the behavioral revolution. Embarrassment alone could not have caused an avoidance of administrative law, not matter how brilliant the critic or hostile the criticism, if the intellectual community had not been so inclined for other reasons. Whether or not the record upholds Dwight Waldo's claim that there was an antilegal temper in public administration,[18] law was in some sense taken for granted, while an immersion in law seemed to offer little profit to academics. Most students of the administrative process in the 1930s were fundamentally sympathetic to the New Deal. The found the purpose of government intervention laudable, especially in light of the Great Depression. Some were even attracted to concepts of democratic socialism.[19] They had a strong interest in government with wide discretion and powers to plan.

The models that emphasize the hypothesis of agency "captivity" to client interests, or the model of decaying energy and effectiveness due to "aging," implicitly or explicitly treated these alleged characteristics as difficulties to be overcome.[20] They were not treated as indicators of the inherent deficiency of government when compared to the marketplace. These models, latterly adapted to market-centered theory, were both used to explain why government agencies were not doing what many scholars then endorsed—directly and controlling the economy more effectively. Inquiry with this bias was aimed at government discretion, not at finding means to impose limits on government power, and thus not at the concepts of administrative law being put forward in the 1930s.

The third reason is that public administration scholars had already begun to seek principles of administration that could be applied independently of the legal system. All the main currents of administrative thought, from the 1920s to the 1970s, were in accord: one thread connects Leonard White, William F. Willoughby and the Taylorites, Mary Parker Follett and John Merriman Gaus, Luther Gulick and Herbert Simon. The predominant interest was in scientific inquiry into administration, or sometimes in value-oriented inquiry, rather than into law.

Forms and Realities in Administrative Law

AUTHORITY BASIS: CONSTITUTION, STATUTE, AND AGENCY RULES

Political scientists can profitably begin with some thought for the authority by which administrative agency action may be reviewed. While the executive and the Congress play a large part in the ongoing system, not merely in initial authorization, the particular authority to be noticed is the federal judiciary. The courts review the actions of federal administrative agencies, or those of state and local agencies, that are challenged under some provision of the Constitution, federal statutes, or agency regulation. Judicial review is a necessary (though not a sufficient) condition that enables the system to work as it does. The courts therefore have wide latitude and many selective opportunities available to them. Cases may be reviewed on many bases. First is constitutionality, the principal means by which a case that is more than a straightforward review of an agency's actions takes on the question of federal powers. However, in the U.S. system, it is the federal courts that decide what is constitutional and what is not. Nothing can preclude a constitutional challenge if a court decides to recognize a claim as a challenge worth considering.

The statutory basis is normally the Administrative Procedure Act of 1946 and the relevant provisions of whatever statutes an agency administers. (The political history of the Administrative Procedure Act is discussed in chapter 5.) Federal agencies must have statutory authorization. The authorizing statutes vary in what they provide, even as to forum. An agency's action may be reviewed on the basis of its consistency with the rules it has adopted.

STRUCTURE OF COURTS

The Supreme Court is so important, and plays so large a symbolic role, that we will not understand American administrative law unless we also take note of the second-ranking courts (the courts of appeal) and the third-ranking district courts. First, to describe the structure of the federal court system: Agency cases are principally heard in courts of appeal at the circuit level. The nation's eleven circuits are groups of states for which a federal court of appeal has been established by Congress. In the circuits, where decisions are made by joint opinion, there are now 162 authorized judges.

Because of wide differences in demographic and cultural mix, educational characteristics, political alignments, and economic structures, the circuits vary in the kinds of disputes that go to court and the attitudes and

TABLE 4.1 Agency Appeals in U.S. Courts of Appeals (Circuits), 1993
(as percent of total circuit business)

Circuit	% of Total Appeals
District of Columbia	46.8
1st	6.6
2nd	6.8
3rd	5.3
4th	7.4
5th	5.6
6th	6.5
7th	4.4
8th	3.4
9th	9.5
10th	4.7
11th	5.6
TOTAL	7.8

Source: *United States Courts: Selected Reports*, "Appendix I: Detailed Statistical Tables: Annual Reports of the Director, Administrative Office of the United States Courts, Twelve Month Period Ended September 30, 1993," AI-3–AI-6, 1993.

outlooks of their judges. These variations account for many differences in how appellate courts handle the cases and issues before them. The courts of appeal commenced 49,511 new cases in the twelve-month period ending September 30, 1993.[21] According to the Office of the United States Courts, administrative agency appeals made up about 7.8 percent of the total during this period. Figures for 1992–1993 are given in table 4.1.

While cases involving administrative agenies are important circuit court cases and what the circuits decide is very important to the agencies, such cases make up only a modest proportion (about 10 percent) of the total load of the courts of appeal.

Table 4.1 shows that the D.C. Circuit, the Ninth Circuit (California, Oregon, and Washington), and the Fifth Circuit (Texas, Louisiana, and Mississippi) jointly account for slightly more than half the administrative agency appeals in the courts of appeal. The D.C. Circuit received 21.33 percent of such cases, the Ninth Circuit 20.62 percent, and the Fifth Circuit some 9.45 percent.

Nearly half the D.C. Circuit's caseload is made up of administrative agency appeals from across the country. Its bench has often been extremely strong. Chief Judge David Bazelon was a leader in trying to enforce a higher standard of scientific understanding in administrative decision making. He was famous for innovations in criminal law that psychiatrists applauded.[22] In the same period, the D.C. Circuit issued the opinion, written by Judge J. Skelly Wright, that made the environmental impact statement (EIS) a crucial weapon in the hands of especially well informed environmentalists—a weapon used against many administrative agency capital projects.[23] Judge Harold Leventhal, who paid great attention to economic issues, probably had as much influence upon the natural gas industry as any commissioner at the Federal Energy Regulatory Commission simply through the impact of his opinions concerning the commission.

That strong bench included Robert Bork, who found the work not to his taste. In the 1970s and 1980s, the D.C. bench began to show internal conflict as a natural consequence of Republican election victories.[24] Justice Antonio Scalia brought to the court his passionate concern for preserving executive power against legislative encroachment.[25] The former Supreme Court chief justice, Warren Burger, sat in that circuit, as did Justice Ruth Bader Ginsburg. Even more notably, the Republican presidents' more recent appointments to the Supreme Court still faced a majority in the Court of Appeals for the D.C. Circuit that was more liberal and more attuned to the jurisprudence of the Warren Court. The majority that began to emerge when Burger was chief justice and William Rehnquist had become an associate justice grew very critical of the D.C. court of appeals as led by Judge Bazelon. The clearest demonstration was in the *Vermont Yankee* case (see chapter 5).

The lag or disjunction in approach between the Supreme Court and the D.C. Circuit is not new. The same relationship, with different content, prevailed in the 1940s, when conservatives complained that the Supreme Court had become too tolerant of administrative agencies, and would not support the D.C. Circuit in controlling the agencies in the interest of "the welfare of mankind."[26]

Below the circuit are the nation's district courts—descendants, so to speak, of the district system created first by Congress in the Judiciary Act of 1789. Depending on the statute, an appeal may also be heard in one of the nation's ninety-four district courts. There are 649 judges in U.S district courts.[27]

VOCABULARY OF ACTION:
KNOWING THE WORDS AND PHRASES

Whatever courts are the venue, vocabulary is a crucial factor. There is a partially closed politics among decision makers within the administrative law process because it is focused on a single profession, it is anchored in the authority of the judge, and it is veiled in obscure language. The vocabulary of action is important because it reveals the degree to which policy and power masquerade as neutral technicalities.

Admittedly, the language is English and some of the terms are those applied to ordinary moral norms. Most people feel that they know something of *fundamental fairness*; most have some idea from high school civics of the notion of *delegation of powers* and might be impressed by the statement of a court that something is *inherently unsuitable* for judicial decision making.

The term *standing* illustrates the point. Standing is, for litigation, analogous to registration in voting. If you cannot satisfy the court that you have standing, you have no role in the case, no matter what your emotional or intellectual interest. It may be uncertain how a court will treat a claim to standing. A claim may be dismissed summarily for matters that courts do not think it necessary to consider or treated somewhat "creatively" for matters that courts particularly wish to consider.

Standing is difficult to define, but the historic test has been whether there was an actual injury to a legally protected interest. This is particularly important in view of the law's resistance to hypothetical circumstances. The concept of standing describes the litigating parties' ability, through the judge, to exclude other parties.

In recent years, the statement that some administrator has been "guilty" of *ex parte communication* conveys the tone of a serious moral offense. Other terms that sound like verbal mush are part of the discourse: *legislative preclusion, final agency action, screening, exhaustion, ripeness, primary jurisdiction, separation of functions,*

These words are, in fact, but terms of art in the specialized community of administrative lawyers, with meanings derived from, or imputed to, the aggregate of judicial holdings at any moment. Using this lexicon, people debate the most intense and painful issues. Lawyers define and make administrative law through their everyday practice. It is the function of lawyers to convert precedents and principles into arguments that will serve their clients. Their briefs set the terms within which administrative decision makers and judges work. Judges, in turn, make decisions within a territory that has been demarcated by briefs as filed. They must be able to make decisions that will be respected both by lawyers and by other judges and that reconcile the diversity of decisions produced.

Agency Processes That May Yield Attempts at Judicial Review

In acting upon administrative issues put before them, judges are dealing with the outputs of previous agency action. Rule making is the favored subject of lawyer writers. Federal administrators may promulgate rules by announcing (or noticing) the subject matter of their inquiries, receiving comments, and publishing (or not publishing) final rules. The rules are law. Under some conditions, rule making requires that testimony be received and subjected to cross-examination, which is to say that the rule-making procedure should be *formal*. If comments are received otherwise, the procedure is called *informal*. Indeed, *informal action* may constitute the largest part of agency action.

Agencies do act by adjudication, more or less, as if they were courts. Administrators may use a wide variety of enforcement procedures, including fines and orders to cease and desist.

There is, finally, a latitude for action that depends upon personality, circumstances, and risk taking.[28] Norman Clapp, sometime administrator of the Rural Electrification Administration, once spoke proudly of his achievements in building physical facilities for rural telephone service. The historic fight between private investor interests and public revenue expenditure for electric service also extended to providing telephone service for rural areas. "I was the most sued Administrator in the history of REA," he said, "but we got those telephone lines built."[29]

Something similar is said about the personal determination of Joseph C. Swidler, chairman of the Federal Power Commission during the Kennedy and Johnson administrations. Swidler became famous for his vigorous persuasion in regulating the facilities and operations of the electric utilities. Swidler was concerned about the utilities maintaining an adequate capacity to produce and transmit power wherever it was needed. The 1965 Northeast power blackout heightened his concern, and indeed gave him explicit presidential sanction.[30] This was a jurisdiction in which he had relatively little authority, at least as reflected in express holdings by courts, and it is not clear how much additional authority he had because of presidential interest. By a great deal of informal persuasion (jawboning), using his limited authority and political influence, Swidler encouraged stronger agreements among electric companies to share and coordinate their physical facilities through power pools. He did not meet any direct opposition at the time, and it is interesting to speculate what he would have done if had there been rulings against him.

THE SCOPE OF REVIEW QUESTION

However formal or informal may be an agency action, on occasion a decision (or sometimes the absence of a decision) will result in a lawsuit. When some group finds a means to activate judicial review, there is the scope of review question: will the review be on the facts, the law, or both? And what, indeed, separates questions of fact from what is law? What will the reviewing courts take as their scope of consideration? Will the court insist upon "substantial" evidence to sustain an administrative decision? Will it accept the evidence of a single witness, or insist on evaluating the record as a whole? These technical questions of procedure are connected to substantive issues and, therefore, to the politics of an issue.

One crucial means of exercising judicial control over administrative action lies in deciding what evidence the agency must have to make its decision valid. In evidence, as in most human matters, one can speak of low, middle, and high standards. The high level is what is called the *preponderance of evidence* rule. A decision rests upon "evidence which is more credible and convincing to the mind . . . [or] that which best accords with reason and probability."[31] In lay terms, the preponderance standard says that a decision rests on the demonstrable superiority of the evidence. The low level is the *scintilla of evidence* rule, saying that if there is any evidence at all, the matter cannot be taken from the jury.[32] The middle level is the *substantial evidence* rule, substantial evidence being defined as such evidence as a reasonable mind might accept as adequate to support a conclusion.

Political scientists, and others, may note the lack of any effective citation by which to weigh the evidence. From the point of view of the exercise of power, what we note is the consequence of the rule. Reviewing courts have to decide what they will accept as a basis for affirming, deferring to, or otherwise handling an administrative agency's case. According to *Black's Law Dictionary*, substantial evidence

> is that quality of evidence necessary for a court to affirm an administrative board. Under the "substantial evidence rule," reviewing courts will defer to an agency determination so long as, upon an examination of the record as a whole, there is substantial evidence upon which the agency could reasonably base its decision.[33]

The discussion continues:

> Substantial evidence is evidence possessing something of substance and relevant consequence and which furnishes substantial basis of fact from which issues tendered can reasonably be resolved. Evidence which a reasoning mind would accept as sufficient to support a particular conclusion and consists of more than a mere scintilla of evidence but may be something less than a preponderance.[34]

The courts have considerable latitude in allowing review, particularly review under the statute. However, the judge has discretion to decide what these criteria mean to the problem, as framed in the pleadings. It is no longer presumed, as it used to be, that an administrative action cannot be reviewed. The contrary is true.

However, review may be precluded by the very words of the statute. The Veterans' Administration apparently thought, during the Vietnam War, that it stood a good chance of denying the claim of the conscientious objector to benefits, on the basis of the statutory language. Not so. The Supreme Court did uphold the VA's action on the merits. The decision means that there will be many other circumstances in which the VA will have to consider the merits issue more carefully before acting, because it does not have the automatic protection of the statute.

A similar case arose during the Vietnam War concerning a theology student who was opposed to the war.[35] The Supreme Court could have relied on statutory preclusion, but did not do so. When the case reached the Court, the decision was that "pre-induction judicial review is not precluded in this case." The draft board had no legislative authority to deny the exemption of a properly registered theology student simply because it did not like his beliefs or activities. Nor could it use "delinquency proceedings" to punish him by denying the exemption.

An administrator might take some comfort in the fact that only *final agency action* is reviewable.[36] This term is found in the Administrative Procedure Act. It appears to mean that if the agency has final authority to act without review, the administrator's action is home free. If the agency's action is reviewable, the court has to wait until action is final and not come tramping about at various stages before the agency decision is made. However, what is *final* is not so obvious. Even final agency action is subject to review if it is shown to be arbitrary, capricious, or an abuse of discretion.

Courts may shut out review on the basis that it is inherently unsuitable. The political questions doctrine may be traced back to 1841 and does not depend upon someone's ability to define *political*. It merely pertains to a situation or issue that the court believes it cannot effectively handle. In this respect, the courts may turn to a separation of powers test, which will allow them to say, "This matter is something better handled by the Congress or the president." The court may act on the basis that there are no judicially manageable standards or judicially enforceable remedies for handling the issue; on the basis of judicial discretion; on the basis that the matter in hand is foreign policy (as committed to the president and the Congress); or on the basis that it involves sovereign immunity.

It may that the test of being "policy committed to the president and Congress" is fairly explicit and has some identifiable content. This may also be true of matters involving the "sovereign immunity" test. On the other hand, it may be that *judicially manageable standards* or *judicially enforceable remedies* are prudential escape hatches for matters that a court may decide it does not know how to handle or a matter that the court may find too dangerous. Judges sometimes find the same problems as other decision makers: knowing when to run.

SCREENING

Even if a court is willing to admit that a matter is reviewable, screening procedures must be overcome—notably, criteria of standing, exhaustion, ripeness, and primary jurisdiction.

Exhaustion and the question of *ripeness* are screens that govern decisions, once a case is taken, regarding the universe of arguably "takable" cases. They are also rules of thumb to decide which cases are definitively reviewable and which are not.

The question of *primary jurisdiction* is another means of screening.[37] Primary jurisdiction answers, in lay terms, the question of who should decide first. The doctrine is typically raised not in a proceeding before an administrative agency, but in litigation before a court. Agency and court jurisdictions to resolve disputes and issues frequently overlap. Primary jurisdiction is a concept used by courts to allocate initial decision-making responsibility between agencies and courts where such overlaps exist.[38]

Primary jurisdiction is based on the principle that when an agency has been created as a reserve of expertise on a given subject, it should decide on the justiciable questions in which it is involved. Richard M. Travis characterizes primary jurisdiction as the idea that an agency, not the courts, should decide on contested substantive issues in which is implicated.

The first case to use the term *primary jurisdiction* was a 1910 Interstate Commerce Commission matter,[39] although the Supreme Court had actually deferred decision in railroad cases at least as early as 1908.[40] In more recent times, the courts have sometimes retrenched to a lesser degree by deferring to an agency proceeding if the agency's prior determination of one issue "would be of material aid to the court's decision-making on another issue."[41] An example was Ralph Nader's lawsuit against Allegheny Airlines in 1976. Nader was denied a seat on a flight from Washington to New England, where he was scheduled to give a speech, because the airline had a purposeful policy of over-booking, about which he had not been told. Nader sued, using the common-law basis of fraudulent misrepresentation, and won both compensatory and punitive damages. The case was appealed. The appellate court remanded the case to the trial court, saying that it should be stayed, or held up, until the matter could be sent to the Civil Aeronautics Board (CAB) under certain provisions of the Federal Aviation Act (FAA).

Nader had no desire to place the matter in the hands of the agency, and so appealed to the Supreme Court. Justice Powell wrote for a unanimous court that there was no irreconcilable conflict between the FAA and the common-law remedy, that the CAB had no power to immunize Allegheny Airlines, and that primary jurisdiction did not apply. Allegheny's "failure to disclose its overbooking practices implicates no tariff practice or similar technical question of fact uniquely within CAB's expertise."[42] (In regulated industries in the United States, tariffs are the published rates and terms of service. They are approved by the regulatory agency and may not be changed by the seller without approval.) In effect, Justice Powell said that overbooking was not a part of the tariff and that, accordingly, Allegheny Airlines could not claim a special need for CAB intervention.

Agencies are not necessarily anxious to assert primary jurisdiction; they are likely to have a severe overload of work already (see chapter 3). Moreover, asserting primary jurisdiction will not cause friends and adversaries involved in a case to focus any less attention on the agency in question than they did before.

This problem arose in the work of the Federal Energy Regulatory Commission (FERC) with regard to the natural gas industry. In the 1970s, the United States experienced a shortage of natural gas for interstate markets under federal price regulation. However, the pipeline companies had contractual commitments to provide gas to the major markets along the East Coast from New England to Florida, and elsewhere. When they were unable to bring enough gas to market, they adopted curtailment (rationing) schemes or curtailment plans that were approved by the Federal Power Commission (FPC) and were in effect when the FERC succeeded the FPC. Some customers, especially large industrial users, sought to sue the pipelines for breach of contract. The question arose whether the FERC should assert a claim of primary jurisdiction as the only agency with a comprehensive view of the whole gas industry. If it had done so, it would have asked the courts to defer their consideration of breach-of-contract litigation until the FERC had resolved the matter in its own mind. The commission decided not to make this claim.

At a later stage, in the 1980s, the FERC did try to make a primary jurisdiction claim in a case where a pipeline was sued by certain customers. Judge Gerhard Gesell, in the U.S. District Court for the District of Columbia, held that the FERC had delayed much too long in making the primary jurisdiction claim. As the *Wall Street Journal* reported,

> The ruling is a blow to the Federal Energy Regulatory Commission, which regulates gas pipelines. The courts ordinarily defer such questions to regulatory agencies responsible for them. But FERC and its predecessor, the Federal Power Commission, failed to act on Texas Gulf's complaints for almost 15 years. Continued deference to the commission, Judge Gesell ruled, "threatened to become an abdication of the duty of the court to decide the case."[43]

Most agency decision makers, most of the time, are not anxious to expand their agency's jurisdiction or to take on more difficult problems. If they are, however, they must consider how to frame their actions in a way that will pass muster if challenged.

These somewhat technical matters have been discussed to remind some political science teachers and lawyers, to identify for political science students, of the quality of these issues as matters in a power competition. This is necessary in order where some the data must be sought in study that is aimed to lead to an empirical political theory of administrative law.

Creating the Administrative Law System

To think about the politics of administrative law is also to think about change. The existing system is not from time immemorial, nor will it exist indefinitely. For that reason, we turn to a discussion of its history.

THE NINETEENTH-CENTURY BASELINE

The U.S. administrative law system is a twentieth-century product. The nineteenth century was quite otherwise. "The interference of the Court with the performance of the ordinary duties of the executive departments of the government would be productive of nothing but mischief; and this power was never intended to be given to them."[44] So spoke Chief Justice Roger Brooke Taney in 1840, when he declined to overrule a pension decision made by the secretary of the navy (*Decatur v. Paulding*, (14 Peters 497 [1840])).

Mrs. Decatur was the widow of Commodore Stephen Decatur, the hero of Tripoli. Congress had provided a pension for Mrs. Decatur specifically. On the same day, Congress had provided a general pension law for widows of naval officers. Mrs. Decatur made a claim to receive both pensions. As an administrative matter, the question could easily be conceived as to whether or not Congress meant her to share in the general plan and had merely granted her a special, additional benefit as a result of her husband's particular service to the nation and her own depressed circumstances. The secretary, a literary man named James Kirke Paulding, denied her claim.[45] The Supreme Court's opinion, written by Chief Justice Taney, specified three things the Court could not do. (1) It could not entertain an appeal arising from the decision of one of the secretaries. (2) It could not revise his judgment in any case where the law authorized him to exercise his discretion or judgment. (3) It could not, by mandamus, so act directly upon the officer, or guide or control his judgment or discretion in the matters committed to his care in the ordinary discharge of his official duties.[46]

In short, the Court took the position that it was precluded from doing anything. The voice of Jackson-era politics is shocking to the late twentieth-century political scientist, or to the editor who sees stories in the daily newspaper or on the television news about judicial decisions on such unexpected matters as government budget decisions.[47]

THE TWENTIETH-CENTURY SHIFT

Administrative law began to have substantial visibility no later than the decade following World War I. William A. Robson, an English lawyer, wrote in 1928, "By administrative law I understand the jurisdiction of judicial nature exercised by administrative agencies over the rights and property of citizens and corporate bodies."[48] He then quotes an American colleague. " 'Professor Frankfurter describes the administrative law as covering the fields of control exercised by law-administering agencies other than courts and the field of control exercised by courts." The system has changed so far since *Decatur* that Robson's characterization is almost obvious; Phillip Cooper stated in a 1983 textbook, "The availability of law courts for appeal and review of administrative actions is one of the primary underpinnings of the administrative justice system."

The Needs of the Bar as Part of U.S. Law Practice

The driving force turning administrative law from an academic idea to a practical result was the U.S. bar and its demand for judicial review of agency actions. As concept, administrative law came into American scholarship with the publication of Frank Goodnow's first book on the subject in 1893. Goodnow achieved dramatic results, however. Eighteen law classes had graduated by the time the entry *administrative law* appeared in the *Index to Legal Periodicals* in 1911. Lawyers did not worry too much about administrative action before World War I. Administrative law itself was suspect. Agencies were being given new functions, of course, particularly in economic regulation, but they were reviewed on the basis of whatever criteria seemed applicable to the courts, both state and federal. In his 1953 article, Kenneth Culp Davis stated, "Twenty years ago, the only instruction in administrative law was limited to a few seminars in a handful of leading law schools."[49] The center of gravity in the study of law is quite different from that of political science. Law is a practice profession, and few law students are interested in learning material for which there is little anticipated demand. When disputes still largely fell within the domain of the courts, clients demanded that their lawyers have administrative knowledge. Those courts were making important substantive decisions, often on the merits of what the agencies had decided. That is one reason why administrative law, as such, was a small matter for so long.

The spirit of Chief Justice Roger Brooke Taney ruled from the grave. The Supreme Court, and the courts below, scarcely changed their position on preclusion during the remainder of the nineteenth century. Judge Richard A. Posner reports that the Court of Appeals for the Seventh Circuit (Illinois and the upper Great Lakes region) devoted 1 percent of its actions to administrative cases in the twenty-year period 1882–1911. Additional studies suggest that other circuits were similar.[50] But the change in lawyers' interest might have been foreshadowed. The reason was that the Supreme Court began to change the basic rules. It showed a willingness to presume that it could review administrative action.

The particular case was heard in 1902, when the Supreme Court ruled against the postmaster general. The case was *American School of Magnetic Healing v. McAnulty* 187 U.S. 94, 103. Advertisements for the American School of Magnetic Healing stated: "The mind of the human race is largely responsible for its ills, and is a perceptible factor in the healing, curing, benefiting and remedying thereof and that the human race does possess the innate power through the proper exercise of the faculty of the brain and mind, to largely control and remedy the ills that humanity is heir to."[51] The firm claimed that its methods "discard and eliminate what is commonly known as Christian Science, and they are confined to practical scientific treatment." To all this the postmaster general said, in effect, "Nonsense." Thus, he took the action to interdict the flow of mail.

The Court said that the post office could try to develop a fraud case if it wished, but it could not declare the "magnetic healing" material fraudulent merely because it disagreed with it. Thus, it had to allow the material to go through the mails.

> While the conduct of the post office is a part of the administrative department of the Government, that fact does not always oust the courts of jurisdiction to grant relief to a party aggrieved by any action, by the head, or one of the subordinate officials of that department, which is unauthorized by the statute under which he assumes to act.[52]

The Supreme Court could have chosen to follow the criterion it specified in the *Decatur* case. If it had done so, the school of magnetic healing would have been out of business. The postmaster general did have statutory powers to prevent the use of the mail for fraud, and it was not imperative for the Court to block his decisions.

The shift continued. Managerial discretion was under some challenge even in Republican administrations. It would be ridiculous to think of business as a suspect category during the administration of Warren G. Harding. But the conflict between one set of interests and another could produce momentous action.

A particular illustration is a case (*Morgan v. United States*, 298 U.S. 468, 1936) brought in a Republican administration and conducted by the Department of Agriculture under Presidents Harding, Coolidge, and Hoover. It concerned price regulation in the nation's stockyards. The stockyards operators were large investors with enormous facilities in places like Kansas City and Chicago and quasi-monopolistic bargaining power over the farmers and ranchers in the surrounding hinterlands. The secretary of agriculture had some authority, under the Packers and Stockyards Act of 1921, to set the prices that stockyards operators charged customers who brought animals to market and who needed a place to hold them until they could be sold or transferred. This was somewhat analogous to utility regulation. Over a protracted period—more than ten years—there was intensive litigation about the *Morgan* case, since the Bureau of Animal Industries, the departmental unit responsible for initially investigating and suggesting that prices should be lowered, was also the unit that organized the data and made price recommendations to the secretary.

The Seventh Circuit in 1932–1941 devoted 32 percent of its actions to administrative review. These were the New Deal years, when controversy was most vigorous over the role of government in the economy, and the Seventh

Circuit drew its cases from the industrial center of the nation, where many such conflicts arose.

THE TRANSATLANTIC COMMUNITY OF IDEAS

The intellectual process within the bar was greatly influenced by outside experience. The administrative law idea came into American practice because of an unusual intellectual collaboration between the legal professions of the United Kingdom and the United States. American legal scholars have long been impressed by the romance of their intellectual descent from English common law, which led them to draw lessons about how to handle the emerging problem of government intervention.[53]

Gordon Hewart, who was made lord chief justice in 1922, was a key figure in the rearguard defense against the growing body of administrative law. Hewart's essential criticism was that government ministries were involved in secret decision making: affected private parties could not know who, in fact, had decided their claims or on what basis. This amounted to decisions made in secret, by no regular procedure or rules of evidence, by civil servants who were subject to being fired at a moment's notice. He argued that they were not free agents and the process was unfair. Hewart went on to expand his bill of particulars:

> It is, apparently, quite unusual for interested parties even to be permitted to have an interview with anyone in the department. When there is an oral hearing, the public and the press are invariably excluded. Finally, it is not usual for the official to give any reasons for his decisions.[54]

The administrative practice in effect made a fiction of the claim of ministerial responsibility under which powers were being delegated by Parliament. Ultimately, Hewart used the term *administrative lawlessness*. The prestige of the lord chief justice was a great asset to those who held to the older pattern. It was joined, however lightly, to another factor that was not logically essential to Hewart's attack, but was certainly politically connected. The administrative discretion that he attacked was to a degree associated with implementation of the social legislation that had come into Britain under the Liberal government. Mitigation of misery and discontent was a big issue for the Liberals (Henry Campbell-Bannerman, Herbert H. Asquith, David Lloyd-George, and even Winston Churchill temporarily) and even for one segment of the Conservatives (as represented by Joseph Chamberlain). In the last decade of the twentieth century there may be little recollection of the controversies associated with its first two decades.[55]

The most conservative viewers saw the widening of administrative discretion, and of law that permitted it, as a severe threat to monetary and social stability. This fear, we see in retrospect, was much exaggerated. But Hewart was received as a voice against the threatening trend.

Hewart's formulation reflected a developing community of ideas among Anglo-American lawyers regarding government intervention in the market and, thus, administrative constraints on the market. Hewart was invited at least twice to deliver speeches to the American Bar Association's annual meetings. Very similar ideas were expressed, about the same time, by U.S. lawyers in the 1920s and the 1930s.

One was James M. Beck, who had been solicitor general of the United States in the Harding and Coolidge administrations (1921–1925).[56] At the end of the Hoover administration and prior to the New Deal, Republican presidential candidates had won six out of eight presidential elections. Congress was usually controlled by Republicans, yet in 1932 Beck characterized the whole tendency of government as socialist. After discussing various issues related to government agencies' ability to promulgate rules with the force of law and to interpret and carry them out, Beck concluded:

> May not the proper solution . . . lie in the enactment of a general statute, which would permit review in the courts of any decision of an administrative officer of the government on both the law and the facts? To hear and determine all such cases there should be an administrative court. As the Courts of Appeal and Supreme Court could not congest their calendars by such litigation, the decision of such administrative court— consisting of judges learned in the law, and independent of all executive departments—should be final.[57]

The administrative court idea had been conceived by Goodnow at least as early as 1903.[58] But it did not then fit into any practical situation. Beck conceived of an administrative court that would review all agency decisions on questions of law and of fact. Such a court, proceeding case by case, would have immobilized government as it then was emerging. Beck would no doubt have found this a satisfactory result. The administrative court was the conservative defense against administrative action under laws that Congress might adopt.

CONFLICT BETWEEN GOVERNMENT INTERVENTION AND MANAGERIAL PREROGATIVE IN BUSINESS

The present system of American administrative law reflects a passage of ideas across the Atlantic and arises primarily from the sharp conflict between the prerogatives of private business and government intervention in the economy. The older, adversarial system was essentially a noninterventionist system. Government administrators did not try to second-guess private decision makers. Only when the latter fell into conflict and came to court were public decisions made, on issues already defined by the private interests.

However, legislatures did grant administrators more explicit latitude, and courts sanctioned that latitude. As relatively more administrative decision making became acceptable to the courts, then there was a demand for a more regular decision-making procedure. Much of this activity initially occurred in state governments, especially in the regulation of public utilities, although some also came under federal jurisdiction. Once the courts made administrative decision making legitimate, the issue became procedural. Administrative procedure, writes Verkuil, was "ironically, both an adjunct to and a reaction against economic regulation. It developed as much from deeply felt objections to government interference with the marketplace as from the necessity to make that interference coherent and credible."[59]

In the 1930s, there was some hope, outside the business community, that "public control of private business" would produce an orderly and intelligent result, on the thesis that it would prevent anything like the 1929 Depression from happening again. Administrative constraints on the market meant control over decisions made by private managers. In this era the concept of purposeful economic planning was both attractive and reasonable, especially in contrast to the wide latitude given to business before that time.

All this must be kept in perspective, of course. Some degree of administrative constraint had existed before. Banks began to be regulated in the 1860s. Railroads came under the authority of the Interstate Commerce Commission by the act of 1887. Food and drug legislation established some regulation at the beginning of the twentieth century. Nonetheless, managerial prerogative enjoyed remarkable freedom before the 1930s. Executives had virtually unlimited power to decide the levels of profit that they would seek, what investments they would engage in, or how much information they would divulge to shareholders. If the *Morgan* case was troublesome, from a business viewpoint the New Deal soon proved far more so.

Roosevelt vigorously asserted government power, and his administration placed decisional authority in a variety of government agencies. His course of action was severely contested by the American Bar Association. This was a part of the role of the ABA's Special Committee on Administrative Law (1934), the concepts of which have passed into common intellectual currency. The controversy was incredibly intense and bitter. Today political scientists correctly note the conservatism of Franklin D. Roosevelt, but at that time the business community scarcely regarded Roosevelt as conservative.

The intensity of the controversy is not surprising. First, there had never been such an acute threat that business's protected terrain would be subjected to various legislative and administrative controls. Within five years, Congress had adopted five new pieces of legislation regarding the securities industry: the 1933 Securities Act requiring that detailed information be made public regarding the issue of new corporate securities; the 1934 act imposing similar requirements regarding the issue of existing securities; the 1935 Public Utilities Holding Company Act, which required the breakup of certain large interstate public utility holding companies that dominated the electric power business— a bill that Sam Rayburn sponsored and described as the toughest fight of his life;[60] the Maloney Act regulating the over-the-counter securities market; and the Glass-Steagall Act requiring the separation of commercial banking from investment banking.[61]

Implementation of this legislation proceeded first through the Federal Trade Commission and then through the Securities and Exchange Commission, the latter chaired successively by Joseph P. Kennedy, James M. Landis, and William O. Douglas. The intellectual merit of this legislation is now under serious challenge, as far as the Glass-Steagall Act is concerned.[62] (The electric power legislation was decisively modified by the Energy Policy Act of 1992.) Meritorious or deficient, this legislation, notably the Holding Company Act, was very controversial at the time. Those who opposed it must have opposed its implementation as well. The major agencies of the New Deal, carrying out such decisions, were seen as making a critical assault on the prerogative of private business management.

In the second place, Roosevelt's 1936 campaign speeches were strong and minatory. A president who stated that "government by organized money" was as bad as "government by organized mobs" threatened a business elite accustomed to respect that was now greeted with contempt and hostility. Roosevelt told the 1936 Democratic convention that in his first administration the "economic royalists" had met their match. In the second, they would meet their master. The record shows resounding cheers from the assembled Democrats.[63]

The Administrative Court as an Instrument for Conservative Counterattack

Between the methods of the New Deal agencies, which may have seemed rather limited to those who practiced them, and the normal disposition of the business community and its influence with the bar, conflict was inevitable.

The president's attempt to assert more control over the regulatory agencies induced counterpressures.[64] Roosevelt's approach would have minimized congressional influence on the agencies. (Congress, especially one in which conservatives were very influential, would predictably resist such reduction.) Congressional conservatives were aligned with the business community, which objected to the possibility that agencies would be used to carry out the executive's (Roosevelt's) policies. Against potential administrative agents, the organized bar sought a sure defense.

The idea of an administrative court became the instrument for the conservative counterattack. The Special Committee on Administrative Law had, in Roosevelt first term, proposed to transfer the regulatory agencies' legislative and administrative functions to the regular departments, to create no more agencies, and to give the regulatory agencies' judicial powers to the administrative court. The conservatives' concern was more intense because the Supreme Court had also lowered its resistance to Roosevelt. The Court, with a shifting majority, could no longer be assumed to support the rights of property.

The struggles over implementing securities legislation, however, were mild compared to the struggles over labor laws. Management's prerogative to control company labor policy was, before the 1930s, similar to managerial prerogative over company financial policy. Business executives had, subject to the constraints of any labor agreements they might make, virtually unlimited power to hire and fire workers and to set rates of pay and work conditions.

A struggle between labor and management had been going on, more or less, since the celebrated strike year of 1877. Strikes ran throughout the industrial system, even when unemployment exceeded 10 percent. The primary dispute was over labor's recurrent efforts to establish unions and the right to bargain collectively with their employers. In the struggle, businesses generally enjoyed the upper hand during periods of unemployment, though this fluctuated. Management also had the advantage that unions were attempting to bargain over contracts, a right that could not easily be won in a civil court, where presumptions regarding contracts tended to favor management.[65] Indeed, among other objectives, power to hire and fire, and under what conditions, had long been used to block efforts at unionization. For their part, unions sought to gain some degree of control over the hiring, pay, conditions of work, and firing of workers, just as management sought to keep such power in its own hands.

Beneath this more formal surface was a complex world of reality: armed with superior financial power, management had could influence local courts and judges, had greater access to National Guard and police forces for strikebreaking, and could hire private industrial police.[66] The firms did not always win. The United Mine Workers had become an organization of some consequence even before the New Deal, and as early as 1881 an array of craft-based unions had formed the foundation of the American Federation of Labor (AFL).

The New Deal emergency measures began to give public sanction to collective bargaining. That sanction was written into the statutes as the National Labor Relations Act (the Wagner Act) of 1937. The central policy was union recognition, based on representation elections, and collective bargaining as a legal requirement.[67]

Administration of this law came under the jurisdiction of the National Labor Relations Board (NLRB). The NLRB had to deal with numerous technical issues. There was elaborate debate about what constituted an appropriate bargaining unit, what were the rights of employers when other entities were agitating to organize their employees. One important fight concerned whether organizations that were created more or less under company sponsorship, or company unions, could validly represent a firm's employees in collective bargaining. Organized labor solidly opposed bargaining through company unions. A very significant issue that divided the union movement was whether employees should be organized on a craft basis (as with electricians), or on an industry basis (as in the meatpacking industry). Craft unions formed the core of the older American Federation of Labor, whereas the latter principle became the basis for unions in the automobile, steel, meatpacking, and other industries.

The NLRB appointed by President Roosevelt, and its staff, were subject to a wide variety of accusations. Firms were strongly opposed to union representation for their workers, whereas the administration clearly favored unionization. The contention was that the NLRB was friendlier to labor than to management and that it bent its procedures accordingly. In their counterattack, business firms acted through their allies in Congress. The administrative procedures of the NLRB, and presumed favoritism toward the newer unions, provided the rationale for their opposition.

In 1935 Rep. Howard W. Smith of Virginia introduced House Resolution 258, for the purpose of investigating the National Labor Relations Board.

Senator Burke of Nebraska introduced a bill to investigate the National Labor Relations Board in 1938; the investigation was authorized and a few hearings were held. In addition, in 1939, thousands of pages of testimony were taken before the Senate Committee on Education and Labor and the

House Committee on Labor relative to the various bills proposing amendments to the National Labor Relations Act.[68]

Thomas D. Thacher, sometime federal district judge and solicitor general during the Hoover administration (1930–1933), probably spoke for many members of the bar when he said he felt "an acute sense of disgust" with NLRB practices.

The Brownlow Committee report of 1937 was an important factor in developing the later doctrines of administrative law. Administrative law became one of the major forums used by the conservative coalition to redefine debate on how government should work and—by so doing—determined much of what it would do. The NLRB became the foil for proposed legislation on administrative procedure after 1937. In 1938 the Senate Committee on the Judiciary held hearings on the proposed creation of an administrative court. In 1939, the Walter-Logan bill, proposing to create an administrative court (an idea advanced by James Beck) was first reported favorably to the Senate. This bill, the subject of intense debate, became a major symbol in the clash between pro–New Deal and anti–New Deal factions. The struggle went on through most of 1940, a version of the bill having been passed in 1939 in the Senate after the usual legislative maneuvers. Rep. Eugene E. Cox, a notably conservative Georgian, announced an attack on the administrative agencies. Sam Rayburn, then chairman of the Interstate and Foreign Commerce Committee, opposed the Walter-Logan bill in debate and supported the administration. Rayburn had, after all, sponsored the Natural Gas Act of 1938 and the Public Utility Holding Company Act, both of which vested substantial powers in administrative agencies. He regarded the passage of the Utility Holding Company Act as one of the most difficult struggles of his career.[69]

House committee action on the Walter-Logan bill took place in February and April 1940, with approval by the House rules committee on February 8. Action then moved to the Senate, after which the House then passed an amended version. From Brookings came a report defending the regulatory agencies and opposing the bill. Arthur Krock, Washington correspondent for the *New York Times*, maintained a steady drum roll of comment. John L. Lewis, then very powerful as president of the United Mine Workers, opposed the bill. So did the left-wing National Lawyers' Guild. Chambers of commerce and Wall Street lawyers were generally supportive. Sen. Sherman Minton (Indiana), one of the hard-core New Dealers, said: "The bill was not written by a Senator, or by the Senate; it was written by a committee of the American Bar Association, who through paid lobbyists, put it in the hopper of the

Senate Judiciary Committee." There was a split among Democratic leaders, but opponents were apparently able to overcome the resistance of Democratic leader Alben W. Barkley.

The bill passed the Senate without discussion on November 26, by a vote of 27 to 25, with 44 absent or not voting. The House concurred in certain Senate amendments on December 6, 1940, by a vote of 236 to 51; 148 members did not vote.

Attorney General Robert H. Jackson wrote a brief to support a veto, and the president did what he had apparently indicated he would do all along. He vetoed the Walter-Logan bill. The president said that litigation was too expensive, that the procedures already being used eliminated legalism, and that the bill served "vested interests." The bill's sponsors had the support of a majority of those voting in the House but could not secure the constitutional two-thirds required to override. More than a third of House members had not voted at all. Were they away on holiday? Even if nonvoting members had divided in the same proportion as those who voted, the override vote would have still fallen short of the required number. The issue was settled as World War II came to the United States. Wartime is not a favorable period in which to speak about restricting the power of administrative agencies.

The Roosevelt administration took cognizance of the political problem by a side-stepping move. In 1938 Roosevelt adopted the damage-containment strategy of the Committee on Administrative Procedure. While this committee, the source of a very influential report, is known as the Attorney General's Committee on Administrative Procedure, it was truly the president's move. "I directed the attorney general to select a committee of eminent lawyers, jurists, scholars and administrators . . . to review the whole situation as to administrative procedure." Final decisions on the administrative structure should await the report of this attorney general's committee.

Presumably, this committee was meant to perform something of a bridging function—a reasonable speculation, given the appointment of Dean Acheson as its chairman. Acheson had been undersecretary of the treasury briefly until he resigned in opposition to the president's wish to change the price of gold in 1934. Roosevelt deemed this a necessary measure to fight the Depression, while Acheson—on a different wavelength—maintained that it simply violated the law. When the Securities and Exchange Commission (SEC) launched a big investigation of the New York Stock Exchange (NYSE), Acheson had been the NYSE counsel. William O. Douglas describes Acheson as one of the conservative forces of the New Deal. Douglas meant the term unfavorably. Choosing such a chairman doubtless gave credibility to a committee about which many people in the business community and their legal advisers might have been suspicious.

The attorney general's committee issued a report in 1941. When administrative procedure legislation was on the agenda after the war, this report became an important factor in the development of the later doctrines on administrative law. When the war was over, the issue of how to govern agency decision making came back to the Congress. The Supreme Court showed signs of deferring to administrative agencies. Justice Felix Frankfurter had long championed the idea of giving agencies wide scope, and his opinion in *FCC v. Pottsville* (1940) said clearly that the court was not the place to second-guess the Federal Communications Commission. The forum was different. So were the circumstances. Franklin Delano Roosevelt was dead on April 12, 1945. The more conservative political atmosphere of the immediate postwar period presumably rendered the issue of increased judicial review over administrative agencies more persuasive. Vincent Barnett wrote in 1948:

> As the Supreme Court in the past ten years or so has taken a more and more sympathetic attitude toward administrative problems and towards the breadth of administrative discretion, both in interpreting the law and in fact finding, those who had been the staunchest supporters of the judiciary vis-à-vis administrative action have turned to the legislature to force the courts to "do their duty" in controlling the administration.[70]

The Administrative Procedure Act of 1946 seems, against this experience, like a ritually agreed-upon solution. It provided a compromise settlement to the old battles between those who wanted to enhance the government's role in the economy and those who wanted to maintain the widest managerial discretion in the private sector. It did not, and could not, overcome basic conflicts. It provided instead new procedural bottles into which the old wine of conflict would be poured.

Conclusion

What we seek is an empirical theory, subject to testing, of the conditions and consequences of administrative law. Political scientists need to explore competing models of the administrative law system. The predominant model is that contained in judicio-political theory. We suggest, in addition, a closer consideration of the potential relationship between political science and administrative law, and particularly an emphasis on interest group models.

Such an approach also entails an acute examination of the forms and realities of administrative law. Seven interconnected topics warrant attention for the political action manifest in them and the political consequences arising from them.

1. The authority on which judicial review of agency action is undertaken requires attention. Broadly, the articulated authority is grounded in the Constitution, in statutes, or in agency rules.

2. Investigating the dynamics of judicial review means asking who is doing the reviewing. This means both a formal appreciation and a consideration of the exchanges within the system from the Supreme Court on down through the circuit courts of appeal and the district courts.

3. How are disputes articulated? Scholars must pay close attention to the vocabulary of administrative law. Examining the words, phrases, and how they are employed in context will help political scientists to comprehend the debate and assess what tactics are being pursued.

4. Reviewability is a crucial issue—whether a court can review a given issue. What are the criteria of reviewability, what discretion does a judge have to accept or deny review, and what consequences follow for affected groups?

5. The scope of review question presents itself: is this a review of the law? Is it a review of the facts? Is it both?

6. Even if a court is willing to admit that a matter is reviewable, screening procedures must be overcome. Questions raised by screening are the tests of *standing, exhaustion, ripeness,* and *primary jurisdiction.*

7. Finally, there are questions of rule making, adjudication, and informal action as the broad categories of administrative agency action. These are the agency action processes that may yield attempts at judicial review.

It seems useful, as well, to bring the U.S. system into perspective by examining how the present federal administrative system was created. The current view is as follows.

1. The courts abandoned the old conceptual baseline, by beginning to exercise review over administrative decisions around the turn of the twentieth century.

2. The bar played a significant intellectual and practical role in developing the concepts and a climate that would favor judicial review.

3. The bar then became notably sensitive to the importance of the conflict between government intervention and private business prerogative.

4. The concept of an administrative court—initially put forth by Goodnow on merit grounds—took on active political life only when it was seen as limiting the power of government.

5. This concept came notably into play when the Roosevelt administration was at its height and business seized upon the administrative court as a means to constrain government interference.

The driving force turning administrative law from an academic idea to a practical result was the American bar and its demand for judicial review of agency actions. The present system of U.S. administrative law reflects a passage of ideas across the Atlantic and arises primarily from the sharp conflict between the prerogative of business and government intervention in the economy. In this process, the Administrative Procedure Act may be seen as a ritual solution to an important problem.

The question, now, is how to think about and evaluate the workings of the new system. Any mode of interpretation that comes from the law we characterize as dogma. But this is not to call the law a bad name; it is a comment on the claims of those who are unwilling to reexamine the foundations of a proposition. Faith in dogma is a means of controlling the disturbance created by dealing with simultaneously contradictory beliefs and claims.

As an alternative, there is some hope for an empirical political theory of administrative law. Such a theory has to explain the social forces that produce a given system—in the present case the system created in the United States in the twentieth century. It has to explain how the system may be adapted, or not, to interests quite different from those for whom the system was generated. It should be grounded in—and in turn guide—research and interpretations of how the administrative law system actually works. Present models do not provide much guidance as to how far the administrative system is actually penetrated by administrative law controversies, what agencies are affected, what proportion of the applicable statutes are affected, to what extent there is either overt defiance or systematic avoidance of legal decisions, or even whether the courts know what they are doing when they issue orders.

In some degree, this problem was anticipated in Kenneth Culp Davis's celebrated article. The empirical theory must encompass how decisions are made about policy (choice of broad objectives to guide other people's behavior), about program (choice of specified actions taken within that policy), and about operational detail (what actions will facilitate the program). Davis specified his concern in an elaborate—some would say overelaborate—research agenda. His question may be summarized as follows: (1) To what extent are legislative choices nullified by administrative failures? (2) To what extent do regulated groups control the regulators? (3) To what extent, if at all, do regulatory agencies represent an otherwise unprotected public interest? How can the regulatory process be made more successful—or less unsuccessful—in carrying out the will of the people's representatives?[71] This is essentially the question now framed in "implementation" terms.

When questions rise to the level of judicial decision through review of administrative action, a meaningful theory must assume that judges prefer success to failure, or effectiveness to vitiation. Therefore, we expect (or predict) that they will desire administrative choices in line with their own preferences as manifested in their orders. Since administrative decision makers will differ in knowledge, values, convenience, estimates of capacity, and so forth, they will sometimes, wittingly and unwittingly, do things they would not have been directed to do if they had been before the court. They will neglect what they had been instructed to do. Therefore, the theory should also expect (or predict) an off-and-on set of perturbations, sometimes a definite struggle, for control in the successive linkages of programs, policies, and operational details. The decisional premises of the courts and the decisional premises of successive administrators at various points down the line may vary.

5

DOGMA, INTERESTS, AND
ADMINISTRATIVE LAW AS
POLITICS, II

The Old Wine of Dispute Is Poured into the New Bottle of Procedure

The traditional model of administrative law, as described by Richard B. Stewart, expressed the moral claims of the conservatives.[1] They expected that the courts would be their shield and protector. They were disillusioned when the Supreme Court, moderating its opposition to Roosevelt, gave wider latitude to administrative agencies. As C. A. Miller, a railroad attorney, expressed it in 1947:

> It seemed necessary to the welfare of mankind that we be saved from these
> administrative agencies. . . . When our own United States Court of
> Appeals for the District of Columbia attempted to curb these agencies, the
> Supreme Court of the United States would reverse it, and give the agencies
> full authority to go merrily on its sinful ways.[2]

Miller's complaint is a prototype for the conservative expectation as to what changes in administrative law, expressed in the Administrative Procedure Act, was supposed to yield.

The result has been different, and great turbulence has emerged. The argument is essentially as follows.

1. Interests are fundamental and do not die because of a change in positive law. The Administrative Procedure Act, as used by parties and sanctioned by the courts, created "new bottles," new modes of action, into which the "old wine," old and continuing disputes, were poured. This is illustrated both in

the case of labor conflict, as expressed in *Universal Camera*, where the technical issue is what constitutes substantial evidence for an agency decision, and in pricing policy, as expressed in issues about natural gas rule making.

2. New interests are always emerging, and the system cannot be limited to initial purposes. Administrative law questions have spread far beyond the issues of labor regulation or of traditional microeconomic regulation. This is shown in the treatment of nuclear power plant construction, on the one hand, versus social benefits issues, on the other.

3. As a result, the courts become increasingly assimilated to the substantive problems so they are more closely related to the administrative agencies over which they claim jurisdiction. In a sense, the courts themselves approximate administrative agencies in their decision making.

4. The end result is that the making and alteration of administrative law itself reveals a political system of which we have often been unaware, half closed and conducting its business in "professional" and "conceptual" language as if the standards were open and accepted by all, and half open by the impact of interest groups made operational through the partisan relationship.

The Administrative Procedure Act of 1946 brought the country closer and closer to an administrative court. It also moved the agencies farther and farther from the wide discretion that was originally asserted to be their forte. Those who used the act enforced it—to speak of the principles of administrative law referred to by Richard Stewart—with the essential feature being the convenience of the court. This is not simply judicial review, but a variety of methods that make judicial review the open-ended vehicle by which the court can choose to either impose or withhold a judgment, to maintain a course of action or alter that course of action. At the same time, the new arrangement was far from the device proposed by James Beck in 1932—an administrative court—that would have virtually immobilized government.[3]

Deference to Agency as Deference to Congress

Deferring to the administrative agencies soon appeared to be an unstable principle. What became apparent was that such deference was judicial acknowledgment of political realities, as expressed in recent litigation. This was displayed in an opinion by Justice Frankfurter in the *Universal Camera* case of 1951.[4]

Conflict between management and the labor unions was particularly bitter in this case. The investigations of the 1930s, mass union pressure through strikes, and the Wagner Act establishing the National Labor Relations Board, all put limits on business managers' old prerogative to hire and fire workers as they pleased. The atmosphere was also affected by charges leveled by business and its friends in the legal community that the National Labor Relations Board staff was partial to unions and exercised administrative discretion in their favor. The power of labor unions was signified, to the dissatisfaction of the business community, by the active role of labor leaders in the Democratic party in 1944. Public relations and public opinion were also affected by the realism of the United Mine Workers, then led by John L. Lewis, in pursuing its members' self-interest at the cost of great pain to virtually all other parties. In those days, when coal was the prime fuel source, a coal strike could close virtually all operations across the country, and Lewis was not a leader to shrink from battle. This background should remind us that some apparently abstract issues have meaning only in their social context.

The external atmosphere of labor-management strife, as reflected in the congressional claim that the National Labor Relations Board was too friendly to unions, became the rationale for a stricter approach to controlling government agencies in the 1940s. The question became: what standard of evidence should a reviewing court pursue and how deeply will the reviewing court go into matters covered by the administrative agency and into those the agency does not consider?

As we saw in chapter 4, a crucial means of exercising judicial control over administrative action lies in deciding what evidence the agency must have to assure the validity of its decisions. At the highest level, decisions rest on a "preponderance of evidence," or "evidence which is more credible and convincing to the mind . . . [or] best accords with reason and probability."[5] At the next level is the substantial evidence rule. At the lowest level is "the scintilla of evidence rule," meaning that if there is any evidence at all, the case must go before a jury.[6]

In the *Universal Camera* case the court had to consider how to apply the substantial evidence rule. This was not an exercise in a seminar; the court was dealing with problems of power in the real world of industry and politics. The case was decided on the basis of events that occurred before 1950, not long after Congress adopted the 1947 Taft-Hartley, which drastically shifted the legal balance of power in favor of management over organized labor. In the *Universal Camera* case, an employee had been fired for giving information to the National Labor Relations Board. (The regulatory process is nullified if the agency does not receive realistic information about the work environment.)

The employee complained that the firing was retaliatory, whereas the employer said that he was fired for giving information. The NLRB held for the employee, giving him what is now called whistle-blower protection. However, in doing so, the NLRB also set aside the report of the trial examiner, which did not support this action.

Justice Frankfurter's opinion in this case reflects his awareness of congressional hostility to the NLRB:

> It is fair to say that by imperceptible steps regard for the fact-finding function of the Board led to the assumption that the requirements of the Wagner Act [the statute under which the NLRB functioned until 1947] were met when the reviewing court could find in the record evidence which, when viewed in isolation, substantiated the Board's findings. . . . Criticism of so contracted a reviewing power reinforced dissatisfaction felt in various quarters with the Board's administration of the Wagner Act in the years preceding [World War II].

This is remarkable language from a lawyer who had earlier made a reputation for knowledge of the administrative process and of public utilities. Frankfurter had long championed the wide scope and expertise of administrative agencies, as shown in his opinion in *FCC v. Pottsville* (1940). Frankfurter found a fig leaf of exculpation in his case materials. Basically, what he now said was, "We are doing this because Congress is making us do it." In his words,

> The scheme of the Act was attacked as an inherently unfair fusion of the functions of prosecutor and judge. Accusations of partisan bias were not wanting. The "irresponsible admission and weighing of hearsay, opinion, and emotional speculation in place of factual evidence" was said to be a "serious menace." No doubt some, perhaps even much, of the criticism was baseless and some surely was reckless.

Note that Justice Frankfurter does not adopt those allegations as his own.

> What is here relevant, however, is the climate of opinion thereby generated and its effect on Congress. Protests against "shocking injustices" and intimations of judicial "abdication" with which some courts granted enforcement of the Board's orders stimulated pressures for legislative relief from alleged administrative excesses.

The opinion also shows Frankfurter's conclusion that Congress had, in the Taft-Hartley Act, so changed the statute that a tougher interpretation of substantial evidence would have to be followed.

The Administrative Procedure Act and the Taft-Hartley Act direct that courts must now assume more responsibility for the reasonableness and fairness of Labor Board decisions than some courts have done in the past. . . . Congress has imposed on them the responsibility for assuring that the Board keeps within reasonable grounds. . . . The Board's findings are entitled to respect; but they must nonetheless be set aside when the record before a Court of Appeals clearly precludes the Board's decision from being a fair estimate of the worth of the testimony of witnesses or its informed judgment on matters within its special competence or both.

In the *Universal Camera* case, we see the effectiveness of congressional intervention. The Supreme Court was pushed to adopt a scope of review it did not want.

High-Intensity Rule Making: The Natural Gas War

Many who deal with administrative issues argue that agencies should make broad policy decisions by rules, rather than case-specific adjudication. However, after virtually half a century's experience under the Administrative Procedure Act, one may question whether there is a significant difference. The phrase *rule making* in federal practice is now a noun, so that people can speak of "a rule making." If a party or group deems itself threatened or injured by a court suit, it will react. In other words, what counts is how important an issue is to the group, its motivation to get into the issue, and its resources in terms of skill, money, knowledge, and time to pursue it. A group will be scarcely less involved if the matter at hand has the same intensity level when subject to rule making. An illustration is the Federal Power Commission's experience with rule making regarding the pricing of natural gas.

The natural gas industry, which began to develop in the 1920s and 1930s, consists of those who bring gas to the surface (the producers); the business ventures that go into the field, get gas, and move it, often over very long distances (the pipelines); and the businesses that sell to the customer or user (the distribution companies). This industry was the scene of an intense, protracted controversy between producer interests and end-user interests.

The Natural Gas Act of 1938 was committed to the jurisdiction of the Federal Power Commission (FPC). Originally, it was interpreted as applying only to interstate pipelines. In the exact words of section 1(b):

The provisions of this act shall apply to the transportation of natural gas in interstate commerce, to the sale in interstate commerce of natural gas for resale for ultimate public consumption for domestic, commercial, industrial, or any other use, and to natural-gas companies engaged in such transportation or sale.

The same sentence states that the provision "shall not apply to any other transportation or sale of natural gas or to the local distribution or to the production or gathering of natural gas." The initial position of the commission, and of Chairman Leland Olds, was that the FPC did not have any authority over prices charged to pipelines by producers, also known as field prices or wellhead prices. (Chairman Olds later showed signs of changing his mind. His change of mind led to a political massacre.)[7]

However, eventually the Federal Power Commission, under judicial direction in the *Phillips Petroleum v. Wisconsin* case (the *Phillips* decision, 1954), had authority. In a matter that fits the interest-group hypothesis,[8] the city of Detroit and the state of Wisconsin, representing residential customer interests in the pipeline company's area, asked the Federal Power Commission to investigate and determine if a particular price increase was "just and reasonable" under the Natural Gas Act. What they really meant was that they found the price increase unjust and unreasonable.

The case arose from a dispute about an escalator clause in contracts to supply gas. An event occurred that allowed Phillips Petroleum to believe it could raise its price to the pipeline company that served Michigan and Wisconsin. The proviso stated that if the pipeline company did not have its lines built to a certain point by a designated date, the price would escalate. (Apparently no one knew why the proviso was there or ever believed the events causing the escalation would occur.)[9] The escalation did occur. Wisconsin and Detroit made their request, and the FPC said it would not handle it on the grounds that it lacked authority. Wisconsin and Detroit then challenged the FPC in court. In the end, the U.S. Supreme Court said that the FPC did have such jurisdiction and that in order to do its job it would have to regulate field prices. (This later came to be so much a liberal-conservative issue in domestic politics that it is interesting that Justice William O. Douglas was one of the dissenters in that case. Perhaps the reason was that, whatever his stance, Douglas was also an expert in business organization and had some sense of operating realities.)

Organized consumer groups with access to congressional members from urban industrial areas of the Middle West and Northeast, acted in just the opposite manner.

One result of the *Phillips* case was to initiate a protracted legislative fight over natural gas pricing policy. As a side issue, producers, using their access to Congress, especially in contacts with the Texas, Oklahoma, and Louisiana congressional delegations, were ever ready to harass any commissioner deemed anti-industry (or proconsumer).

The FTC moved, as some influential administrative lawyers advocated, to rule making. Case-by-case, company-by-company rate regulation for two hundred companies, in the conventional utility manner, soon proved unworkable. In 1960, it began to experiment with, among other approaches, area rates—that is, setting "just and reasonable" prices on the basis of five production areas.

The transition to area rate making occurred over a nine-year period, and over the next five years the commission made a further transition to national rate making. During this period, there was continuous debate about basic gas policy. A difference of emphasis emerged between the attitudes of the commissioners and those of the professional staff. The staff was committed to allowing a return on equity while keeping producer prices down to keep customer prices low. The commission subsequently moved in 1974 to national rate setting. In 1976 it adopted a major and controversial order just before President Carter's election and the rise of a new national concern with energy policy that developed in the winter of 1977.

Gas moving through interstate commerce fell under FPC jurisdiction, but gas moving within a state came under state authority. As the FPC later interpreted its jurisdiction, once gas was regarded as interstate commerce, it was forever in interstate commerce unless the FPC decided otherwise. At one time, the interstate price, which FPC was holding down, was about two-thirds the price in the intrastate market.

In the twenty-three years between the *Phillips* decision and the election of Jimmy Carter, virtually every important FPC decision was appealed to the courts. Different circuits proved sensitive to different arguments, even given the same statutory language and the same financial figures.[10] The industry's relationship to the courts is illustrated by one of the critical orders sustained by the Court of Appeals for the District of Columbia Circuit. The technical question was whether rate making by rule, rather than by adjudication, was agreeable:

> The FPC official responsible for the preparation of order No. 411 wrote . . .
> with the possible reaction of the courts in mind. He anchored the order
> and the justification . . . in an opinion written by Judge Harold Leventhal
> in 1966. The FPC official had in mind . . . a familiarity with Judge
> Leventhal's thinking over the past several years.[11]

Generally, consumer interests were better off in the Court of Appeals for the D.C. Circuit than in the Fifth Circuit. whereas only the naive thought the industry better off in the D.C. Circuit than in the latter.[12]

In general, the industry won a lot, and its losses were not apparent in the near term. This reinforced the idea that the FPC was their captive, as it also reinforced the idea of the aging of agencies, which was partly the basis for the liberals' abandoning a strong interest in the regulatory agencies.[13] The political fights were extraordinary, and even more so after the 1973 oil crisis dramatized awareness of a national energy crisis and focused new attention on energy policy. All this came to a head in the extraordinarily cold winter of 1977, when natural gas was in short supply. Enforced reductions in supply were undertaken, under a plan approved by the FPC. Life was extremely unpleasant for many consumers. Under the Natural Gas Policy Act of 1978, the Federal Energy Regulatory Commission (FERC), which had replaced the FPC, was given a new charter. In establishing the new agency, Congress took away the old agency's right to set wellhead prices and stripped it of virtually all authority except in some categories in which price controls remained. The statute set up categories of gas, set prices for each category, and mandated inflation adjustments that called for automatic monthly increases.

The rule-making process, a process by which administrative agencies make law, is most turbulent and most intense when the interests in conflict cannot achieve some resolution in the primary branches and must use the administrative agency as the forum. Conflict will remain, but becomes manageable, when some of the forces in contention come in over others in the primary branches. This is what happened with FERC and the natural gas controversy after 1978. Since the mid-1980s, FERC has changed its regulatory approach dramatically. What no one foresaw, judging from the legislative record or anything ever presented to FERC, was the complete shakeup of the pipeline industry that was to occur later in the decade. In one sentence, the Federal Energy Regulatory Commission, from 1984 on, and especially from 1987 on, chose economic efficiency as its criterion for setting gas rates. There were three critical years and three decisions: 1984, when FERC altered its requirements on minimum bills in distribution pipeline transactions; 1985, when it issued the far-reaching Order no. 436 that provided for open access; and 1987, when it issued the policy statement on rate design.

Various features of the law, and changes in the economy, led to a great concern with what few people had discussed before, namely, "take-or-pay" contracts. The Natural Gas Policy Act (1978) shifted attention from regulation of producer prices to an increasingly free market for producer prices. Pipeline companies were concerned with avoiding the legal and public relations exposure that might accompany future gas shortages and curtailments. They bought any gas they could get, often being forced to pay very high prices under contracts that obliged them to take the gas or to pay for it in any event.

This pushed high gas prices on to the distribution utilities and their customers, just at the time of the 1982 recession. One response in some quarters was to demand corrective action by FERC; and in 1984 the commission did act to the extent that it issued Order no. 380. FERC was reluctant to venture into the take-or-pay thicket, but was pushed into it by consumer interests. The Maryland People's Counsel besought FERC action against such contracts, to prevent having charges passed on to Maryland consumers. The end result was a decision, Order no. 380, that eliminated the minimum bill requirements for distribution company purchases from pipelines.[14]

The next major landmark was the imposition of open access requirements via Order no. 436. On June 23, 1987, the U.S. Court of Appeals for the D.C. Circuit sustained the commission's action. The opening paragraph of the opinion conveys the importance the court attached to the order under review: "Order [no. 436] envisages a complete restructuring of the natural gas industry. [It] may well come to rank with the three great regulatory milestones of the industry: the passage of the Natural Gas Act . . . in 1938, the imposition of price controls on independent producers' wellhead sales under *Phillips Petroleum Co. v. Wisconsin* [1954], and adoption of the Natural Gas Policy Act [NGPA] in 1978."[15] Judge Mikva, who concurred in part and dissented in part, also referred to it as "this massive and historic order."

Order no. 436 was followed by a policy statement issued on July 27, 1989, entitled "Order on Rehearing and Clarifying Policy Statement Providing Guidance with Respect to the Designing of Rates." The commission took the policy statement seriously. The statement discussed in detail some specific issues to be treated within a preferred framework. The essence of the policy is to reduce the buyer's contractional dependence on any particular pipeline, to force pipelines to provide transportation for any purchases made, and to market each service separately (or to practice what is called *unbundling*). The effect is to displace pipelines from the characteristic mercantile function of buying and selling gas. Instead, the pipelines are largely converted into transportation companies.[16]

Despite the magnitude of the change, the matter becomes manageable administratively because the forces in contention have resolved their major battle elsewhere.

High-intensity rule making has been seen in other policy areas besides natural gas, when it has been impossible for the contending forces to settle their differences at a lower level. The potential for conflict has been strongest, in recent times, in disputes involving the quality-of-life issues of the affluent society.

Michael Pertschuk, Carter's designee as chairman of the FTC, had twelve years' previous experience on the Senate staff, much of which time he was involved with issues under FTC jurisdiction. As FTC chairman, he was an aggressive advocate of various consumer issues, notably offensive television advertising. The Federal Trade Commission had received petitions from Action for Children's Television (ACT) and the Center for Science in the Public Interest, asking it to promulgate rules limiting the content of commercials accompanying children's television programs. The petitions contained evidence on the amount of advertising for sugared products directed toward children, the limited ability of young children to recognize the commercial intent of such messages, and the health risks of excess consumption of sugar. Pertschuk led the commission to propose a rule that would ban television commercials directed to young children who are too young to understand their purpose or otherwise comprehend or evaluate them. Similar concerns were raised about advertising for sugared products directed to older children. The commission, led by Pertschuk, held that such commercials were unfair and deceptive within the meaning of section 5 of the Federal Trade Commission Act, requiring appropriate remedy.

The rule, vigorously opposed by the advertising industry, received a judicial defeat and a stinging opinion by Judge Gerhard Gesell.[17] Indeed, a shocking element was that Judge Gesell, a highly regarded member of the bench, had once been William O. Douglas's trusted emissary in proceedings against the New York Stock Exchange, where his adversary was the more experienced Dean Acheson.[18] In the end, however, the advertising industry lost their battle, with the court of appeals ruling:

> We hold that the Cinderella standard is not applicable to the
> Commission's rulemaking proceeding. An agency member may be
> disqualified from such a proceeding only when there is a clear and
> convincing showing that he has an unalterably closed mind on matters
> critical to the disposition of the rulemaking. Because we find that the
> appellees have failed to demonstrate the requisite prejudgment, the order
> of the district court is reversed.[19]

Indeed, Judge Leventhal not only supported the decision, but also wrote a concurring opinion in which he advanced the exhaustion of administrative remedies argument as a reason not to overturn the FTC proceeding.

The fight between Pertschuk and his business adversaries went on, however, in the legislative process. Pertschuk's actions had elicited heavy lobbying from the business community, and legislation to curtail FTC authority was much feared. Pertschuk's problem was to get legislation that would sustain his authority, or limit it to the least degree possible. He also needed the support of the executive. Norton Long used to recite an anecdote of the agency official who earnestly besought support from a White House official during the Roosevelt administration. The White House staffer said: "You are right; now go out and get some support, so the president can afford to come out in favor of it." Pertschuk built up a public relations campaign.

> Our strategy and our lobbying of the White House was designed to stimulate a firm and timely presidential veto threat; . . . we knew that the president was in the midst of a bitter primary campaign and that his political advisors would in large measure determine the extent of his involvement.
>
> We had forwarded a steady stream of favorable editorials and clippings to every White House staff member who might have say in shaping the president's speech. We had been striking a responsive chord in the White House, but "60 Minutes" galvanized White House staff support for both the president's appearance and an unequivocal stand in support of the commission.

The end result was that the president did invite the conferees working on anti-FTC legislation to the White House. "The president . . . spelled out his bottom line, issue by issue, and he promised that a bill that fell below that line in any of its particulars would be vetoed. The Senate conferees backed down."[20]

Consumer issues and various kinds of environmental issues, such as nuclear power plant policy, reveal how administrative law as political strategy extends far beyond the confines of traditional regulation. High-intensity rule decisions enable us to reevaluate the theoretical and empirical foundations of rule making. Lawyers and political scientists once seem to have concurred on the desirability and legitimacy of rule making. Following the view of Kenneth Culp Davis, rule making was seen as a superior method by which to decide broader policy issues. It may be that, but, on the basis of experience under the Administrative Procedure Act, its superiority is not definitive. The empirical studies that Davis once urged political scientists to make might still be of value, though preferably with a stronger theoretical core than Davis was willing to contemplate.[21] The incorporation of empirical theoretic work into law, as urged by Judge Richard Posner, would be even more valuable.[22] If lawyers know little about the process of legislation, as Posner argues, neither they nor political scientists pay much attention to the actual process of rule making.[23] Turbulence is a product of contending forces pertinent both to public law and to public administration.

Administrative Law Expands Far Beyond Microeconomics

The judicial review process, particularly reinforced by the experience of American business, became fairly well understood, down to the 1960s. Whether it is so now may be open to debate. Change came as administrative law was adapted to include interest groups. Interests averse to unlimited power of business, or who sought still other purposes, made use of the same rules and procedures. The administrative law process—the 1946 settlement of the old 1930s fight—has been opened to new participants.

The common tendency is to accept the judicial mode of decision making as a means of governing administrative agencies. Congress, like most other participants, appears to accept the settled judicial determination to control the administrative process. This allows those with something at stake to challenge decisions, often on the grounds that the right procedures are being neglected. Each side tries to insert its preferences into the judicial format, or at least into a format that a reviewing court finds acceptable. Each side challenges what an agency has done for the other side. The most persistent, skillful, and successful of these new participants have been environmental protection groups.

Environmental regulation illustrates the opening of the administrative law process to new participants who previously had little or no legitimate access at all. Environmental protection policy is essentially a constraint on business's prerogative regarding the disposal of hazardous waste products. This movement has been particularly powerful in the D.C. court of appeals. Environmentalists were particularly successful when their cases fit with Judge David Bazelon's leadership in the D.C. Circuit on science-related issues, though their success was not owing to Bazelon's influence alone.

The Nuclear Regulatory Commission (NRC) is perhaps the most important independent agency other than the Federal Reserve Board. Civilian nuclear power plants are constructed, owned, and operated by various electric utilities across the country. They are all under the jurisdiction of the Nuclear Regulatory Commission, from design through construction, through operations, and ultimately decommissioning. NRC authority is comprehensive and virtually total. NRC proceedings have become intensely controversial, and the decisions resulting from them are virtually certain to be appealed to the appropriate circuit court.

CONSTRAINTS ON ENVIRONMENTAL DECISIONS

Calvert Cliffs Coordinating Committee, Inc. v. United States Atomic Energy Commission (1971) and *Duke Power Co. v. Carolina Environmental Study Group* (1978) both illustrate the tendency to use judicial review to enforce administrative decisions.[24] In the *Calvert Cliffs* case, the Supreme Court expanded the reach of the National Environmental Policy Act by demanding a much broader view of alternatives to be considered when an environmental impact statement (EIS) is made, as required by law.

In the *Duke Power* case, the environmentalist group was granted standing, but it lost on the merits of the constitutionality of the Price-Anderson Act. This act sets up maximum damages to which any utility with a nuclear plant would be exposed if a nuclear accident occurred. The act required such a utility to waive all other defenses, and it promised that if a problem were bigger than the liability, Congress would pay for the rest. When a group of parties in North Carolina sought to block Duke Power Company's plan to construct nuclear power plants in 1978, their killing blow would have been struck not at Duke Power Company, per se, but at the Price-Anderson Act.

Of course, no crisis had yet occurred. There had been no Price-Anderson defenses, so the situation was purely hypothetical, although not trivial. The plaintiffs claimed that Duke Power's nuclear construction plans would jeopardize their rights under North Carolina law. Since Duke could not act without Price-Anderson, they should be allowed to challenge the law. The Supreme Court, in an opinion by Chief Justice Burger, sustained a lower court's decision to grant standing, then went on to sustain the constitutionality of the law.

In a 1978 case involving an application for a construction permit made by the Vermont Yankee Nuclear Power Corporation, the court of appeals overturned a rule on procedural grounds and remanded it to the commission.[25] The rule concerned the disposal of spent nuclear fuel. In effect, the appeals court said that the NRC's procedure should encompass more than the minimum requirement for informal rule making. Apparently, the court believed that the commission might make a bad judgment in the absence of a more fully developed record.

The Supreme Court reversed the court of appeals decision in extraordinarily blunt terms. Justice Rehnquist found nothing of merit in the decision:

To say that the court of appeals' final reason for remanding is insubstantial at best is a gross understatement. Consumers Power first applied in 1969 for a construction permit—not even an operating license, just a construction permit. The proposed plant underwent an incredibly extensive review. The reports filed and reviewed literally fill books. The proceedings took years. The actual hearings themselves over two weeks. To then nullify that effort seven years later because one report refers to other problems, which problems admittedly have been discussed at length in other reports available to the public, borders on the Kafkaesque. Nuclear energy may some day be a cheap, safe source of power or it may not. But Congress has made a choice to at least try nuclear energy, establishing a reasonable review process in which courts are to play only a limited role.[26]

The Rehnquist attitude in the *Vermont Yankee* decision contains an interesting irony. It is rather similar to that of the "old" Frankfurter in the *Pottsville* case. There, in the absence of significant congressional pressure or direction, the Court was asked to use its own discretion to control the Federal Communications Commission. Frankfurter said, in effect, let the FCC do what Congress gave it authority to do. Rehnquist, in *Vermont Yankee*, belittles the appeals process when he says it concerns to "just a construction permit," as if there were a realistic likelihood that, once constructed, a nuclear plant would not get an operating license. Bazelon might reply, in terms reminiscent of C. A. Miller, that the courts had given too much latitude to regulatory agencies, but that also is about a policy, not a principle. It is about what the judge thinks the agency will do with the latitude.

SOCIAL BENEFITS ISSUES

The litigation process conceived for the protection of property has been extended to other purposes. *Goldberg v. Kelly* (1970) dealt with the technical issue of whether someone could be removed from the Aid to Families with Dependent Children program without a hearing. *Mathews v. Eldridge* (1976) dealt with the difficult problem of declaring a man able to work when he claimed a disability. On its face, the *Mathews* case appears to be the total opposite of the *Goldberg* case.

Then, in 1974, 133 years after Mrs. Decatur's case, involving a navy widow's pension claim, the Supreme Court came to another benefits case. It is not quite parallel. In *Johnson v. Robison* (1974), the man bringing the appeal was a conscientious objector who was opposed to the United States' involvement in the Vietnam War.[27] Having been exempted from military service, he had performed alternative civilian service instead. Now he wanted certain educational benefits available to veterans of military service under the terms of the Veterans' Readjustment Act of 1966. He challenged the actions of the Veterans' Administration (VA) on the ground that to deny him this benefit violated his constitutionally guaranteed religious freedom and his right to equal protection under the Fifth Amendment.

The Veterans' Administration said that he was not entitled to the benefits under the terms of the statute, nor was he entitled to bring suit to try to get them. His suit was legislatively precluded because the statute, 38 USC no. 211(a), expressly prohibited judicial review of VA decisions on "any question of fact or law under laws administered by the Veterans' Administration providing for veterans' benefits."

The Supreme Court agreed with the VA: the litigant was not entitled to the benefits under the Veterans' Readjustment Act, and Congress had not infringed his freedom of religion. However, the Court held that the VA was wrong about the right to sue:

> Section 211(a) does not extend to actions challenging the constitutionality of veterans' benefits legislation but is aimed at prohibiting review of those decisions of law or fact arising in the administration of a statute providing for veterans' benefits, and is hence inapplicable to this action, neither the text of the statute nor its legislative history showing a contrary intent.

An important question for administrative law, to be addressed in chapter 6, is a contractor's or supplier's right to earn money when the government is a customer. This is a critical issue in a nation-state committed to a strong military defense. These cases exhibit both the constraints imposed by a given party on others and constraints that a given party is subject to and which it wishes to be relieved of.

Administrative law also involves the liability of public officials. It also involves the rights of government employees. Finally, in more recent times, we should add another set of claims—namely, the right and opportunity of citizens to influence decisions before they are made.

The Half-Closed Politics of the Administrative Law World

The politics of administrative law is a broad concept. As both decision makers and parties recognize, procedures and results are closely intertwined. Intense conflicts occur between different interpretations of the law about what the law means and what is to be done.

The driving force of American administrative law is the bar's demand for judicial review of agency actions. The existing system was formed through specific political combat in the New Deal years, when there was a critical conflict between business firms' prerogative to make decisions without external constraints and government intervention in the economy.

The conservative coalition redefined the debate on how government should work and sought to limit the power of government agencies by creating a sort of administrative court. The conservatives both lost and won. They lost in their attempt to suppress the growth of government and to exclude public intervention in market decisions, through the mechanisms of an administrative court. They won a partial victory by establishing and incorporating an administrative procedure act that was integrated into many substantive statutes.

The Administrative Procedure Act of 1946 was itself a working compromise between giving government agencies wide administrative discretion and curbing their power by an administrative court. It has come to be accepted as part of the political and administrative culture in the United States.

Richard Stewart maintains that, under the Administrative Procedure Act, courts developed three techniques that could be adapted to selective application and could be used to trim agency powers without intruding upon the major bulk of delegated authority implicit in a statutory scheme. The first technique is to undertake substantial scrutiny of what supports a substantial evidence claim. The second is to require "reasoned consistency" in decision making. The third is to require a clear statement of legislative purpose.[28]

After the 1946 act, this working compromise, now said to have come unstuck, apparently existed the courts and the agencies. Courts came to adopt an abstemious view of agencies' decision making and substance, if the "cabining" principles were followed. The courts are now seen to have withdrawn from the compromise because of "unlawful and abusive exercise of administrative power in areas where the traditional model has seldom applied and the private interests most directly at stake had not enjoyed its protections."[29] However, it is a mistake to see courts and administrators as parties to a working compromise, just as it is a mistake to think that the compromise has failed because "the courts have gone too far" or because the agencies have resorted to "regulatory excess" or have failed to carry out legislative mandates and protect collective interests. Rather, both developments reflect social demands, but the sources of demand are different.

COURTS AS QUASI-ADMINISTRATIVE AGENCIES

Agency decision making entails constant pragmatic adjustment to the environment—which includes the court system. Agency decisions must accommodate, as far as possible, what the agency believes a reviewing judge may demand. As the courts are drawn more deeply into substantive matters, does this make the courts into another aspect of the administrative process? Much attention is assigned to the diligent pursuit of objectives to which judges have become committed.[30] Whether courts become "too ready" to intervene in a policy vacuum, especially where judges perceive a vacuum, is a value judgment one need not make. However, judges do bring deep intellectual, emotional, and psychological convictions to their decisions about the law.[31]The availability of judicial review enables plaintiffs to force attention on an issue even when the technical legal basis may be debatable. If agencies are not subject to review until their action is final, then we must ask about the cases involving the secretary of agriculture, as well as the administrator of the EPA, on the subject of allegedly dangerous pesticides such as DDT. In the late 1960s the D.C. court of appeals indeed tried to force action to start proceedings to cancel the use of DDT and to suspend the registration of DDT while the proceeding was conducted. The secretary of agriculture and the head of the Environmental Protection Agency had petitioned for this. But because they did not act as the EDF wished, they were sued. Each argued, among other things, that no final agency action had been taken by their refusal to initiate certain proceedings over which they had jurisdiction.[32]

Pierce, Shapiro, and Verkuil note that in some highly controversial cases, "no matter how important a legal rule may be," judges who are outraged by the evidence brought before them will try to find a means to correct an abuse. The judge in the District of Columbia Circuit said that the health hazards posed by DDT were so large than even a temporary refusal to suspend its use "results in irreparable injury on a massive scale." The judge may also "have believed that the Secretary of Agriculture was dragging his feet solely because of pressure from his constituents in the agricultural community and among pesticide manufacturers."[33]

The extensions of judicial review may, by now, have reached such a point that federal district judges sometimes approximate administrators. The judge's problem sometimes is to find or to fashion a remedy that can be implemented.

In 1987 and 1988, in an Alabama case of great national interest, *Jaffree v. Wallace*, both the pedagogical and the administrative interests of the public education system were at stake. Some parents challenged the school authorities' choice of textbooks because they promoted secular humanism. The U.S. district court received expert testimony maintaining that secular humanism was a religion. On that basis, textbooks allegedly promoting secular humanism were determined to violate the students' First Amendment rights to freedom of religion.

Once the judge made the initial determination, the purely administrative question—convenience—arose. "U.S. District Judge W. Brevard Hand, who ruled that 44 texts were promoting humanism in violation of the U.S. Constitution, by promoting a godless humanist religion, rejected pleas of state school officials to allow the texts to be used for the rest of the school year [1991]."[34] The banned books were first removed from a school in the state's largest single school district, Mobile County, with the other school systems awaiting orders. The judge said forty of the books should not be used, and the remaining four, on home economics, could remain in the classrooms only if offensive portions were not used. But the state argued that removing the books would disrupt the education process and prove costly to financially strapped rural school systems. The state did not have to comply, and an appeal was processed swiftly through the Court of Appeals for the Eleventh Circuit, which reversed the trial court decision.

DISTURBANCE FROM CONFLICT AMONG THE PRIMARY BRANCHES

The semiclosed character of the process (which gives it continuity) is from time to time disturbed (or disrupted) by outside pressures. Legislative-executive controversy has an impact on agency decision making. The present reality is that these independent regulatory agencies are treated somewhat like "arms of Congress." One should emphasize, of course, that each agency is different and that the precise terms of the statutes applying to each must always be considered. Nonetheless, Congress quickly adapted to the "arms of Congress" theory. The relevant congressional committees and subcommittees, and particularly their chairs and senior staff members, take an active interest in their agencies.

However, we should remember Justice Scalia's emphatic assertion that congressional committees exercise too much direct control. But we cannot accept that view in simple terms. Congress has limited the power of such agencies when their actions threaten to impose political penalties on members of Congress themselves. The Federal Trade Commission has, more than once, found some investigation or rule making unacceptable. This was often visibly so when the FTC sought to enforce a policy that affected small businesses that are widely represented throughout the country—for example, controlling the sales practices of used car dealers and the information they supply about the quality of their vehicles, or the pricing practices of morticians.

It is not quite true that Congress commands and agencies obey. Other considerations are pertinent, not the least of which are other actors such as the White House or the courts. Although Rep. John E. Moss, a Democrat from California, always advocated tough regulatory policies, he had only partial success in enforcing his preferences, even though he was an important sub-committee chair. When in 1975 the FPC adopted a major change in natural gas rates that strongly favored the producers, Congressman Moss tried unsuc-cessfully to initiate a criminal action against Richard Dunham, then FPC chairman.

For many years, Democrats in Congress have tended to be more liberal and Republicans more conservative, though this difference can be exagger-ated. Even during the Carter administration, some of the FTC's most severe critics were Democrats, and some of the most severe critics of FPC natural gas policy were producer-state Democrats.[35] In the Reagan administration, there were running battles between the pertinent House committees and the Se-curities and Exchange Commission (SEC). It is hard to measure the influence of the committees on the SEC. While there is some, the SEC does not take direction as if it were under the control of House committees.

The courts themselves represent important limits not only on the agen-cies, but on Congress' control over agencies. Congressman Moss again pro-vides a useful illustration.[36] In 1975, as chairman of the Subcommittee on Oversight and Investigation, Moss demanded a variety of data from the in-dependent regulatory agencies, which were then headed by Republican ap-pointees of Presidents Nixon and Ford. The agencies did not comply but, advised by the Justice Department, sought and received a restraining order from the federal district court. Moss could not now enforce his demand for agency documents without risking contempt of court. He thereupon crit-icized the judicial intrusion, but withdrew the subpoenas, saying that the court "failed to take account of the co-equal status of Congress with the Judiciary." Moreover, he said the district court ignored a Supreme Court decision that the "Speech or Debate Clause protects against inquiry into acts . . . in the regular course of the legislative process" and that the "wisdom of the congressional approach or methodology is not open to judicial veto."

However, Moss withdrew the contested subpoenas. Even though he as-serted confidence about the eventual result, any further (appellate) judicial proceedings, he said, would not "subject the Subcommittee's actions to the unwarranted assumption of jurisdiction by the Courts." Perhaps the subcommittee might have prevailed. However, it could have prevailed only by allowing a court to decide its jurisdiction, including the risk of a still less favorable decision. In this case, therefore, the subcommittee's inquiry was simply stopped, the court being the vehicle by which others, including the president's supporters, achieved this victory.

The D.C. court of appeals has, on at least a few occasions, decided cases in which congressional pressure on the agency allegedly harmed some private party. The court held in 1966 that a congressional committee had improperly interfered with the Federal Trade Commission while there was an adjudicative procedure regarding the Pillsbury Company before the commission.[37] Moreover, the agencies are intensely subject to judicial review, and the courts take an active interest in maintaining regulatory agency decision making in a form they can review.

In this regard, the legislative veto issue has been almost entirely misunderstood by many commentators. The courts have formulated their decisions in language that protects the prerogatives of the executive against congressional encroachment. But the practical effect, if not the intended and unstated purpose, is to protect a claim of exclusive judicial prerogative to say what the laws mean.

Finally, a word on the mystery of presidential influence: It is generally agreed that the centralized budget controls, legislative clearance, presidential selection of agency heads, and chairpersons' control of administration enhance White House control over the agencies. The fear that this would happen was certainly expressed both in Congress and by members of the bar, and in the intersection between them.

The dogma of executive leadership is fully consistent with this expectation. Americans have a romance with the idea of presidential leadership. No matter what important problem arises, policy entrepreneurs urge the president to exercise his moral authority and provide leadership. With this goes the assumption that nothing is important until the president is engaged. One should never undervalue the chief executive's role, nor neglect the surprising suddenness with which it may be activated. Nonetheless, scholarly studies and the testimony of officials in cabinet-level agencies show that the relationship is much more complex than the dogma of judicio-political theory indicates. There is command in the purely executive side, but there is also a good deal of bargaining, some of which is bargaining from above to induce assent from below.[38]

What should we expect of the regulatory commissions, where the claims of "law" may be invoked, and where the role of Congress is always a present consideration? Krasnow, Longley, and Terry—observers of the communications field—write that the FCC, like most government departments and agencies, does not deal with the president (except on matters of the greatest national and international importance) but with the White House staff.[39]

My own observation, during four years of official responsibility, was similar. The Federal Energy Regulatory Commission was not a trivial entity in 1977–1981, when energy was a major international topic. Nonetheless, the relationship between the White House and FERC was vague and uncertain.[40] The chairman shared with his fellow commissioners a good many items indicating congressional interest. But those from the White House, to the extent they existed, were stated circumspectly. This could, of course, have been mere caution. But, in the politics of the federal government, officials with close relationships to the White House more often find it advantageous, for reasons of power, not personal egotism, discreetly to let those relationships be seen from time to time.

However, scholars should remember that present habits of mind are shaped, in large measure, by the remote experience of the early New Deal. When FDR took office, the government was much smaller and executive institutions were less developed. In domestic economic affairs, people seemed to have bigger expectations of the Federal Trade Commission than could be realized. Part of the objection to Commissioner Humphrey was not that he was an abrasive man, but that he was deemed pro–big business in an agency when the political demand of the time was that the agency should control big business. This is a much better explanation of why Roosevelt wanted to be rid of a man whose mind did not go along with his.

At the same time, the nation's financial system was in virtual collapse. Roosevelt recommended securities legislation to Congress not merely within his first hundred days, but in his first month. It is not surprising that he worked closely, and personally, with his first three chairmen of the Securities and Exchange Commission: Joseph P. Kennedy, James M. Landis, and William O. Douglas.

Because the regulatory commissions were regarded as so important, people expected them to have close connections to the president, though such connections might inherently conflict with the idea of agency independence. This early expectation survives in the language that administrative lawyers still use: "the Big Seven" refers to the Civil Aeronautics Board (now abolished), the Federal Communications Commission, the Federal Energy Regulatory Commission, the Federal Trade Commission, the Interstate Commerce Commission, the National Labor Relations Board, and the Securities and Exchange Commission.[41]

No one appears to have studied presidential archives for evidence on the presidents' relations to regulatory commissions. Krasnow, Longley, and Terry sum up the state of research-based knowledge on the formal reporting procedure. "Under most recent administrations the FCC and other regulatory agencies have sent detailed monthly summaries of their principal activities and pending projects to a key presidential aide."[42] Presumably, the summary would have no significance in the policy-making arena until the recipient caused someone to do something that would reveal White House interest. There are very few indicators of such interest. Of course, the president's interest might be prudently disguised. But this seems implausible, beyond a certain point. The reason is that official agency sources are so often penetrable, by outsiders, or leaked by insiders.

There are a variety of small episodes, but it is difficult to generalize from them. Chairmen are unquestionably the most important members of such commissions, as they are official points of contact with the White House. (At the same time, do not underestimate the kinds of resistance and circumvention that individual members can employ if a chairperson seems to be trying to override the others.) Five chairmen have committed some observations to the public record once they were free of the constraints of office.

Justice William O. Douglas has been the most forthcoming, writing about his time as chairman of the Securities and Exchange Commission. Although Douglas did not know Roosevelt before 1935, when he was brought to his notice by Joseph Kennedy, he became an intimate member of the president's advisory and social network. According to his account, the president thought the economic downturn of 1937 was the result of a Wall Street plot against himself, while Douglas saw it as the result of a curtailment of public spending. Roosevelt took his advice, seconded by Marriner Eccles and by Harry Hopkins. On the specific issue of SEC business, Douglas asserts that he had to get the president personally to overrule Bureau of the Budget Director Bell and provide the funds that he thought the SEC needed. "Dan Bell was mirroring the big-business attitude. The powers-that-be wanted a hands-off policy when it came to their preserve. The Bureau of the Budget may have been reflecting only its own prejudices, or it may have been responding to pressures from the Establishment."[43]

Douglas was reconstructing in the 1970s what happened in the late 1930s. We have no way of knowing whether he consciously or unconsciously reconstructed the experience into something other than what it was. But some of what he says might be the language an agency official in the 1980s, when the Office of Management and Budget used its powers to constrain agencies to various degrees. Douglas's account of what he did, however, is perhaps different:

> Whatever the reason, my rebellion was instant. The bureau had no rightful concern with policy. It had no expertise in the manifold phases of the financial world, which was under our jurisdiction. My position was that the Bureau of the Budget could tell us how much we had to spend in the next fiscal year but that it was up to us to determine how that amount was to be expended. The battles were intense and recurring. I always won in the end, but I usually had to go to the President for help.[44]

Edward Howrey writes an entertaining account, chiefly about internal administrative matters, about his relations with Congress and his desire to convince President Eisenhower (through Sherman Adams) that he knew something about administrative law, nothing about air law, and should thus be left to manage the FTC and not be moved to the Civil Aeronautics Board.[45]

William L. Cary recalls that, as chairman of the Securities and Exchange Commission, he never saw the president on business, although he was invited to meet Kennedy at the time of a severe fall in the stock market in 1962. The secretary of the treasury, the chairman of the Council of Economic Advisers, and the chairman of the Federal Reserve were also invited. However, having a prior commitment to testify on the Hill, he sent an alternate.

> To a regulatory agency . . . the White House was a collection of people, and to most of us it was primarily Ralph A. Dungan, an able assistant who participated in choosing us. Even Mr. Dungan was so heavily involved in matters of greater national and political importance (such as the Foreign Aid program) that he literally had no free time to talk with us. There were, in addition, the equally brilliant but equally busy assistant counsel in the White House, and the Bureau of the Budget, an arm of the Executive. There were also a number of second-echelon political assistants who telephoned, but the brief conversations with them quickly warned one of the dangers of becoming too intimate.[46]

This is as specific as Cary gets as to how White House–agency relations were managed. In general, relations were nonexistent or marginal. The presidential staffer charged with appointments led nominees to believe they were chosen to "make things better," which may reflect criticisms of agency backlog and planning failures circulated by James M. Landis before Kennedy took office. White House staffers seemed to say if there was any unhappiness, they would have heard. Encouragement came only obliquely.

The best study is that by David Welborn, which shows that while President Lyndon B. Johnson did have some contact with regulatory commissions, it was limited and erratic.[47] James L. Baughman, who has studied the president's relations with the FCC, notes that whereas various journalists attested to Johnson's personal interest in the mass communications industry, Johnson played no major role regarding the agencies, apart from his appointments.[48] It was known, of course, that Caspar W. Weinberger came to Washington after his experience in California as chairman of the Federal Trade Commission and quickly moved to the role of director of the Office of Management and Budget. It is improbable that he would have secured the second crucial post if he had been deemed unsatisfactory in the first. The OMB directorship is not the position to which people are kicked upstairs.

Michael Pertschuk shows that the president can take an active interest in a regulatory commission's business if he and the chairman are sympathetic. But the president must also see a political advantage in taking an interest. Moreover, there must be no ethical doubts about his involvement. (Since the misadventures of the Nixon administration, one of the tasks of White House counsel is to assure that the president and the entourage are not inadvertently drawn into regulatory commission matters where they do not belong.)

James C. Miller, Pertschuk's immediate successor, chaired the Federal Trade Commission from 1981 to 1985. His account offers even less operational detail about the president's involvement or that of the White House entourage in commission business.[49] It is obvious that he was satisfactory to the White House, for he then was moved to the vastly more important position of director of the OMB. He speaks of his chairmanship as a capacity in which he "served President Reagan," an understandable expression, but not that of one who is careful to maintain an appearance of courteous independence from the White House.[50] Miller is well aware that he aligned FTC policies with those of the Reagan administration, but perhaps he did so simply because he believed in them. There is no sign of disagreement on any significant issue, hence no problems to be reconciled, and the references to the Antitrust Division and to Assistant Attorney General Baxter would justify a belief in full intellectual agreement.[51]

An emphasis on the independent regulatory agencies neglects the executive regulatory agencies. Presidential influence should in theory apply more to the agencies that exercise substantially the same type of regulatory function, but are located wholly within the executive branch.

If agencies are controlled by judicial review, and if some procedures are deemed by courts inherently unfair, then it matters little by whom those procedures are undertaken or applied. The *Morgan* case arose in no independent agency, but in a subunit of the U.S. Department of Agriculture; and it was the secretary who had to approve, in form, orders whose contents he could not have known well. This case started long before Roosevelt was president or Humphrey a commissioner. The ramifications are still present. The greatest volume of administrative decision making takes place in the Immigration and Naturalization Service and in the Social Security Administration.[52] The Environmental Protection Agency is fundamentally important not merely because of its case volume but because its functions relating to production processes and hazardous waste disposal necessarily permeate the whole industrial and government system.

Very little direct evidence exists, moreover, of White House influence on the process. In some clear cases, the outcome is consistent with White House preferences, though we cannot say the result is because of that direction. In September 1992, for instance, the FAA rejected recommendations that airlines should be required to provide restraint devices for children under two years of age.[53]

The dogma of executive leadership is, intriguingly, part of a "new conservative" challenge to the independent regulatory structure. At this stage, the challenge is still at the level of ideas and ideology, not associated with the practical interests of economic enterprise. The bearers of the challenge are a generation of law professors, some moving from government to the academy and some from the academy to government, who seem dedicated to overturning or eroding regulatory authority. The leader of the root-and-branch overturners is Justice Scalia. He placed this approach squarely before the Supreme Court in the *Synar* case, and the Court as squarely declined to do anything about it.[54]

If the bold approach has failed, we may well see more subtle efforts by those who proceed by distinction and reinterpretation. Pierce, Shapiro, and Verkuil point out various respects in which the FTC removal statute, under which Humphrey was found to be protected in 1935, was already narrower than the Tenure of Office Act invalidated in the *Myers* case. They maintain:

It only imposed a for-cause requirement upon presidential removal, not a senatorial concurrence requirement, Thus, to satisfy Humphrey's Executor, a President would need only to assert cause for removal. . . . This is an important theoretical distinction between the Myers and

Humphrey's Executor removal contexts if (as no President has yet done) cause for removal is asserted.

This leads to a second, as yet untested, proposition. What is "cause"? If . . . "cause" may be a failure to follow the policy directions of the President, then "cause" would exist when the President seeks to replace recalcitrant commissioners. Since implementation of policy is more an executive function than is adjudication, the failure to implement properly (or "efficiently" in terms of the FTC removal requirements) might justify removal in the President's, and even in the Court's eyes.[55]

Pierce, Shapiro, and Verkuil express opposition to *Humphrey's Executor*:

Humphrey's Executor is venerated precedent, but it is also a lonely one. It is the case upon which the entire "constitutional" theory of agency independence is constructed. Because the idea of agency independence is, or can be, at war with prevalent notions of presidential supervision of agencies, and because it thereby encourages enclaves of agency discretion, there is valid reason to rethink the question of independence.[56]

This approach, grounded in the dogma of executive leadership, proposes fundamentally to change the terms of discourse. The intellectually and politically interesting question is whether the three scholars advocating this approach can constrain their choices within satisfactory limits. If executive control over one set of independent regulatory agencies is achievable, as under this theory it is, then the question arises whether they can avoid similar executive claims over other portions of the governmental system. It would be interesting to see a theory of executive control based upon removal for "cause" that pertains to communications or natural gas, but can exclude a similar claim for finance and banking.

Courts versus Courts

Dispute within the system can be very intense. This is true when courts of appeal review the decisions of regulatory agencies. It is also true when the Supreme Court reviews decisions made by courts of appeal. If a court deals with a closely related set of issues, over some time, judges will inevitably develop a particular approach. They will come to an intellectual consensus about how to employ their decisional authority. This clearly happened in the Fifth Circuit with regard to public school desegregation, when district courts were resisting the order or responding too slowly. It happened with regard to criminal law and the rights of the mentally ill in the D.C. Circuit.[57] There is a striking problem, however, when a court at one level develops a strong and consistent approach that a higher court frankly repudiates.

Such conflict is virtually inevitable when electoral change brings new administrative appointments, so that the two levels of the judiciary are no longer in concord. This is what happened with the D.C. Circuit, generally characterized as liberal, when its settled majority was led by Chief Judge Bazelon. Some have speculated about a conflict between Judge Bazelon and Warren Burger, when the latter was still a judge in the D.C. Circuit. A *Washington Post* reporter wrote: "In 1962, when Bazelon became chief judge of the court, eligible to serve until 1979, Burger reportedly fumed at 'another seventeen years of this.' The relationship between the two was, at best, icy." The D.C. Circuit was generally supported by the Supreme Court. However, "support from the high court began to unravel in 1969, when Burger replaced Earl Warren as chief justice. When he heard the news, Bazelon had every reason to be, as remarked to friends at the time, 'speechless and sick for a week.' "[58]

Indeed, the D.C. Circuit began to experience more frequent reversals by the Supreme Court, as still other, more articulate and more purposefully conservative justices were appointed to the Supreme Court during the Nixon and Ford administrations. The result was high-intensity politics within the judiciary, distinctively shown in the unusual and sharp attack by Justice Rehnquist against the D.C. court of appeals, or at least against Judge Bazelon's approach. This was the burden of the *Vermont Yankee* opinion.[59] From the tone of the opinions, the Supreme Court might be presumed to have thought the circuit court guilty of "organizational contumacy" beyond the bounds of proper disagreement.[60]

What are the strategies and tactics available in the rather closed world of judicial decision making when intellectual convictions about substance and about the authority structure of the judiciary run into conflict? What is a Judge Bazelon to do when a Justice Rehnquist blasts his opinion on *Vermont Yankee*?

Partisanship and the Half-Open System

We have not stressed in this book the close connection of partisan politics to public administration. Yet the administrative law process reveals a close connection to electoral, partisan politics. American scholars generally adopt the view that partisan politics should not be found in the administrative process, and should have nothing to do with anyone in Washington, D.C. In a crude way, however, partisan politics is a source of disturbance, and thus relative openness, in a system that otherwise would tend toward stabilization and being closed.

When top-level administrators are chosen, given the differences in ideology and opinion between parties, agency nominations understandably reflect those differences. Democratic and Republican appointees to the courts also differ in their dispositions and attitudes. So do Democratic and Republican appointees to cabinet and subcabinet office. We should, therefore, expect different behavioral tendencies according to which party is in the White House. It is as difficult to imagine Michael Pertschuk being appointed to the Federal Trade Commission by a Republican president as it would be to imagine James Miller being appointed by a Democrat.

Appointees may have systematic philosophical biases toward narrower questions of administrative law. Some have a disposition toward legislative preclusion. These individuals will generally align themselves with those who can afford politically to hold similar views. We are back to partisanship.

Richard M. Dicke, for many years a partner in a major New York law firm, made this point in discussing certain pending changes at the Securities and Exchange Commission early in the Reagan administration. "Well, they will loosen up some, and then the Democrats will come in and they will put in a bunch of guys who will tighten up some. Then after a while, the Republicans will come in, and their guys will loosen up some again. I've been around this business for nearly fifty years, and that is always the way it happens." Securities analysts who follow regulated industries take it as given that, on the whole, Democrats will be less inclined to favor investor interests and more favorable to small customer interests than will Republicans, and vice versa.

Agency administrators also have ideological predispositions, and sometimes they are partisan. But their biases are generally related to the interests with which officials identify. An agency may or may not wish to claim primary jurisdiction. Those with something at stake are likely to prefer to have judgments made by someone who understands many of the subtleties. This may seem like "narrow" self-interest if it is claimed by the natural gas industry or the chemical firms. If the parties at interest are universities, medical schools, or other institutions in which scholarly interests were engaged, there may be a similar preference for judgments made by people who understand the system.

Consider the powerful effects on public administration when the court process and public opinion converge. One could argue that, except for the business community, environmental protection advocates have been most successful at using the administrative law system. Access to the courts, and the strong backing of public opinion, have been crucial to their success.

Summary and Conclusion

There is a deep conflict, in principle, between the dominant doctrines of the bar—judicio-political theory as the dogma is here designated—and the observations that would follow from a careful empirical-theoretical analysis in political science. The essentials of this approach are stated by Richard B. Stewart. They amount to the proposition that the polity is best governed when judicial review of administrative determination is the final mode of decision making.

This approach ignores the reality that administrative law itself—its interpretation and implementation—is a form of continually changing political strategy. The strategy once seen to be effective in maintaining political control in private institutions and outside government was the product of Stewart's "traditional model."[61]

Stewart maintains that, under the Administrative Procedure Act, courts developed three techniques which could be "adapted to selective application, and could be utilized to trim agency powers without intruding upon the major bulk of delegated authority implicit in a statutory scheme." The first technique is to undertake a substantial scrutiny of what supports a substantial evidence claim. The second is to require "reasoned consistency" in decision making. The third is to require a clear statement of legislative purpose.[62] Even under this "working compromise," as Stewart calls it, administrative law remains itself a vital factor in administrative turbulence.

The major cleavages that divided the U.S. economy and society before the Administrative Procedure Act could not be dissipated merely by adopting a "new bottle" of procedure. Rather, the new procedure became the format within which old fights were continued and redefined. Principles elaborated in decision making are applied not only to well-known interests, but are extended over time to the benefit of others.

The initial disputes were about the prerogatives of big business, with the bar as the principal intellectual expositor, and about attempted government intervention in various aspects of the economy, which means attempts by other interests acting through government authority to constrain business. This struggle dominated questions of financial control, but crucially questions of employers' power to hire and fire workers and related decisions about the work force and labor efficiency. The struggle is exhibited in the Wagner Act, in the latitude exercised by the National Labor Relations Board, in business's counterattack through the Taft-Hartley Act, and the redefinition in administrative law as expressed in the *Universal Camera* decision. What *Universal Camera* shows, from an empirical-theoretical analysis, is that even technical issues regarding the choice of evidence and whether a particular decision accords with a certain standard (e.g., substantial evidence) can be conceived in group struggle terms. So conceived, administrative turbulence is also perceived as natural.

Administrative law in the United States has expanded far beyond issues of microeconomics. The same processes have been engaged in various other features of social combat, as in the adaptation of the procedures imposed for earlier purposes in the protracted struggle over environmental controls and science-related issues, of which the nuclear power controversy is most notable. The same kind of struggle can also be seen in the use of the administrative law process in questions of entitlements and social benefits, and many other domains of public policy.

The administrative law world is both half closed and, as a matter of logic, half open. It is half closed in the sense that it has a relatively stable set of participants, bounded by complex rules and a language that only the participants speak and comprehend. At the same time, it is half open, as a field of contest in which claimants from many parts of society enter indirectly, through the leverage of the primary branches. In this process, there is a certain turbulence due to the function that courts often assume, acting themselves as if they were administrative agencies, and in the contest between different courts over the resolution of the same issues, as in the contest between the D.C. Circuit court of appeals manifested in *Vermont Yankee*.

The half-open quality of the system is a function of political partisanship. Partisanship is present, even if participants are unaware of it or minimize its presence. William L. Cary takes his explicit purpose to be "to present the Federal regulatory commissions in their political context."[63] Yet Cary explicitly downgrades partisanship:

> In considering "balance" and potential differences within the
> commission, I minimize the role of political affiliation. During the
> Kennedy years neither Newton Minow, Chairman of the FCC, nor Alan
> Boyd, Chairman of the CAB, would have mustered adequate support
> without some of their Republican colleagues. Indeed, many of their
> Democratic members were in the opposition. An incoming chairman can

achieve far more by appreciating the talents and experience available, including his predecessor (who may remain as commissioner), than by adopting an immediate "new broom" approach.[64]

This is a plausible case. Nonetheless, party bias does enter in three ways, owing to the differing tendencies of the clusters of interests and interest groups that make up a political party.

1. The result that the same pressures (e.g., claims as to the importance of capital or the rights or workers) have different meanings to different presidential administrations.

2. Accordingly, there are notably different choices in administrative appointees. The illustrations in Richard Dicke's comments, from commonsense experience, about how the SEC regulates securities practices are in point. The different appointments tend to produce fairly rapid effects in what top level agency people attempt to do as they articulate what they believe, how they act in accord with career ambitions, and so on. There will be, inevitably, less rapid reaction from subordinates and some dissent from colleagues who remain as expositors of earlier policies and group preferences.

3. As there are different choices in administrative appointments, so there are differences in judicial appointments. The result is, among other things, a delay effect. Courts are engaged in conflict with other courts, to the extent that one court is dominated by the appointments of a previous administration and party, and this delay plays a major role, since courts are a critical instrument for changing the direction of agencies.

4. Finally, the different ways in which congressional committees exert pressure, extend protection to, or otherwise deal with administrative agencies are part of the same pattern. Administrative law is closely related to the organization of control. Insofar as control itself is in debate, turbulence is a consequence. From the viewpoint of the political scientist who seeks to understand rather than to enforce a dogma, this adds potency to the research agenda long ago suggested by Kenneth C. Davis. It also suggests, for those who seek to structure decisions, that we pay closer attention to Judge Richard Posner's point that law should seek to incorporate the empirical work of recent and contemporary political science.

III

External Sources of Disruption

6

POLITICS, TECHNOLOGY, AND ADMINISTRATIVE HISTORY

A TRIBUTE TO LEONARD D. WHITE

Administrative history offers a means of identifying many topics worthy of more discussion. And it reveals three important crossover or exchange relationships between the politics of administration and the technology of administration. The first concerns the equipment with which work is done and decisions are made—the subject of this chapter. The other two exchange relationships, administrators' choices about technology and their need to cope with and regulate the consequences of technological change, are discussed in the next chapter.

Leonard Schapiro, a British Sovietologist, once observed that the obvious often escapes students of politics, past and present.[1] It is obvious to everyone that technology and technological change are sources of turbulence in the working atmosphere of administration. When we consider force, money, information, or some combination of these elements of power, the necessary questions are: By whom are they used? From whom are they derived? To whom are they applied? In what manner? To what purpose? Administration involves both moral judgment and labor-saving devices. Technology always involves the latter, and often becomes entangled with the former. By the late twentieth century, when the computer has become virtually universal, it is clear that sophisticated technology is indispensable to public administration.

Leonard D. White was the intellectual pioneer on this topic, and we may yet follow his example in depth. In the first edition of his textbook (1926), he wrote: "What differentiates the modern public official from the scribe of antiquity, is the marvelous material equipment with which he works, and the contribution which science has made, and continues to make, to his profession."[2] Strictly speaking, he might have said that nothing else counts. "Marvelous material equipment" is the only thing that differentiates ancient from modern administration. In a later edition, he wrote: "The whole technique of present day administration rests upon science and invention, and the effectiveness of governmental action has been immeasurably increased as a result."[3]

In more contemporary methodological language, White might have described technology is an exogenous variable, a determinant from outside the process that governs what happens inside the process. Technological issues connect the study of administration to the study of society and culture. The equipment used for public administration is a source of pressure in all political systems, regardless of culture. The implications of this view are manifold, yet we have no orderly body of data with which to test the more or less explicit hypothesis. This reinforces the importance of approaching the study of administration from a perspective that considers many cultures at the same time and multiple units of culture in different periods of recorded history.

Politics—the organization of power—is influenced, first, by equipment or physical technology that enables social technology to meet demands that could not be met before. Time- and effort-saving issues are always quick to come to the surface, though moral judgment issues are always present too. The rural sheriff who beat confessions out of his prisoners in the Kemper County jail had made a moral judgment as to who was within his community, or shared moral order, and who was not. He was merely applying a rather crude technology to achieve his ends.[4] The record of the twentieth century, in places where scientific education is higher, is replete with grim accounts of technologically more sophisticated torture.

Moreover, change in particular capabilities comes so fast that our political discourse often fails to keep up with emerging political facts. That is why, for instance, literature about public administration has barely begun to mention expert systems, even as the Department of Defense pays both for research on the subject and for symposia about the application of expert systems in government.[5]

Leonard White's language may overenthusiastic. But we have no reason to abandon the presumption of his good judgment. He knew that the ancient Egyptian scribe served a *god*-king. The peasant was mere raw material of no greater value than straw. He also knew, I expect, that government in fourth-century Athens required little qualification from elected citizens as it was helped out by the technical knowledge of the state slaves employed as assistants in most offices.[6] The Egyptian scribe had no moral or ethical duty toward the peasant. It is doubtful that the slave functionary felt morally or ethically obliged to the Athenian citizen. Therefore, White presumably knew of the profound changes in the moral structure of the political unit and of the administrative functionary's place within that moral structure that have occurred over the centuries.

In his administrative history of the United States, with which he concluded his publishing career, White returns to the theme. He discusses the influence of inventions on public administration, stressing improvements in the physical instruments of communication—notably steamboats, railroads, and the telegraph—and of warfare.[7] Setting aside enthusiastic excess, White's emphasis on technology in administration is extraordinarily important. Why would it be fruitful for political scientists to study this subject further? We should start with a more fundamental understanding and clear our minds by applying it to historical experience.

Students of public administration are familiar with the technological dominance of the West. Since World War II, the technology transfer has moved from west to east (or, in more contemporary terms, from north to south), but until the thirteenth century it was quite the reverse. The earliest known technology transfer was from the East to Europe. The mechanical skills and technological literature of the East were distinctly superior, and Marco Polo felt like a "barbarian" when he visited China. The situation was changing, however, and two centuries later "the technological preeminence of Western Europe over Asia was an accomplished fact."[8]

In a certain sense, the relationship between East Asia (notably Japan) and the countries of Western Europe and North America brings this to our consciousness once more. Equipment is an aspect of one culture that is most readily received and used in another, although sometimes its reception reinforces old authority structures and sometimes it undermines them. Equipment is important to public administration because it extends the power of administrators, for good or ill, to act within the scope of whatever authority they have. (It also enhances their ability to act beyond the scope of their authority.)

Equipment and Structure: The Physical "Framework" of Administrative Decision Making

History reveals a highly dynamic exchange between the creation of intellectual tools and physical tools. Contemporary social scientists can learn much from archaeology and classical literature. The earliest technologies are symbols in the mind, not physical tools. The visual symbols for language—characters or letters—are very powerful; as soon as people agree that "A" is not "not A," the symbol is a tool that can be used indefinitely. Writing was one of the most crucial advances in technology. Dating to at least the fourth century B.C., writing was used by the Sumerians "for the consistent recording of numerous daily transactions." Without "the written record administration would have lacked the one technique vital to its extension."[9]

The technologies of the mind depend vitally upon physical technology. Records could not be kept until materials were found on which to keep them—beginning with stone tablets. Almost simultaneously with writing came the significant technological innovation: more flexible and portable surfaces on which to write: papyrus in the fourth century in ancient Egypt, and parchment (or animal skin), which was very expensive. Paper, which was notably cheaper, came into use in China not later than the first century A.D., but did not come into wide use until Arab adaptations of the paper-making process in the eighth century.[10] The papal bureaucracy, and its global extensions, was built upon a foundation of written records that would have been impossible except for the flexible instrument of paper. Concurrently, social technology was being ever more refined by the use of mathematics.

Equipment and structure have a compulsive, coercive effect on human action—hence on administration—similar to other aspects of ineluctable nature. Administration has a *framework*, not in the metaphorical sense normally used to describe administrative action, but in the literal and physical sense. Structural steel, indoor plumbing, central heating, air conditioning, and elevators are all part of the development of administration, even the atmosphere of administration. The modern office skyscraper exists because we have structural steel with which to build it and elevators that allow vast numbers of people to occupy the same land area—literally stacking people on top of one another, like a physical manifestation of hierarchy. Indoor climate controls enable large numbers of people to in small spaces.

Ecological Adaptation

The adaptation caused by modern technology is *ecological*, in that it affects how persons and practices adjust to one another. Technological change also directly affects the ability of administrators to perform their duties. The increase in the nineteenth-century administrator's power to apply force is brilliantly illustrated by the revolver. The revolver is a lightweight device; a five-year-old can fire one. This weapon has become a vital part of police culture, enabling a lone police officer to confront a threatening crowd and enforce the law. It is also imperative to meet the armed force of the lawbreaker.

Cheap photography and cheap printing contributed to the information-providing and information-seeking functions of administration. The poster on the post office wall reduced the scope of sheer rumor about what the "wanted" person looked like and what the charge was. The installation of streetlights had similar relevance in deterring crime and helping to apprehend lawbreakers.

The office, as a setting for large-scale, intense activity in both commercial enterprise and government, came into its own in the nineteenth century. But the problem of large-scale reproduction of documents is much older. Before the typewriter and carbon paper, before the photocopying machine, duplicates of important handwritten documents were made by copyists. In the eighteenth century, for instance, the merchant John Hancock used copyists for correspondence regarding overseas shipping. For the sake of security, duplicate copies were sometimes sent by a separate ship, in the event the first was lost at sea.[11]

Thomas Jefferson, who often found himself without the services of a copyist when at home in Albemarle County, and who had a fascination with the newest technology, tried to use a copying machine made by the Philadelphia artist and inventor Charles Willson Peale. This machine, the "polygraph," was a "mechanical apparatus whereby one or more extra quill or steel pens simultaneously copied on separate sheets of paper whatever the writer was writing with the first pen." Despite Jefferson's enthusiasm, he could not make it work, and as a commercial proposition it was a failure: its manufacturing cost remained twice its selling cost. Jefferson owned another copying press invented by James Watt, as did James Madison, Benjamin Franklin, and George Washington.[12]

There is a record of a slave copyist, Isaiah Montgomery, owned by the brother of Jefferson Davis on a plantation near Vicksburg. At age ten, Isaiah was taken into the Davis household and trained as valet and private secretary. In later years, Isaiah Montgomery described his duties: "There were no typewriters in those days, and frequently four or five copies of a long speech or plea or account would have to be made by hand."[13]

The invention of the typewriter indicates how long it once took to bring a technical innovation to fulfillment. This remarkable instrument was attempted in Great Britain in 1714, but not until 1867 did Charles L. Sholes, an American, build the first practical machine. The typewriter only gradually displaced the copyist, which were still used long after the Civil War. "The slow retreat of the letter copyist from the federal scene is illustrated by President Harrison's experience," White tells us. "He dictated his correspondence to his stenographer, Edward F. Tibbott. The latter then usually wrote out in long-hand the letter to be sent, and also made a typed copy for the files."[14]

Before the copying machine, duplicating typed documents was made possible by carbon paper.[15] Like the typewriter itself, this bit of technology increased the dissemination of information both within and outside an organization. It also created a security problem, making it more likely that un-authorized persons might see sensitive documents—a problem that has exploded with advances in photocopying. Indeed, copying is now so cheap and easy that maintaining confidentiality is much more difficult. As one technology succeeds another, certain elements are carried over. While the typewriter–carbon paper coalition, once the state of the art, has virtually disappeared, the word processor retains a vestige of the typewriter in its keyboard, just as the automobile body is a vestigial version of the horse-drawn carriage.

Changes in equipment may become associated with other interests, so that important changes in social organization occur as essentially ecological adaptations. The introduction of new equipment changes the personnel requirements of an organization in many ways. Doubtless, some people who were skillful with horses and maintaining carriages made the ready conversion to driving and maintaining automobiles. Many others did not. Similarly, the men who dominated the nineteenth-century office as stenographers and copyists were ultimately replaced by female typists and secretaries. This was true not only in the United States, but abroad. The Russian word for typist is *machinistka*, a feminine form. The shift from a male to a female office force occurred just as the office began to expand and the typewriter was introduced.

Sociologists and historians disagree about the reasons for the feminization of office staff. Margery Davies denies that it occurred because of the typewriter; she asserts instead that it was because the typewriter, which coincided with the changing character of the office, had not yet become stereotyped as an instrument to be used only by men. Once women began to enter the work force in increasingly large numbers, their supposed superior dexterity came to be the rationale for placing women before typewriters.[16] Since typists required training, both urban public schools and entrepreneurial business colleges introduced business courses for women. Similarly, the automobile also brought with it a need for school-trained competence. The automobile required a driver and, even more, a trained mechanic. Today the concepts of position classification, recruitment, selection and training, promotion and compensation, discipline and removal are staples of modern personnel administration that are direct responses to the rise of the technician.[17]

Ecological adaptations create new structures of interest, thus changing the politics of the office and of management. Thus, one source of stress, at least at the level of micropolitical decisions, is that changes in work patterns lead to changes in the prestige and compensation attached to particular work functions. Before the availability of air conditioning, supervisors in New York allowed workers to leave early on hot summer days. Even after air conditioning became common, the custom of taking off early had become so ingrained that workers treated it as a right and resisted managers' attempts to revoke it.[18]

New equipment constitutes both a source of stress for those who are so deeply committed to old patterns that they cannot adapt to new ones, and a source of opportunity and profit for those who can grasp the new. If this is a commonplace about office work, it also shows up in larger skill categories. In the civilian electric power industry, the most sought-after officials are those who have received training in the nuclear navy. They are reputed not only to know the reactors, but also to have developed a high degree of organizational skill in the navy mode. In turn, this phenomenon may be socially patterned in that it opens opportunities for members of social groups that otherwise would be less welcome in the work worlds they enter.

Equipment and Administrative Communication: Enhancing Control and Reducing Overload

The parametric function of physical technology is shown more specifically in the problem of administrative communication. When Norton Long urged practitioners and students of administration to study the attainment, increase, use, maintenance, dissipation, and loss of power, his reference was to the social world outside the administrative agency. Yet that set of questions also applies to the internal problem of administrative communication, which is necessarily related to authority and power patterns. The very concept of a *chain of command* implies who is entitled, permitted, and forbidden to communicate what to whom. It involves both express rules, such as the various security classifications (Secret, Top Secret, and so forth) and concepts such as "need to know." It also involves implicit criteria such as deniability (which might be interpreted as the "need not to know") and a subtle web of ideological, cultural, and other understandings that give meaning to words, spoken or written.

Administrative communication entails both the span of control problem and the depth of control problem. *Span of control* refers to the capacity to oversee those who theoretically report directly to a superior. It may be impossible to identify an optimal span of control.[19] By *depth of control*, I mean the pattern of administrative communication between central decision makers, intermediate officials, and the Nth field functionary, from top to bottom, and the reverse.[20]

Thus administrative communication is both social and cultural. However, administrative communication is also a problem of physical technology. Communicating with one's subordinates is one way of exercising command over them. As a military officer once put it, "Without communications, I command only my desk."[21] Some central control must be exercised. At the same time, overload is always a danger for those at the center. The search for ways to enhance control and reduce work overloads may be the most common reasons for people in power to be interested in physical technology.

Large-scale central government with a great capacity for rapid action is possible because of changes that have freed central decision makers from dependence on natural-resource technology. Modern technology has enormously increased the capacity of central officials to find out what their subordinates are doing and to give directions in real time. Until the early nineteenth century, administrative communication over long distances relied on essentially unprocessed natural resources: human muscle (or the ability to speak directly to another person), animal muscle (the horse that Paul Revere rode to spread the alarm), the wind and water that carried ships, or—at the outside—the carrier pigeon with a message attached to its leg.

Some governments, such Rome and various European empires, did cover vast physical territory. The Roman Empire extended from Scotland to the Middle East. The imperial highways formed a great chain of communications some 4,000 miles wide, making it possible for armies to move when and where needed. Edward Gibbon wrote, "Houses were everywhere erected at the distance of only five or six miles; each of them constantly was provided with forty horses, and by the help of these relays it was easy to travel an hundred miles a day." The road system thus gave the emperor "the advantage of receiving the earliest intelligence, and [of] conveying their orders with celerity."[22] Under these conditions, devolution or delegation was inevitable. Ancient empires overcame slowness to the extent that current technology permitted.

The Roman Empire died in the fifth century. A thousand years later, European nations began to extend their empires over the seas. The communications problem was more severe for these empires than it had been for Rome.

Geographic relations were so different that the knowledge required for administration was far more uncertain. The problem can be illustrated by speculating on administrative or managerial control in the Spanish Empire. When Ferdinand and Isabella authorized the first expedition of Christopher Columbus, they took on a distinctive venture with high financial risk.

If such a matter were placed before a government today, the debate would entangle prudent common-sense judgment, sophisticated policy analysis of the kind that graduate programs now teach, and the self-interest of parties who thought themselves to gain or lose by the choices proposed. Samuel Eliot Morison says that royal advisers initially opposed the plan because of mathematical uncertainties in calculating distances, not because educated people adopted "flat earth" theories. They did not doubt the sphericity of the earth, but they thought Columbus's mathematics were wrong.[23]

Albert B. Donworth, describing the discussion of the Columbus project at court, theorizes that Columbus had learned of the Scandinavian voyages across the Atlantic, but his knowledge was purposely kept secret from his potential European competitors. However, he offers no citation whatsoever as to a source of evidence or process of reasoning.[24]

Given what we know of administrative practice generally, we can guess that if Ferdinand and Isabella had indeed overruled their advisers, the latter would not have given up easily, even after the fact. They might wish to persuade their majesties to reject such foolishness a second time. And might not the king and queen have had second thoughts? This presents the problem of administrative communication. Once Columbus set sail, he was beyond the bounds of immediate control. Suppose the king and queen wanted to send someone to check up on him; where in the maritime vastness should the agent have gone? *They did not know where to look.* Even if they had known, they and the distant agent could not have understood the same facts the same way at the same time.

The inherent limits of natural-resource technology also affected the British Empire prior to the American Revolution. When Benjamin Franklin first went to London in 1757, he served as lobbyist-negotiator on behalf of the Pennsylvania Assembly in a dispute with the proprietors, heirs of William Penn, about taxation of their property.[25] On the voyage Franklin was more than a month at sea. On another voyage in 1764, his "friends had wished Franklin thirty days fair wind and he gratefully reported to [his wife] that their wish had come true."

As passage took a month or two from America to London, an agent was often out of touch with what his clients were doing or wanted, and they with him. It is easy to imagine a bargaining session in which Lord North replied, "Well, Dr. Franklin, there really is no point in discussing that, for your people in America have shown their stubborn resistance to His Majesty's wishes. *HMS Overshoot* just arrived with the news that the Adams cousins burned your very memorandum on the steps of the governor's mansion in Boston four weeks ago, the very day you gave the memorandum to us. How can you possibly deal with us in such bad faith?" What could be Franklin's answer?

The time lag would cast doubt on Franklin's credibility. While some might find him reasonable, hard-liners might easily respond, "Wrong! Our latest reports from Philadelphia not only show that he is deceitful, but that sound thinkers in Pennsylvania already are repudiating him." Indeed, something like this happened. While Franklin was away, one of his Philadelphia adversaries spread numerous assertions in England that Franklin had lost popularity in Pennsylvania. This would explain why Franklin was almost triumphant, as he wrote an English ally, as soon as he returned home:

> My Fellow Citizens, while I was on the Sea, had, at the annual Election, chosen me unanimously, as they had done every Year while I was in England, to be their Representative in Assembly; and would, they say, if I had not disappointed by coming privately to Town before they heard of my Landing, have met me with 500 Horse. Excuse my Vanity in writing this to you, who know what has provoked me to it.

The colonial governors represented the crown in North America. As Franklin and his clients were necessarily out of touch, so the government in London and the colonial governors were out of touch. In each case, the natural-resource technology made inevitable a major disjuncture between the information available to principal and agent.

Who can tell what the negotiating situation would have been if the conflicting interests and beliefs had been communicated instantly? The situation remained basically the same in the first years of the republic. Leonard White emphasizes how poor communication was in those early days.[26] It was possible to get letters between Philadelphia and New York in one day, with horses and riders moving in relays, and in the 1790s mail could be sent between Boston and New York in three days. That must, however, have been more or less the equivalent of express mail. The regularly scheduled mail from the east coast to Kentucky called for nineteen days in the late 1790s, and it could sometimes take as much as a month.

Overseas communication was obviously worse. Diplomatic correspondence was often lost because ships went down at sea or were intercepted by the enemy. The hazards of the time produced their own managerial problems in the American government. President Washington, apparently something of a "tight ship" administrator, took Secretary of State Jefferson to task "for failure to send [William] Short [minister at the Hague] his commission and instructions." Considering that Short was already abroad, it is not clear how Washington learned that Short did not have the documents. Perhaps Short—who had good enough political connections to be promised a Senate seat while still abroad—had some friend or connection who came across the water and went straight to Washington with the complaint. "It appeared finally that the vessel carrying these papers was wrecked." Washington's instruction was that, to avoid such complications in the future, duplicates or even triplicates of letters should be forwarded separately. President Adams had the same troubles during the French Revolution. "By 1797 the losses were so great that Pickering and Pinckney, in Paris, sent quadruplicates." It took about six months, on the average, to complete a round of communication with Europe, excluding the time required for preparation of documents. White concludes, "In considerable measure Washington and Adams were forced to conduct their foreign policy on the basis of conjecture or probability rather than solid fact."

Virtually identical difficulties still existed in the first decades of the nineteenth century. When Napoleon found it necessary to abandon his forces in Russia and hasten to Paris, that obviously was a moment of crisis. But it took his army nearly two weeks, traveling at forced draft pace. He started on December 5, 1812, and was in Paris at midnight on December 18. The message of his defeat (in a bulletin issued from Russia on December 3) reached Paris on December 16 and was published on the morning of December 17.[27] When, at a later stage of the Napoleonic crisis, Lord Castlereagh, the British foreign minister, decided that negotiations warranted his presence in Europe, he too moved at a fairly swift pace. Even so, he still required fourteen days to get from London to Basle.[28] There were not many people more important at the time than Castlereagh, and only a handful of people who could claim peer-level standing with Napoleon. We thus may suppose that the horses and conveyances were as comfortable and swift as the technology of the times would allow, given the missions on which they moved. They obviously could command more attention than a letter sent by the U.S. postal service from Washington, D.C., to Kentucky. Yet their travel was hardly more expeditious. The reason lies in the limits of technology. The means available were those provided by nature, and little more.

The eighteenth-century invention of the steam engine, hence the artificial production of power, was a crucial break from natural-resource technology.

Castlereagh was dead by his own hand and Napoleon exiled for a decade before George Stephenson got his first train to run at the momentous speed of fifteen miles per hour. It was nearly two decades more before the first ocean-going steamship functioned. The railroad engine in the 1820s and the seaworthy steamship in the 1840s represented the first dramatic breaks in a long time. Both allowed the movement of bulk—people and goods, as well as the messages that people might carry with them.

However, the communications lag was still there, and on this account the federal government was administratively weak until the Civil War. (Other governments were in the same general condition.) This was not so much because it lacked authority to issue orders. In some respects, the government's claims may have been stronger than they are today, for the courts had not yet asserted much power of judicial review.[29] But the government was weak because it often lacked the practical ability to back up its claims. The number of federal employees throughout the country was modest. Moreover, Washington's communication with, and control over, the field force and its ability to back up the field force was weak, for technological reasons at least as much as the asserted legal ones.

With the railroad and the steamship, one could move messages by sending the human messenger more rapidly, or even by sending the packaged message (letter) more rapidly. The next decisive change was the invention of the telegraph. The "capacity of government to direct and control its agents," L. D. White tells us, "was obviously vastly increased by the revolution in the means of communication," notably by the telegraph.[30] Samuel F. B. Morse, its inventor, could see the possibilities. In 1844 he anticipated the time when "all the agents of the government, in every part of the country, are in instantaneous communication with headquarters—when the several departments can at once learn of the actual existing conditions of their remotest agencies, and transmit at the moment their necessary orders to meet any exigency." In ordinary federal civil administration, the technology was rapidly absorbed. The General Land Office had a field force that received monies in the western states. By 1860 the General Land Office was connected with its field offices, and it used the telegraph routinely to require reports when receivers were more than five days delinquent. The telegraph was brought into service for military communication during the Mexican War and was used for very high-level political communications in the next few years. Although Abraham Lincoln, as congressman, had been a staunch critic of President Polk's action in the Mexican War, he also turned out to be a strong supporter of the war hero, General Zachary Taylor, in his 1848 presidential campaign. We may reason that something was afoot politically, thus, when in September of 1849 the telegraph wires carried this message to Springfield for the former congressman: "Is Mr. Lincoln in Springfield? The President desires to hear from him immediately."

When Lincoln was president, he found the telegraph crucial to his direction of the Civil War. As an undergraduate I learned of Lincoln's insistence on going to the telegraph office himself to see the dispatches from the front. I did not grasp how much this was a product of the president's need to assert command directly, as well as the usefulness of immediate information and of the direct opportunity to send messages expressing his concern with various aspects of the war.[31]

William Seale, historian of the White House, offers us a clue at a very human level. July 21, 1862, was "a scorching Sunday." From time to time the president descended the winding service stairs to the basement, following what would become a familiar path to the War Department's telegraph office. He passed under the west wing colonnade and through the small contingent of soldiers camped on the lawn between the White House and the War Department. In the telegraph room the president anxiously read the dispatches that came in regularly over the wires.[32]

Lincoln needed to *know*, not to satisfy nervous curiosity but as decision maker. Even with such communication, Lincoln still had considerable difficulty enforcing his preferences on some of his generals. Nonetheless, the president could deal directly with his military problems.

The new equipment not only was useful to the federal government but also was rapidly fitted to local administration. Within three years of Morse's demonstration, the New York City Council authorized a telegraphic fire alarm system.[33] This system was operational in about four more years (1851). Other cities probably acted similarly. Over the next twenty-five years, New York City had about 600 signal boxes, and these were so improved that by 1870 a policeman could be summoned or a fire alarm transmitted instantly. The system spread to about seventy-five major cities and towns by 1876. Fire was so serious a problem in the growing city that Delos Franklin Wilcox, with aesthetic and emotional intuition, spoke of the fire force as a delicate barrier between the city and its destruction. Remember that he wrote only twenty-six years after the Great Chicago Fire in which some 300 people died in a twenty-four hour period.[34] The frightful phenomenon of almost uncontrollable fire was still a threat in the twentieth century, as shown in the San Francisco fire after the earthquake of 1906.

However, even in the late 1860s, the feedback loop was still incomplete.

This was true whether for high politics and grand strategy, for routine administration of the Land Office, or for local government. Even if, as a general proposition, senders knew that the written message had been received, they could not know whether it was understood. Nor could they know if or why the agent might urge a different view. In the absence of direct speech, the feedback loop is necessarily incomplete. For example, telegraph messages were usually too short to communicate a message in its full complexity.

Who has yet comprehended the impact of the telephone as a method for direct contact between superior and subordinate, so that each knows what the other has said—instantly? In some circumstances, immediate communication is urgently necessary. When Bell said to his assistant in 1876, "Watson, come here, I want you," people knew that the telephone would work. Its use in some conditions was mandated almost at once. By the following year, Pennsylvania law was requiring anthracite mines to have some form of aural communication with the surface. Three years after Bell's experiment, a telephone was put in the White House telegraph room. President Hayes apparently did not have much interest in it; he spoke with Bell by telephone during a trip to Providence in 1877, but apparently was not much impressed. Treasury Secretary John Sherman (whose name survives in the Sherman Anti-Trust Act) was impressed, however. He had a telephone installed in his Washington home and another in the Treasury. The lines from the White House telephone ran out the window and across the street to the Treasury. "The new communications was but little used at the White House," reports Seale, "because there were so few other telephones in Washington."[35] McKinley was said to be the first president who *liked* to use the telephone—which means that it was nearly twenty years after the device became practical before a president really found it to his taste and needs.

Telephone communication makes it impossible to use the excuse, "I did not get your message," a standard feature of administrative routine. It does not eliminate the possibility that a subordinate will misunderstand a superior's message. It does enhance the opportunity for checking below, provided that a superior is willing to take the risks of skipping over layers in the chain of command. Early in the Kennedy administration, stories circulated that he would call State Department desk officers directly to get the accurate information he needed. These stories may be manufactured myth, but the relationship that they indicate is important for students of public administration to keep in mind.

The telephone proved to be not merely a means for internal control, but also a means for lateral coordination. The working relationship between

Franklin Delano Roosevelt and Winston Churchill during World War II was very close. They sent written messages to each other at the rate of about one a day for nearly six years, beginning on the eleventh of September 1939 and concluding only with the president's death.[36] Some part of that relationship was aided by the fact that they talked with each other directly, their telephone conversations protected by devices to scramble the transmissions so that interlopers would understand nothing being said.

Radio offers still greater power as a general means of communication in administrative organizations. In the first two decades of the twentieth century, the United States Navy adopted radio, even though ship commanders initially resisted the radio due to their subsequent loss of autonomy at sea. Radio came into use not only for military purposes, but also for a variety of civilian administrative purposes, some of which necessarily deal with emergencies. The Forest Service, in which the prevention of forest fires was a high priority, learned to adapt radio to its uses. So did a variety of other organizations, including fire and police departments in local government.

Central decision makers, given the potentiality, will tend to intervene at successively lower levels of detail. One of the most dramatic demonstrations can be found in the decline of diplomacy and in the rise of "summitry," or its kin practice of high-level consultations by others at the ministerial level. In any event, the reduced number of independent decisions made by the professional representatives of nation-states may be attributed in part to changes in technology, which may help to push the disputed issue to the highest level of decision making.

Ecological adaptation is essentially the same as incremental decision making. Adjustments are made at the margin to accommodate the environment. The aggregate of such adjustments often is that some new pattern emerges before people recognize it. In a sense, it is analogous to the case-by-case marginal adjustments that yield substantial changes in the content of the law. When this shows up in the behavior of individual decision makers, people first criticize the individual who seems to deviate from the norm, not recognizing that the old norm itself is collapsing. Such was the situation of John Foster Dulles, secretary of state during most of the Eisenhower administration. Dulles traveled the world frequently, attending to the network of alliances that the United States sought to create around the borders of the Soviet bloc. Critics deemed this unnecessary, often attributing it to Dulles's presumed egotism or his distrust and disrespect for the professional diplomats in the United States foreign service. Dulles may indeed have been distrustful of his professional subordinates. However, his global travels surely have been matched by those of Kissinger, Vance, and Schultz, among his successors. Therefore, we must search for a broader explanation, unless we explain the action of each secretary idiosyncratically. The more plausible hypothesis is that the airplane made it possible for the secretary of state to visit his counterpart in other countries with which relationships were deemed critical. The proposition is that combining high-speed airplanes, making it possible to go almost anywhere on very short notice, with other technologies of communication creates a pressure for centralizing decisions.

President Lincoln's close attention to his military problems exceeded the effective attention he could give to diplomatic problems. It was important to keep the British from cooperating with, and certainly from recognizing, the Confederacy. Minister Charles Francis Adams, in London, was substantially on his own. The president had little chance to coordinate his decisions with any advice or information that Adams might give him. There was no transoceanic communication to match the land telegraph. Samuel F. B. Morse was interested in an undersea telegraph, and a congressional resolution was passed authorizing the study of such an idea. There was a failed attempt to initiate a transatlantic cable in 1850. When the undersea cable was laid in 1866, "the State Department was then as close to its ministers and consuls as the General Land Office to its agents."[37] By that time, however, the war was over and Lincoln dead.

President Kennedy was in a very different position at the time of the Cuban missile crisis of 1962. The reports are that Kennedy paid close personal attention to minute details during the crisis.[38] This may not have been made imperative by the technology, but given the president's anxieties, it may have been close to imperative, as he thought he might well have to issue orders for nuclear attack. It is not surprising that he wished no detail to be overlooked, since the crisis itself revealed to him important matters in which things had gone awry.

Very similar emotional engagement has been reported for at least four of his successors. Lyndon B. Johnson selected targets in the Vietnam War. The same technology made possible, and may have made imperative, a conscious decision made by Gerald R. Ford to be the point of control in the Mayaguez episode. The same technology made possible, and perhaps the rest of the political atmosphere made imperative, President Carter's 1979 decision to control the rescue operation for American hostages held in Iran. The White House, with Lieutenant Colonel Oliver North standing in for the president, directly monitored the *Achille Lauro* episode. Whether the end results in fact reflect this degree of detailed control may be greatly doubted. The question for students of contemporary public administration is whether central decision makers can avoid direct intervention in matters where the communications technology regularly brings knowledge to their immediate attention.

Conclusion

I do not here propose a theory, although theory is much needed. My purpose is to suggest lines of inquiry, of exploration, and it will be adequate if my own speculations should be overturned by more definitive investigation. Administrative history seems to support the belief that there is a dynamic exchange between technology and administration. Equipment and structure have a coercive effect on human action. As a source of pressure on political systems, equipment is to some extent substantially independent of culture. It is the one aspect of culture that is most readily received and used, although the effect of the reception on old authority structures may often be problematic.

If equipment generally controls much of structure, it is especially important in field administration, notably in reducing the "span of control" problem. Changes in equipment not only change structural organization, and accordingly the exercise or loss of power, but also lead to pervasive ecological adaptations and conscious, planned adjustments. Finally, the most important change effected by sophisticated equipment is the enhanced control that comes from freedom from the limits of natural-resource technology. Physical technology has increasingly raised the capacity (or competence) of central decision makers to find out what their subordinates are doing and to give directions in real time. In this sense, the effectiveness of central government is to a large degree a function of the burgeoning technology of the nineteenth and twentieth centuries.

Technology enters our thinking in another way, if we consider the means of administrative action. To what ends are force, money, and information applied? An administrative entity may deal with the world around it according to three fundamental techniques. The first is the absolute hard core of government—*regulation*, or enforcing the authoritative mandate of *shall* and *shall not*, and the softer versions of *may* and *may not*. The second is *facilitation*. Rather than relying upon direction and permission, governance may proceed by assisting persons (or other entities) to do what may be deemed desirable. (In the contemporary United States, the facilitative side of government is enormous, so that most of the blame for the large size of government is assigned to regulation, but it is actually the facilitative side that accounts for it. Public schools and public hospitals, agricultural research in the U.S. Department of Agriculture, and support for medical research—along with in-come support expenditure programs—may be classified in this way. The third means is *entrepreneurship*, in which the government entity acts essentially as if it were a commercial venture. Entrepreneurial administration is designed to be the most fully independent of nonmarket considerations, so that agency managers' perceived needs and the constituency's perceived needs are theoret-ically identical in the relevant organizations. These techniques involve judg-ments about purposes and understanding of consequences, to which we now turn.

7

POLITICS, TECHNOLOGY, AND

ADMINISTRATIVE HISTORY

A TRIBUTE TO JOHN MERRIMAN GAUS

One can only wonder what the discussions must have been like when John M. Gaus and Leonard D. White were colleagues in the same department. On the subject of technology in administration, their interests overlapped and at the same time diverged. White repeatedly focused on the first of the three cross-over (exchange) relationships between technology and administration. His tendency, though with a full knowledge of politics, led toward the technocrats. He focused repeatedly on how equipment was used in the administrative process. Gaus placed "physical technology" among the seven factors that were "useful in explaining the ebb and flow of the functions of government."[1] (The other six were people, place, social technology, wishes and ideas, catastrophe, and personality.) In Gaus's terms, physical technology may produce results that cause shifts in demands on government action. This raises the second crossover relationship between politics and technology—the purposes that people (including administrative decision makers) undertake to serve as they lead to choices of technology—and the third such relationship, actions of administrators in coping with the consequences of technological change.

The Administrative Choice of Technology

The growth of technology is not autonomous. Equipment and choice of technologies do not occur simply by the accretion of knowledge and its logical commands. Decision makers, acting either on their own judgments and de-sires or as surrogates for private demands, seek to produce some new technology. The launching and deployment of technology, in W. Henry Lambright's terms,[2] is a significant activity in which administrative acts play a crucial role. It is essentially decision making about the actual use of money and information as a means of influencing or controlling the choice of a particular technology. A technology can be created only if the principles underlying it and the means of practical application are understood. But such understanding does not lead directly to application. Not all technologies can be developed simultaneously. Either physical space does not permit it—one cannot build a railroad yard and an aviation terminal on the same spot—or financial limitations preclude it, as when there is insufficient money to provide for railroads and airplanes at the same time; or intellectual resources are inadequate, if those with knowledge of railroads and aviation lacked time to work on both.

The choice of which knowledge to pursue to another level of practicality is often made through the direct purposes of officials. Someone must decide which technologies are to be preferred. Those choices may reflect the values that someone attaches either to the interests (hybrid seed corn or new chemical processes) or to the belief that one method is more promising than another.

Lambright aptly summarizes: it takes a favorable political climate to make coalitions of support superior to coalitions of opposition.[3] Technologies may be combined for political reasons, of course, if the backers of each are too powerful or persuasive to be ignored. Values lying outside the technologies are not necessarily superseded by the technology; although once a given technology receives pride of place, its logical processes may override any values that stand in the way. Moreover, every technology is associated with investors who expect to get their capital back with suitable interest, people who seek careers and an earned income stream, or other people who simply are convinced that their lives will be enhanced by something significant.

The chief means for launching and deploying technologies is through purchasing. Decisions to add new equipment are capital investment decisions that are known at all levels and scales of government. Political science would benefit from an effort to develop hypotheses and collect data about government sponsorship of technology. If the government and the economy are not coextensive, then government must acquire what it wants either by appropriation or negotiation, commonly some form of purchasing. Purchasing was recalled to us by James McCamy's discussion of administration-under-contract.[4] Whether privatization and third-party government are efficient modes of service delivery may be debated. What is not debatable is that purchasing is a means of exercising and achieving power. That connection would have been obvious to any city boss of the early 1900s—the time of Goodnow and Wilson. When American reformers spoke of separating politics from administration, they often meant to exclude highly discriminatory partisan benefits derived from public purchasing. Municipal government literature used to include a reformist slogan, "There is no Democratic and no Republican way to pave a street." Among other things, this meant that decisions to purchase rock, gravel, asphalt, and other road construction materials should be allocated on professional, engineering, or efficiency grounds, rather than on the partisan attachments of the sellers. Such a slogan is used to advocate the moral norm that those with power over capital investment should not be allowed to enrich themselves or their friends.

Capital investment involves purchases of conventional technology, currently available, as with the purchase of automobiles for departmental use. Our present interest, however, is capital investment to inspire, generate, or invent equipment that is not already on the market. The necessities of government sustain, as well as ride upon, new technology. This often involves creating a market or buying what is not conventionally available. It means the creation of demand.

It also means the creation of rules for buying and selling. When the necessary studies are done, they will almost surely reveal the real economic history of the United States. Contrary to much doctrine, the U.S. government has consistently provided capital to create or sustain new technology. Indeed, one instructive means to study government departments would be to compare their rankings in the scale of public capital investment. The ability of an administrative unit to secure what it "requires" is a measure of the importance that decision makers attach to its functions. The implicit proviso, of course, is that the acquiring unit will not use it to the disadvantage of those who have provided it. By the same criterion, we might examine systematically the allocation of capital investment to programs and activities.

It would also be valuable to learn how telephones and radios, so indispensable to police work and fighting fires, were acquired by local governments. Such a study of urban government should reveal more clearly the treatment of police and nonpolice needs as surrogates similar to the military and civilian needs in national government. A similar study could be made of the spread of computer equipment. Universities make a distinction between administrative computers (for payrolls, other financial records, purchasing) and academic computers for faculty and graduate students, for undergraduate instruction, and so on. The capital requirements of university medical schools,

compared to those of liberal arts colleges, should provide evidence for thinking through similar results.

The early nineteenth-century postal service was impressed to aid the
emerging steamship industry. On rivers within the United States (constitutionally subject to the power of Congress, whether interstate or not), steam-
ships were soon declared to be postal routes, and as such fell under the
protection of the U.S. government.[5] When the railroads developed, similar
protection was given—even to the extent of government intervention in railroad labor disputes in the 1870s, though according to article IV, section 4, of
the Constitution, federal troops were to be used only at the request of the
states. Administrative decision making supported the research and experi-
mentation that led to the development of the U.S. aviation industry. In the
twentieth century, the U.S. mail contract was essential to the civilian air
transport sector and was vigorously promoted by the Post Office. In this case,
the Post Office–sponsored business provided the foundation for the commercial business. The two combined sustained the aircraft manufacturing industry, which turned out to be available for military production in World War II.

The office machine industry has been similarly, and perhaps more profoundly, influenced by administrative decisions. Today there is little need or
use for the punched card; however, thirty years ago, the punched card—
generally called the IBM card—was the state of the art for industry, though the
frontier lay in computer research. A form of punched card was first used in
cloth manufacturing in the early 1800s in France, with holes cut to control
certain weaving operations. In 1886 Herman Hollerith, an employee of the
Census Bureau, adapted the idea for data collection. Hollerith devised an
electromagnetic means to cause pins to fall through holes in cards representing particular items of information, thus enabling swifter tabulation. As a
result, the 1890 census was tabulated in about one-third the time required for
previous censuses.[6]

Hollerith's reputation was established on a vast international scale, and he
soon had a commercial career in a firm that the late Thomas J. Watson
developed into the International Business Machines Corporation. The Hollerith inventions enormously enhanced the U.S. government's ability to know
about a variety of conditions within the country and to use that knowledge in
decision making. In contemporary terms, we have moved from punched-card
tabulations to computerized models in which the economy is estimated in
vastly finer detail for government purposes than for academic purposes.

One could also inquire into the administrative technology for the physical production of money, a rather technical issue. A crucial problem is pre-

venting whatever society uses as currency from being debased or counter-feited. Among the problems is assuring that each coin is precisely the same as every other in content, size, shape, and weight. This problem drew the attention of Leonardo da Vinci in the fifteenth century, and remains of some consequence today.[7] Paper currency, a creation of the seventeenth century, involves enormous problems of security and protection against both theft and counterfeiting. Thus the technology and operating codes of the Bureau of Engraving and Printing are kept secret.

Domestic or "Routine" Requirements and Large-Scale Purchasing

Later in this chapter we shall emphasize war and war preparation. But preparation for and waging war are not the only situations that stimulate a government's engagement with technology. The routine requirements of government are also important, such as the humdrum question of finance. Money issues necessitate a technology for physical production of money, for its storage and for its recording and counting. Modern government also involves a technology of decision about expenditure objectives; econometric models to assist in choosing what ought to be preferred are very recent developments.

The search for a means of assuring that money is properly collected, stored, recorded, and dispensed is fundamental to bureaucracy.[8] Equipment changes have always been critical to this process. Cash registers, adding machines, calculators, and computers contribute to financial record keeping. The administrative decisions entailed are not about the use of money, but about the collection and use of information on the state of money. The movement from memory, and from presiding over a physical store of wealth, to a system of recorded symbols has been crucial in financial administration in ancient Rome and in the Saudi kingdom of the early 1930s.

The matter is dramatized in modern governments, where the sums of money collected and spent and the forms of transactions are colossal when measured against any past standard. Some of the most critical issues are those concerning the Social Security Administration and the Internal Revenue Service. The SSA, for instance, underwent a major alteration in 1982; its computer systems had become obsolete, difficult to maintain and adapt, and vulnerable to fraud and failure. The General Accounting Office issued a series of reports on the SSA computer problem and summarized it as follows:

> The potential and/or actual consequences of . . . grave system deficiencies were described as including grave risk of failing to pay Social Security

benefits, inadequate responsiveness to legislative changes, exposure to the risk of fraud, and inadequate services to the public. SSA itself cited such examples of inadequate services to the public as: (1) delayed posting of earnings for up to the 3 years, (2) slow issuance of Social Security cards, and (3) erroneous benefit payments.[9]

In 1982 Congress approved and SSA moved to implement a Systems Modernization Plan that included four tasks:

1. Capacity upgrade: Purchase computers and peripheral equipment to replace the inadequate hardware and to correct problems caused by insufficient and obsolete hardware.
2. Data communications utility: Build a modern telecommunications system that would make the automated systems interactive, thus providing quicker service to the public.
3. Data base integration: Move the data files from a slower recording medium (tape) to a faster one (disk); document a state-of-the-art environment in managing data, which would be more responsive to change and better protect the data.
4. Software engineering: Establish an incremental process through which SSA would first document and analyze its existing software and then develop new software and systems to replace inefficient software.[10]

The plan was estimated to cost about $500 million and to be completed in 1987. By 1985 the estimate was up to $863 million and the completion date revised to 1989. Six months later, at least one committee chairman (Congressman Jack Brooks) requested that the GAO answer whether the plan should be canceled or redirected, and whether there was validity to SSA's position that it could reduce staff by virtue of the automation effort.[11] GAO's study reported that over the past five years, SSA had spent $400 million without meeting the objectives of modernizing its software or establishing an integrated data base. (Presumably, this meant that SSA had achieved the improved telecommunications systems and had bought new hardware, with expenditures equal to about 80 percent of the originally estimated project cost of 1982.) GAO described the software problem as the most critical and said that without a solution the SSA would have to rely on the old, inefficient software systems into the 1990s; spend over $190 million more for equipment that might be obsolete before fully used; and delay the development of the integrated data base. In addition to its recommendations to the agency, GAO said Congress "should consider limiting SSA's future ADP [automated data processing] appropriations . . . until SSA demonstrated its ability to complete software redesign, . . . determined its system configuration requirements, and . . . had its revised plan reviewed by appropriate committees of the Congress."[12]

These are crucial practical matters worth serious academic attention. Among other things, they involve problems of how rapidly changes should be made, what is truly the state-of-the-art *requirement* for government decision making under severe financial limits, and the extent to which proposed changes should be frozen, once a decision about the path of development is reached. Similar issues will arise in the FAA's proposed air traffic control system for the 1990s, to be produced by IBM at a cost of $3.6 billion.[13]

The case is still stronger for administrative sponsorship of the computer industry. Although the concept of the computer, like the concept of flight, is very old, the computer was developed for military use. World War II demanded the financial investment and the allocation of human effort necessary to turn the concept into working reality. The first large-scale electronic digital computing instrument, ENIAC, was developed at the University of Pennsylvania during World War I, specifically for military purposes. The army needed equipment to calculate the firing tables necessary for accurate use of artillery. Vannevar Bush, a pioneer in computers, presided over the National Defense Research Committee, which promoted work on equipment suitable to support antiaircraft defense. Military application created a variety of interests, during and after the war, that fostered computer development.[14] Investment for the needs of war and preparation for war supplied the basis for development, from which computer pioneers moved into entrepreneurship. The pattern then appears to have been the adoption of computers, as they were refined, for important industries, notably banking, where they were domesticated for the rest of the business culture. The third step was ever more rapid absorption of computers into the profit-making sector, where their acquisition could be treated as part of the cost of doing business, and where their contribution to profits could be appraised in some crude measure. Their absorption into the nonmilitary part of government has lagged the most, except in some crucial areas where the paper load is intense and where the penalty for failure is very high. This is why, I dare say, that the most important nonmilitary uses in government have been in federal tax collection and in entitlement payments, notably Social Security.

Two computers appeared in the civilian sector of the government within four years after the University of Pennsylvania computer, ENIAC, was operational. In 1954, the first fiscal year in which the president elected in 1952 had full control over the budget, there were ten. Four years after that, there were

250; and by 1962, the first fiscal year in which the president elected in 1960 had full control over the budget, there were 531.

The needs of wartime administration also led to the development of a more far-reaching information system than existed before. During World War I, the War Industries Board became the central policy-formulating agency, organized on the basis of the various commodities. "President Wilson called for the presentation of a weekly 'Conspectus,' as he termed it, of the state of the nation and of the war preparations in particular, to be prepared by . . . a staff of economists and statisticians, and based upon pertinent data supplied by all the agencies of the government."[15] (This report was prepared under the direction of Edwin F. Gay, an economic historian who later became dean of the Graduate Business School at Harvard.) The salient fact is the war required an intensive data-collection effort, and engaged specific and personal interest of the president.

In 1963 President Kennedy directed a major review of computer policy through the Bureau of the Budget. That report, completed after his assassination and sent to Congress by President Johnson, raised issues that return to our present-day discussion of computer use in the federal government.

The Need for Attention to the Military Case

Purchasing is indicated in Willoughby's use of the military term *materiel*, which means weapons, supplies, and tools, in contrast to personnel. Military requirements have been so important that we need to inquire into the history and recent practice of purchasing decisions in military matters. War and war preparation have been notable incentives for government to authorize capital investment for new technology. Tracing the growth of this process from 1940 to the present would reveal major changes both in the economy and in the polity. The United States and its allies have developed a major industrial structure, especially since the Korean War, dedicated to maintaining competence for military production. An aspect of administration of utmost importance is the vast expenditure of funds for the Department of Defense and the armed services. There is, of course, an ideological problem: those most sympathetic to such an inquiry are likely to be antimilitary and opposed to current U.S. policy in world politics. Conversely, those inclined to respect the military and to support U.S. policy—or who see it as no more immoral than that of other nations—are likely to resist such an inquiry. Both are unnecessarily distrustful of the scholarly imperative to follow data wherever they lead.

Whether the preoccupation with war-oriented research has been economically productive is a matter for debate. John U. Nef, an economic historian, argues that the societies showing the best adaptation in war technology were also those with the best capacity for technological development for peacetime purposes.[16] The dismal fact, however, is that a far more purposeful pursuit of technology has been undertaken for preparation for and conduct of war than for virtually any other purpose. Leonard White notes that war was one of the two big stimuli for applying scientific principles to administration in the United States even before the Civil War.

The interpenetration of purpose and consequence is most dramatic in large-scale ventures where technological decisions and large capital investments go together, and it is particularly important in decisions relating to the military. Erroneous assumptions, missed delivery dates, and cost overruns have become recurrent features of the military industrial structure. Controversies about what should be bought, sponsored, or encouraged are framed as matters in which information (scientific or professional judgment) and its extrapolation are crucial.

In the late nineteenth century, for instance, a fierce dispute ensued about the future of the submarine vessel, a struggle that divided naval professionals from their civilian allies in the 1890s. It was in some respects similar to the air power struggles of the 1920s. Then in the next twenty years, debate extended to the issue of converting ships to oil-burning engines. This conversion produced the problem of assuring a secure supply of fuel oil. The British government's commitment of money to Middle East oil was a direct consequence of its decision to have an oil-powered navy. The U.S. government was strongly influenced, for a time, by the navy's interest in securing domestic oil reserves for future military use and protecting them against normal market demands.[17]

Naval officers' interest in radio communications played a part in decisions about the organization of the radio industry in the United States. At the end of World War I, General Electric—then a major player in the emerging industry, to which it has since returned—negotiated with British Marconi about certain important elements of equipment (Alexanderson alternators) that GE controlled. Marconi wanted to buy; GE wanted to lease on a royalty basis. Marconi came back with a much sweetened financial offer on condition that it be given exclusive rights.

GE's representative, the famous Owen D. Young, known to students of interwar diplomacy for the Young Plan on German reparations, disclosed to Franklin Roosevelt, then acting secretary of the navy, the full details of the deal. The navy was interested in the alternator to maintain communications with its ships and bases around the world. Naval officers caucused with one another, and someone apparently even took the matter to President Wilson. There were domestic complications caused by the competitive posture of the telephone company and of Westinghouse, and what Young sought was control of Marconi's American subsidiary.

The issues were almost entirely issues of control. Marconi would rent, but would not sell equipment on which it had patent control; however, the navy was determined to have a completely American system.[18]

Secretary Josephus Daniels, unlike his second in command, preferred government ownership of overseas communication, but government owner- ship was not in the cards. The directors of the General Electric Company purchased a controlling interest in the American Marconi, the British also agreed to terms, and the Radio Corporation of America was formed.

Perhaps the most dramatic debates were those over the development of radar in Great Britain, from 1934 onward.[19] The evidence suggests that similar controversies occurred in the Soviet Union, colored by the environment of terror and conspiracy that characterized decision making under Stalin.[20]

Major administrative issues also arise about what level of risk should be accepted, or for what purposes. One is how quickly the production techniques of one type of industry can be adapted to the production needs of another under urgent conditions. It is virtually inevitable that group A, coming into what has previously been group B's terrain, will deprecate B's approach and enshrine its own. It is also highly probable that, at first A will make disastrous mistakes, which it may or may not ever overcome.

COMPETITION OF *MASS* AND *CRAFT*

The controversy that first stood out in this area was over *mass* versus *craft* production of airplanes. This issue arose during World War I with boat build- ing; it was hoped that auto manufacturers could get results with mass produc- tion methods. But in the end the results were no better. One reason could be that they had too little time to learn how to do the job before the war ended.

These issues were presented anew in the manufacture of a fighter aircraft during World War II. When French and British needs became extreme, Presi- dent Roosevelt called for annual production of 50,000 planes. This order was far beyond the capacity of the aircraft industry. (Until 1939, the American air- craft industry was a modest venture that produced goods worth $279,497,000, roughly the value produced by the confectionery industry.)

Automobile industry leaders had confidence in their mass production methods. However, when manufacturers began to work on airplane production, they discovered technical design features, such as surfaces milled to 5 millionths of an inch, or equipment differences whose significance they had underestimated.[21] In one situation, Ford agreed to produce Pratt and Whitney radial air-cooled engines under license. When the company tried to do so, it broke the available equipment, and it took six months to get delivery of a special tool they had first declined to order.

THE GOVERNMENT'S FRAMEWORK: DESIGN-PRODUCTION SPLIT

As the complications became more apparent, the government decided that airframe firms would remain prime contractors with responsibility for design, while auto makers would produce subassemblies and components. However, the auto makers continued to seek responsibility for manufacturing whole airplanes, and Ford succeeded eventually in producing B-24s at the rate of one per hour, for a total of 6,792 planes. If Ford could do this much, General Motors could not willingly do less.

The General Motors XP Contract

In September 1941 General Motors proposed a fighter aircraft using structures, controls, and accessories already in production for other aircraft. The responsible agency for the government was the Army Materiel Command; under the contract, the government would supply the engine. Only the fuselage would have to be developed anew. "As visualized the new fighter would attain a high speed of 440 MPH at 20,000 feet, and a rate of climb estimated at 7 1/2 minutes to reach 30,000 feet."[22]

In the end, the Materiel Command canceled the contract. When things did not work out, final settlement came to over $9 million on the completion of eight planes and a final production contract cost of over $40 million. For this, General Motors delivered a plane with a rate of climb reduced by about 44 percent, from 5,600 feet per minute (as specified) to 3,000 feet per minute. This meant that the government paid ten times as much as initially estimated for a plane that would perform at slightly more than half the speed anticipated.

The government and General Motors reached an original contract for two planes (XP-75) at an estimated cost of $428,271 for delivery in six months. This meant two planes cost about $215,000 each for delivery by June 1943.

The delivery date embodied Materiel Command's first major concession, apparently. (The original idea had been for April, then May delivery.) After the experimental planes had been delivered, costs apparently were expected to go down drastically. The total cost of the production contract, not merely for the experimental planes, was $325 million with a unit cost of $100,000 (or 3,250 planes), exclusive of the engine to be supplied by the government.

Materiel Command's next major concession was to increase both the number of experimental planes called for and the unit price per plane. The Materiel Command, perhaps to expedite the program, increased the number of experimental models from two to eight, at a contract cost of $4,550,702, and a unit cost of something more than $500,000 per experimental plane (in contrast to the original $215,000). The plan for using ready-made assemblies began to fall apart for a series of technical reasons. Design changes proved necessary. The manufacturer had to switch from wings of one type of craft to another type. The landing gear for one of the planes proved too heavy. Each change required redesign of equipment used to maintain uniformity on the assembly line.

As a practical matter, Materiel Command had to accept design and equipment changes—essential to the process—that further postponed the date for test flying the experimental craft from May to November 1943.

When testing began, the pilot reported that the plane lacked stability and displayed a tendency to stall and spin when making tight turns, "the maneuver most essential to fighter aircraft."[23] The instability could have been overcome by altering and enlarging the tail surface, but this precluded off-the-shelf stock and shifted the plane's center of gravity backward, "adversely affecting its flying qualities." After a crash killed a test pilot, the remedy was to extend the ailerons out to the wing tips, but this delayed production and added weight.

Materiel Command also gave General Motors a letter of intent for a mass production contract of 2,500 planes, with deliveries to begin in May 1944. When it became clear that correcting all difficulties would push the peak production date into mid-1945, at least thirteen or fourteen months beyond the initial delivery date, the contract was canceled.

The XP project illustrates some recurrent difficulties in technological development under high pressure. The problem was urgent. The manufacturer had a strong incentive to proceed beyond patriotism—its own reputation, for possible spillovers into the civilian aircraft market after the war, and because the government was the customer of ultimate financial reliability. Pressure was intense. At the same time, automobile manufacturers lacked both the knowledge and the standards to apply to the problem. They simply did not know what they were doing. Inevitably, estimates about what production techniques would work were often wrong. In turn, delivery dates were wrong and costs underestimated.

Donald Kettl writes an interesting account of this matter in the case of the Divad (or *Sergeant York*), a highly computerized tank that was thought able to locate and strike down enemy aircraft before they could bomb American tanks. The Divad project became excessively expensive, and Defense Secretary Weinberger canceled the project in 1985. It was the first time the Defense Department (DOD) had closed a weapons production line in fifteen years.

> Divad production was to be a model of efficiency. To save time and money, Army planners decided to buy "off-the-shelf" components for the gun. The Army started with its M48 tank chassis to propel the gun. Then it added twin forty-millimeter Swedish Bofors guns, radar from the Air Force's F16 fighter, and a laser range finder.[24]

The objective in this composite approach was to save money and cut the time for producing the new weapon from fourteen years to about seven. By the time DOD closed down the project, it had cost $1.8 billion, and an additional $3 billion would be required for the total of 618 guns the army wanted. Instead, it bought 65 guns to be used for experiments, but they did not meet initial expectations.

Decision Making About Technology—The Regulatory Problem

Administrative decision making also entails coping with technological changes that generate a wide variety of pressures and opportunities in social life. The political process takes cognizance of technological change. Legislators have wide discretion about whether to take up or postpone technological issues. Legislation, on the whole, probably reflects resistance to change, so that the first legislative ventures in technology tend to reflect efforts to defend the status quo ante. The courts must sometimes cope with technology as the source of litigable issues, but adjudication is more controlled by the initiatives of litigants. Public administration must cope with technology all the time, and it has the responsibility for initiative and not merely for response.

The automobile is a different example of ecological adaptation. Its development fed the demand for roads on which it could be used. Henry Ford's membership on the Wayne County Road Commission in the early 1900s requires no elaboration. As public highways became more common and use of the automobile more widespread, other coercive political forces emerged naturally. "Interests," in the narrowest sense of the word, were much in contention: users, manufacturers, builders, machinery suppliers, and so on. Writing in 1947, Gaus noted that "the original causes—a combination of physical inventions such as the internal combustion engine and the vulcanization of rubber—get obscured in the ultimate disputes over taxation, jurisdiction, requirement of liability insurance and examination of drivers' licenses, or over the merits or demerits of systems of traffic control or the financing of over-head crossings or express highways."[25] If Gaus were alive to revisit the auto-mobile industry in the late twentieth century, his reference to the automobile and the internal combustion engine would encompass pollution control, lead-free gasoline, and the airbag controversy, not to mention the energy supply and the question of an oil-import fee. White also emphasizes

> the change in the nature of administrative tasks introduced by invention
> and technological change in the life of the people, and by a wider
> application of our rapidly increasing scientific knowledge to everyday
> problems of community welfare. A century ago public health
> administration was limited only to port inspection of incoming vessels at
> the largest ports only. Since the establishment of air line transportation to
> Central and South America, the United States Public Health Service has
> been obliged to devise vacuum cleaner methods of safeguarding against
> the importation of a single yellow fever mosquito in a Pan-American
> airship. The clipper ship has renewed the possibility of yellow fever
> epidemics under circumstances peculiarly difficult to control.[26]

James McCamy puts this concept on a grand scale when he conceives of public administration as handling "the social consequences of science."[27] Technology can be disruptive, if it enables individuals and entities to violate rules effectively. New technology contains within itself the source of new problems. These disruptive effects may come on a large and bold scale or they may come in small, saturating modes. On a large scale, consider the par-ticularly violent period in criminal history when the Thompson machine gun was developed. Although the 1920s underworld used the machine gun exten-sively, for mysterious reasons police evidently did not often adopt the weapon. In 1926, a chief of detectives in Chicago called for volunteers from among police officers who had served in France during World War I. He told them, "The war is on," that they were to hunt down underworld gangsters "without mercy." They were told that their cars were equipped with machine guns so that they could "meet the enemies of society on equal terms." This cannot have been true, because three years later the Chicago Police Department had only five such guns in its possession.[28] On the other hand, federal agents seem not to have had the same limitation.

On a smaller scale, consider the combined effects of the automobile, the condom, and the motion picture. The drives of human sexuality are always a source of stress on the social order and evoke problems for law and its administration. The automobile is a small, mobile space in which a couple may escape the vigilance of those most anxious to control them. A boy and girl may go where they will, then lie to their parents about where they have been. The condom, reducing pregnancy risk, makes it far less likely that the lie will be detected. The motion picture, endlessly conjuring visions of sensual delight, teaches by example that everybody is enjoying the satisfaction of self. The aggregate is a changed pattern of behavior in violation of the existing rules governing sexual behavior. Once it is admitted that rules are not being followed, those committed to an older moral order argue, "No matter what you say about morals, it is better to face the facts." A similar translation takes place in the administrative practices of school systems, police departments, welfare departments, and the courts, which had previously acknowledged the traditional moral code.

Regulating the consequences of technology has been very visible in American administration in the twentieth century, particularly in its last decades. Influential American scholars have perceived a major difference between economic regulation and social regulation. The former, said to be the "old" or "traditional" form of regulation, applies to the control of prices, investment, rate of return, and profits—expressly calculated. Social regulation applies to production processes, conditions of work, and other such matters, where economic calculations are less obvious. It is fashionable now to criticize social regulation as excessive, costly, and burdensome, particularly in an intellectual atmosphere where Chicago School economics has come to be the reigning orthodoxy.[29] But whatever its merits as economic theory, it is unhistorical to denigrate social regulation. If administrative regulation is a surrogate for what was formerly legislative and judicial decision making, and if we keep in mind what activities legislatures and courts used to undertake, social regulation seems far less novel. It is a natural consequence of technological development.

Nineteenth-century technological development, both in the United Kingdom and in the United States, provides ample clues. In his study of how courts build up and discard precedents, Edward H. Levi offers a set of cases from which to make this inference. They concern the development in England of judicial criteria to determine the liability of persons for injuries caused by equipment they have owned or produced. The courts had, at one stage, to build up criteria to determine liability for want of care; and they ultimately moved to criteria regarding what equipment was dangerous in itself or because of some latent, unknown defect.[30] Leonard D. White treats the same problem in his account of congressional legislation and the creation of administrative agencies regarding steamboat inspection, overseas passenger vessels, and the qualifications of pilots.[31]

Each technology produces a different set of interest relationships and a different administrative pattern. The development of natural gas pipeline technology offers an interesting illustration. The United States has more than 250,000 miles of underground pipe to transport natural gas. Some of these involve very large firms and long-distance lines running from the Gulf Coast to New York and New England. Other lines are shorter. Problems occur only with the creation of a particular technology that allows the transmission of gas. Petroleum and natural gas—both hydrocarbons—are associated in the earth. Whereas liquid petroleum can be put in pipelines or tankers and transported easily, natural gas is extremely volatile and cannot be transported unless refrigerated to absolute zero or contained in a high-pressure pipeline. Essential requirements are a system of powerful compressors to apply intense pressure to the volumes of gas being brought in (up to something in excess of 1,000 pounds of pressure per square inch) and pipes (that may be as much as four feet in diameter) that will contain the gas without suffering ruptures and the consequent explosions. Until this technology is available in any given oil and gas area, natural gas cannot be transported; and producers have little choice but to flare off (burn) the gas—which is patently wasteful but necessary because otherwise the petroleum product is also contaminated.

When the technology suitable for long-distance natural gas pipelines became available, firms were organized, capital made available, and the urban markets of Boston, New York, Philadelphia, Washington, Detroit, Chicago, and so on were linked to the producer areas of the Southwest.

The economic regulatory issues pertaining to natural gas production and distribution are directly related to pipeline technology. When federal price regulations were in effect, prior to the 1978 Natural Gas Policy Act, the term *pipeline quality gas* had considerable legal and financial significance. The Federal Power Commission (and, to a small degree, the Federal Energy Regulatory Commission) had to decide who should bear the cost of removing impurities. At what point is gas of pipeline quality?

In the 1970s, problems arose concerning a proposed natural gas pipeline to transport gas from Prudhoe Bay in Alaska to Chicago and California. The construction project was under the aegis of a statute, the Alaska Natural Gas Transportation Act of 1976. The producers were certain major oil companies that were not entitled legally to participate directly in ownership of a natural gas pipeline. The company authorized to build the line had been selected by the government, within the constraints of the statute; and taking action to make the project financially feasible was of major public importance.

At one stage, the Federal Energy Regulatory Commission was obliged to make judgments about the size of the pipe and the pressure at which the line would be operated. The issue shows how fragile the line is between control (regulation) and facilitation or entrepreneurship. These issues were an off-shoot of the physical technology, in the sense that there were some technological alternatives with different economic consequences. The issue was whether to remove liquids of potential economic value from the gas at Prudhoe Bay or at some point farther south in Alaska. The companies deemed Prudhoe Bay the most realistic point, and Alaskans desired operating pressure to be set at a level consistent with building an extraction plant at Fairbanks, then suffering 13 percent unemployment. It was theoretically possible to operate the line at 2,000 pounds per square inch, but that would drive the gas stream to the lower forty-eight before liquids were extracted. The decision was also governed by considerations relating to the size of the pipe, which had various international ramifications and was largely governed by a decision already made by the president.[32]

The consequences of technological development may be adverse, favorable, or even both. Thus, we may think of two sorts of peacekeeping, one within the domestic polity and one at the international level. Technology facilitates a degree of peacekeeping by providing some procedure or mode of decision making that each distrustful side can believe is more or less tamper-proof. That is the significance of the voting machine.

Like weapons, votes are means of combat, votes being the more civil way by which people may agree to resolve disputes. The voting machine can assure suspicious antagonists that they will not be damaged by cheating at the polls. This fosters trust in the results of balloting to an extent otherwise quite impossible. In American politics, at any rate, the difficulty has not been overt coercion (although most scholars have probably underestimated this abuse) but widespread electoral fraud.

Fraud was relatively easy with paper ballots and was fairly well known in U.S. state and local elections until the late 1950s. Methods of fraud were numerous. The precinct agents of a given candidate might clandestinely mark a blank ballot and give it to a reliable voter, who would deposit it in the box. The voter would secretly give his or her own blank paper ballot to the precinct agent on leaving the polling place. The agent would mark it and give it to another reliable voter, and so on. Ballots might also be invalidated by dishonest election judges. One device was to hide a small piece of graphite under a fingernail and "accidentally" make another mark on the ballot. Polling judges, seeing more than one mark, would be confused and put the ballot aside. Nor is the voting machine proof against collusive election officials, but it is much more difficult to tamper with. Thus it has enhanced the influence of those who believe that administering elections can be a relatively simple technical matter not influenced by partisan considerations.

At the international level, the nation-states have not yielded their arms to votes, but sometimes they agree to arms control or limitations. The great barrier, as reflected in Soviet-American relations, was fear of being deceived by the other side. The development of technological means of verifying arms control efforts may be somewhat similar to the development of the voting machine. The existence of independent means of verification appeared to give both countries sufficient confidence that they could take some chances on negotiations.

At the intermediate level of interpersonal conflict and threat, no known technology is applicable. It has been estimated that something in excess of 100 million handguns are in private possession in the United States. It is, however, utopian to believe that the society could be rendered arms-free in a short time, even if that were deemed desirable. The scanner can be used at airport gates. It cannot be used on every street corner.

Modern technology that overrides natural-resource technology produces significant side effects that invite government regulation. The administrative process has begun to act, on a massive scale, to replace many of the actions that might formerly have gone to court, or to take up actions that have not yet developed into a form suitable for adjudication. One example, as discussed, concerns the sheer physical requirements of the natural gas pipeline operation. What should be the requirements for the materials in the pipes? Where may pipes be safely laid? What notice is to be given to what other parties? These issues are of the same character, though far less dramatic or controverted, than are those related to civilian nuclear power production in the United States. They are issues concerning the acceptable levels of physical risk and the validity of the evidence submitted concerning any given proposition.

Concluding Observations

Administrative decision making is also engaged with the choice of technology, notably through the purchasing mechanism. It is thus also involved in the creation of markets, not merely adaptation to existing markets. In American experience this is verified notably in creating markets for computation equipment, from the nineteenth century until now, and in the creation of markets through military research and development. In high-pressure, high-necessity situations, the routine requirements of government are also very important. The matter is dramatized in the many situations where the routine necessity is to collect, store, and maintain money in some form.

The military case is particularly worthy of attention. The purposeful pursuit of technology for military purposes has been the most critical area for technological-administrative relationships. Regulatory decision making about technology arises from the massive spillovers from new devices. Such spillover sometimes creates possibilities for behavioral change far beyond previously existing rules. A deeper inquiry into this form of regulation will likely render suspect the distinction between economic and social regulation that has come to be common in recent political science.

8

PUBLIC ADMINISTRATION
AND THE PLURAL SOCIETY

In this volume we are concerned with achieving an empirical political theory of public administration. Two methodological points should thus be reemphasized. The first is that this is an exercise of discovery more than of verification. Our objective is to get from practice into theory. If action is known to occur frequently, but theory does not attempt to explain it, then theory is deficient in that respect. The second point is that in searching for material it is legitimate to search broadly, in current phenomena and events in history, and even by disciplined imagination, for the points that may help us to frame future inquiry.

Recall, as well, an essential fact about the discipline of public administration. Political inquiry is far from home. It merely sets the field of administration aside, whereas administration cannot be understood without regard to the logic of power. Public administration consists in the exercise of discretion about the use of force, information, and money or money surrogates—the basic resources of politics. It is thus the central process for the organization of power, the surest operational indicator of what a constitution contains because it is the never-ending record of social transactions between governments, those who willingly accept government authority, as well as those who seek to evade, resist, and capture or control governments. It is the most persistent indicator of the degree of integration and/or disintegration in a political system.

Whatever introduces major change into that process is a source of turbulence. Chapters 6 and 7 focus on physical technology and administrative turbulence. Whereas technology is applied in the effort to attain continuity, it is simultaneously a continual source of disruption, as old practices give way to new ones. Technology, while obeying physical laws, is subject to social choices and depends on the pictures that people have in their heads at any given time.[1]

This chapter turns to an even more obvious source of continuing turbulence in administrative action, one also related to the pictures that people have in their heads: ethnic identity. Theories about public administration are notably deficient. Although ethnic difference is crucial to administrative practice virtually everywhere in the world, it is essentially absent from administrative theory. True, it is minimally introduced into American textbooks under the rubric of *affirmative action*, a policy whereby some classes of persons, primarily African Americans, members of other ethnic minorities, and women, are given preference in hiring and personnel policy.[2] Our purpose in this chapter is to indicate some directions in which political science might go, to observe and document practice more precisely, thus to move from practice into theory. Although the chapter relies heavily on the African-American experience, its intention is not to focus on "the plight of the blacks," but to identify some points of departure for the study of ethnicity as a major source of turbulence in the administrative process everywhere in the world.

Groups and Public Administration

Group action is fundamental to political systems, although political science for the most part limits its inquiry to the constitutional democracies. Interest is even more fundamental.[3] This view does not apply merely to the United States, or major governments, or the governments of Western Europe, East Asia, and Latin America, that receive the most attention from scholars. If this view is correct, then it is fundamental and should be observed in forms of government that do not even approximate democracy,[4] in remote times,[5] and in places distant and almost unknowable.

Thus ethnic groups must be taken into consideration when we seek a theory of public administration. Administrators may attempt to ignore basic social facts, if their beliefs, resources, or strategies so dictate, but over time they will discover that there is a high price to pay in resistance, lack of cooperation, and withheld information.[6] The means of administrative initiative and response will vary according to time, place, agency, and culture. Ethnic groups must be taken into account as we construct theories about administration and social groups in general.

Ethnic Groups and Cleavage

Social cleavages based on ethnicity, as well as those based on wealth and social class, are the most persistent divisions found in human collectivities. The multiethnic polity tends to be a plural society. The behavioral relationships, the intellectual and practical problems of such multiple groups are substantially similar, whether the demarcations are said to be tribal, linguistic, communal, national, religious, or racial.[7]

The ethnic group tends to be described by its members and its folklore as a shared moral order and in that sense is a community. Its members claim to have a reciprocity with each other at a deeper level than with nonmembers and perceive a vital interest in sustaining one another.

There is much pretense in the claims of most ethnic groups. Yet there is also a degree of reality, which social scientists can explore, involving some crucial problems of organization theory. John Merriman Gaus asked, "What keeps members in this organization working together?"[8] March and Simon present half of the question when they identify "the decision to participate" as a crucial decision for membership in any organization.[9]

The decision to participate is largely preordained by social rules that exist for the individual before birth, and these rules are reinforced from the nursery to adulthood. The ethnic group is one of the most important variants of the communal group, as designated by Max Weber, in contrast to the associative group.[10] Members think and feel, on various emotional or traditional grounds, that they belong together. However, the decision to participate in a group is not explained by superstitious notions of "instinct" or "primordial" sentiments. Ethnic identity is a form of organization based upon social fictions regarding a common ancestry and reinforced by rules of marriage, procreation, and the education of children. It is an organization based ultimately on the community of birth and death.

People do, however, cross ethnic group boundaries, explicitly or by silent withdrawal. The pursuit of careers, income, and wealth, the choice of personal friendships and life styles, the selection of potential marriage partners all play a role. The complications are severe. Most African Americans have some skin tone, facial structure, or hair texture that reveals their ancestry. But the fit is by no means perfect. Persons whose physical appearance reveals no African ancestry do withdraw, to live and work in circumstances where their heritage cannot be ascertained. A premium is placed on discretion, if not absolute secrecy. Spouses are not told, children have no reason to suspect, and the passage of time means that the idea of some other heritage would be a shock to grandchildren. A court in a Louisiana case accepted expert testimony that about 25 percent of African Americans have some genes from white ancestors and that about 5 percent of ostensibly white persons have some genes from African ancestors.

The determining factor in the decision to leave the African-American ethnic group is that there are greater advantages to being known as white. By normal criteria, it is entirely rational to seek another identification. This, presumably, was the rationale of the Louisiana woman who sued in 1985 to have her birth records amended. She brought suit against the agency that maintains birth records (Louisiana Department of Health and Human Resources) to seek a mandamus on the basis that her records had always been wrong. The court ruled that "individual racial designations are purely social and cultural perceptions" and that "those subjective perceptions were correctly recorded at the time [the] birth certificates were issued."[11]

The case was peculiar, arousing more curiosity than empathy. Any ostensibly white person with a birth certificate that classified her as nonwhite might rationally follow this woman's course. However, the African-American social norm probably would be deeply offended if a person known to be African-American decided upon a strategy of exit rather than group loyalty.

This concern with the ethnic group relationship is designed to establish grounds for discussing the dynamic interplay between ethnic differentiation and public administration. Public administration in the plural society is our subject. Implicit in this concern are questions about the mutual relationships of social groups. To what extent are groups entirely separate in social transactions? If separate, to what extent are groups merely neutral and to what extent actively hostile? A second set of questions concerns the power situations of groups vis-à-vis each other. Do they share the same kinds of power resources (voting power, economic power), or are they complementary? Does one group have the power to overwhelm and then suppress the other? Is this power recognized by the other? A third set of questions concerns a group's institutions and its capacity to mobilize and use resources when dealing with other groups or with public officials.

Whatever their resources, groups all make implicit and explicit demands upon each other. The aggregate of these demands constitutes the administrative behavior of the plural society.

The Plural Society

How is the behavior of administrators in the plural society affected by the idea of pluralism? The ideal of pluralism, as used by most social scientists, has become an approved civic virtue, at least in the United States. No one respectably opposes cultural pluralism. The plural society is one in which more or less parallel ethnic groups are joined primarily by the coercion system and the economy, through which the most essential physical human needs are provided.[12] In the plural society groups may coexist spatially, in the same economy, and under the same polity, yet their members have very few crosscutting relationships in a minimal number of settings. There is little true reciprocity and sharing of values.

In a plural society, officials commonly make different decisions and undertake different actions toward different groups. If ethnicity were not closely associated with people's behavior, fates, and social roles, then ethnicity would have little to do with public administration. Reality proves that this is not the case.

In contrast to the embattled leader he later became, the young Woodrow Wilson, in his 1886 Cornell lecture, was unique and analytically far ahead of the crowd in recognizing the importance of ethnic and cultural variation for administrative practice. At that time, the United States had not yet received the great flood of immigrants from southern and eastern Europe. Nor had the white South succeeded yet in excluding blacks from national politics. On public opinion as a variable in administrative reform, Wilson wrote, "To know the public mind of this country, one must know the mind, not of Americans of the older stocks only, but also of Irishmen, of Germans, of Negroes."[13]

Wilson recognized a world in which ethnic variation counted. So did Max Weber. Europe did not have the racial divisions represented by black-white relations in the United States, although it was nurturing a virulent anti-Semitism that would soon be shown to the world. Weber, who seems to have anticipated little of what anti-Semitism would do, was concerned with other problems. In the 1890s, Weber was troubled about conditions in West Prussia, "where local landowners were finding it increasingly profitable to employ Polish day laborers instead of German agricultural workers and where, in consequence, a remorseless Colonization was taking place."[14] Prussia's population was 10 percent Polish before World War I, and there were 1 million foreign workers in the Ruhr, one-third in agriculture and the rest mainly in manufacturing.[15]

The world in which Wilson and Weber were educated knew ethnic diversity. Goodnow and Willoughby, Gulick and Simon, like all major contributors to the theory of administration,[16] lived in a world where ethnic differences were as obvious as class stratification, industrialization, professionalization, or any of the other variables that play so large a role in administrative theory. The fact of ethnic diversity is even more apparent in late twentieth-century Europe, as observed in debates about "guest workers." Ethnic diversity is an obvious characteristic of the postcolonial Third World, from which some of the most instructive studies of ethnic politics have come. Diversity is also a factor in parts of the world beyond Europe in which European populations are dominant. The absorption of a large volume of white, non–Anglo-Saxon immigrants into Australia, since World War II, is part of the pattern. Ethnic differentiation is particularly noteworthy in Canada, since the rise of francophone separatism did so much to disestablish older alignments. (In addition to the complexities caused by distinctions among white groups based on language, both Australia and Canada have significant non-Caucasian populations.) In all these circumstances, the scholarly literature shows remarkably little attention to ethnicity and cultural differences as factors relevant to administration. (See chapter 2.)

Yet ethnic differentiation has long been a feature of human organization. This chapter, therefore, offers provisional suggestions as what new inquiry into this subject might explore. The first major topics are the strategies and choices that administrative agencies make as they confront ethnic differentiation.

Administrative Technique, Strategy, and the Relevance of Differentiation

In the United States, the administrative process is centered in agencies (departments, bureaus, boards, commissions) with a wide range of mandates. These may come from external demand (forces in the society at large that impinge on the agency), from organizational demand (internal doctrines, practices, habits, and commitments), and from the free choices made by the agency's leaders and personnel, depending on their values and judgments.

A fundamental problem is that free choice is usually very constrained for administrators. An agency must achieve a certain level of power within its environment. Power is related to the constituencies or interest groups that can offer support when needed and—conversely—can punish the agency when dissatisfied.

An agency has a prime mission that emerges from among many demands.

Its prime mission is not necessarily the same as its formal legal authority. It is the actual performance of services essential to the constituency that, so to speak, holds a first mortgage bond on its time, energy, and resources.[17] The role of public administration in the plural society is strongly influenced by the basic techniques that an agency, department, or institution normally employs in pursuit of its mission: regulation, facilitation of approved social activities funded by the public treasury, or of entrepreneurship when government enables people to achieve these ends by functioning like a commercial enterprise.[18]

Just as there are different ways of defining a prime mission, agencies also approach ethnic differentiation in different ways. Agencies can choose a concept of mission that will allow them (1) to ignore ethnic differentiation, (2) to expand their sense of mission to include ethnic differentiation, (3) to stabilize their existing missions, or (4) to retrench and surrender potential claims to jurisdiction.

In some government policies and institutions, ethnic differentiation is presumed to be irrelevant. This is said to be true in foreign policy, although this presumption is daily proved wrong. If ethnic differentiation is important in a society, it will affect administrative discretion within the entire government system, including how foreign policy decisions are made. Those who guide national economic policy also treat ethnic plurality as irrelevant. This phenomenon is reflected in policy concerns about the level of unemployment. British policy between World War I and the Depression was profoundly influenced by the fact that unemployment persistently hovered around 10 percent of the population, what A. C. Pigou characterized as "the intractable million." This was thought to be not merely an economic problem but a moral problem, as it is in current times by so market-centered a writer as Samuel Brittan. (See chapter 6.)

The unemployment problem in the United States was so intense at the depths of the Depression that it reached about 25 percent and was still in the teens when World War II broke out. The goal of full employment has been an important part of national policy since, though the goal of 4 percent in the Employment Act of 1946 has been abandoned by most commentators and surely by policy makers. However, the unemployment rate for African-American men has always been around 10 percent. This fact means an enormous disparity between blacks and whites in income or savings. The department of the Treasury, the Council of Economic Advisers, and the Federal Reserve Board are all aware of this fact. But the idea that the economic policy-making agencies should pay specific attention to how that ethnic-based separation might be reduced is not taken seriously.

Of course, some agency strategies are intended to control a group that another group wishes to subordinate. Such control is either open or hidden from view, depending on the character of the society, the relative power of groups, constitutional doctrines, and the extent to which controlling a given group imperils other groups more commonly accepted as legitimate.

In U.S. history, at least four minority groups have been subject in varying degrees to federal coercion, not protection. The Mormons were one such group. In the 1850s, a dispute about how the Mormons would be governed in Utah, with Brigham Young and President Tyler as principals on either side, led to the full-scale invasion of the Utah Territory by the United States Army.[19] However, the Mormons were in too strong a position to be coerced by the U.S. government; the price was simply too high.

A second group were Japanese Americans in World War II. The U.S. government rounded up 110,000 Americans of Japanese ancestry, foreign-born and native, from their homes on the West Coast and moved them into concentration camps, where they were confined for much of the war. The attitudes and methods of the federal administrators under whose authority the Japanese were placed are worthy of study within the conceptual frameworks of political science and public administration. How the people responded to this control is also worth examination, including the remarkable phenomenon of a high-performance Nisei combat unit in the army.[20]

The problem of the plural society is also well illustrated by the relationship of Native American peoples to other groups, especially whites, within the larger polity. Westward expansion of the United States was founded on clearing regions that had long been peopled by natives, called Indians, even including the wholesale movement of tribes to other states. There were disputes about whether Indians should be exterminated, permitted to die, confined to reservations, helped to assimilate, or even forced to assimilate into the rest of the population. Moreover, these disputes continue to affect Native Americans today in ways quite unknown to other nonwhite peoples.[21]

Finally, we should take note of U.S. federal agencies' relations with African Americans. The Justice Department's role in advocating the rights of African Americans has been particularly emphasized since the civil rights movement of the 1960s, as it was before the 1890s. However, scholars have generally ignored the fact that the lawyers' side of the Justice Department found limited scope for such work between the 1890s and the 1960s.[22] More to the point, the investigative side of the department has long exercised surveillance and control over the African-American population. This surveillance dates at least from World War I, when the General Bureau of Investigation (GBI) explored the possibility of sedition in the black press and produced a report on the subject.[23] Also worthy of reflection is that on at least one occasion the department's role was sought by one set of presumptively influential African Americans against another whose influence was not in doubt, namely Marcus Garvey. The federal prosecution of Garvey in the 1920s was not merely induced by white racial hostility. Indeed, though white leaders were often vocal and caustic about any threat to their regime, there is little evidence that they sought action against him. However, there is proof that the African-American opponents of Garvey were subject to rough condemnation, which may have caused them to fear for their lives, and that at least one fallen-away member of the Garvey entourage was shot and killed, apparently by Garvey supporters.

As a matter of normal political calculation, an agency tends to move away from subordinate groups. An agency must gather the support of a powerful constituency. It is seldom possible for an agency that adheres strictly to a mission associated with a weak group to achieve the power necessary to defend its interests. One strategy is to expand services to bring in a more comfortable constituency; this explains why the Labor Department restructured the mission of the job referral service for European immigrants so as to create the basis for the United States Employment Service. In 1907 the government created a Division of Information within the Bureau of Immigration and Naturalization whose purpose was to help immigrants to find jobs beyond the Atlantic seaboard cities. However, it could not serve its own political needs if it adhered strictly to its original mission. By administrative interpretation, the agency sought to get outside the bounds that seemed to be set by statute. Francis Rourke points out, "The strict letter of the law allowed only for the administration of an employment service program for the immigrant population."[24] It chose, in effect, a constituency with a bigger political stick. The agency's 1914 annual report reads:

> This division . . . has been specifically empowered by Congress to
> promote a beneficial distribution of immigrants . . . [however,] that
> function may be regarded as having been so far inferentially enlarged to
> include citizens within the scope of its intended benefits. The department
> has, therefore, through the Division of Information entered upon plans of
> work for improving the opportunities of the wage earners of the United
> States, whether citizens or aliens, for profitable employment.[25]

The Labor Department case indicates how redefining a prime mission can improve an agency's chances.

An agency takes political risks, however, when it diverts attention from its mission, or even appears to do so. The more plural the society, the more risk that any administrative initiative toward the interests of a secondary or subordinate group will be penalized. Charles M. Hardin characterized this problem, which arose regarding the former Bureau of Agricultural Economics (BAE), as "whether a constitutional democracy [the United States] can maintain publicly supported research and educational agencies which are fairly free to probe controversial issues."[26] The BAE was controversial from the start (about 1921), as it was involved with debates about price controls on farm products, various land planning issues, and the possible role of farm cooperatives.[27]

However, the BAE was particularly censured when it conducted a "sociological study allegedly raising the race issue." This study dealt with "anticipated rural migration problems in 71 counties representative of the major type-of-farming regions of the country."[28] Because Coahoma County, Mississippi, a predominantly African-American, cotton-growing area, was one of the study sites, the report attracted the unfavorable attention of the Mississippi congressional delegation. The study was apparently seen by very few people, but the bureau director came under intense criticism at a hearing called by members of the House Agriculture Committee. As Hardin describes the event, the bureau director repudiated two offending paragraphs "on the matter of the race question" excerpted from the report.

> [The bureau director] maintained that this part of the report comprised only 3–5 percent. [Two congressmen] thought it comprised 40–50 percent. The only excerpts were read into the hearings by [one congressman] as follows: "At present the militant Negro leadership in urban centers of the North" is making its opinions felt on the rural Negroes of Coahoma County, "for a number of them subscribe to northern newspapers which do not hesitate to emphasize injustices done to Negroes"; and "The city of Clarksdale has a highly rated white high school and a junior high school for Negroes. The municipal swimming pool for whites is located on the campus of the white high school. The school system maintains a free kindergarten for white children of preschool age. The superintendent of the white school is strongly opposed to employing Negro teachers who come from the North or who have been educated in northern schools."[29]

If the dominant social order admits to some responsibility for the "less fortunate," such responsibility will also manifest itself in policy areas and institutions where custodial or remedial functions are at stake. The departments of Housing and Urban Development and of Health, Education, and Welfare have come to be regarded more or less as the national trustees for blacks and others "less fortunate." If an agency's functions are custodial, members of subordinate groups will be able to work in those agencies without loss of self-esteem. Indeed, many will be motivated positively to seek such occupations because they want to serve human needs. This desire has become so deeply ingrained that U.S. black professionals are taught that they ought to entertain such aspirations. Of course, they wish to increase their own incomes and rise in the world. But professional occupations allow them to do so without feeling that they are "sellouts" or remote from the aspirations and needs of their "poor brothers and sisters on the street."

Moreover, those who control the agencies may find it convenient to incorporate minority group members at levels somewhat higher than they would attain in organizations that did not have that group-specific function, even though the function is only latent. It was once easier for a black person to become a welfare worker than a police officer. The welfare worker's function is specific to an assigned case load and could be confined to the black community. The police officer's function was generic and could not be so easily confined without making the emptiness of the promise of full responsibility more apparent, with other bad side effects. These realities could explain many occupational choices for blacks, at each enhanced level of education, until the recent collapse of unofficial apartheid. Black people could become public schoolteachers, case workers, and so on, with less difficulty than they could enter other public careers.

Because administrative agencies may hire persons from subordinate populations to fill positions that perform line functions, such as welfare case workers, teachers, school principals, police officers, and station command personnel, there may also be openings for staff positions such as ethnic adviser or ethnic specialist.

It may appear strange that an office that is politically weak to begin with could afford to take any interest in a weak constituency. Yet now and again an individual, even one belonging to a group relatively remote from power, can make a difference when sufficiently motivated. The United States Office of Education, though it had very little budgetary or other decision-making authority, once took a strong interest in the education of blacks—even directly providing common schools when states could not or would not do so.[30] The original commissioner of education, Henry Barnard, president of St. John's College and sometime chancellor of the University of Wisconsin, included education for blacks among his wide-ranging concerns and interests. This interest was accentuated when Ambrose Caliver, an African-American specialist, joined the office in the early 1930s. According to Harry Kursh, Caliver "would eat his lunch at his desk rather than in the segregated government dining room," an indicator of his group status at the time.[31] He became a bureaucratic missionary, "a veritable one-man factory of information, who directed hundreds of conferences and authored or co-authored scores of major Office studies and reports."[32]

Caliver's freedom with his time is a curious phenomenon, especially as federal interest in education for disenfranchised groups always involved some threat to the system of racial stratification in the South. There is no evidence, however, that Caliver's studies got anything comparable to the hostile reaction to BAE's Coahama County study.

The best expectation is that the high-prestige agencies can assume that ethnic differentiation is irrelevant to their mission. If agencies wish to redefine their missions, they will try to reconstruct their constituencies so as to minimize the cost of service the weaker group (as in the Labor Department example). Some agencies will find it easier to deal with issues that permit them to represent the stronger side (as in the case of the General Bureau of Investigations). Agencies that permit their staffers to take up ethnic issues that disturb some prime constituency will pay a severe price (as in the case of BAE and the Coahama County study). Finally, agencies defined as custodial will have greater latitude. Even in this case, however, we should expect another source of turbulence.

The authority, pay, and prestige structures of the custodial agencies tend to reflect the same stratification found in the rest of society. In the Office of Education, for instance, a sympathetically critical reporter found that females and blacks were relegated to relatively unimportant positions, though the office atmosphere was congenial. That point could be made of virtually all public agencies. It is apparent that, though the absolute number of whites is larger, a large proportion of the welfare-receiving population is African-American; the proportion of white case workers is larger still; and the proportion of whites increases as one mounts the administrative ladder.

We may approach the problem of how administrative agencies function in the plural society with this question: How are basic social resources be used? How does ethnic plurality enter into the process? Answers to these questions involve the structural relations among groups; their history and demography; the cultural, economic, and educational capacities of group members within the larger society; and the groups' sheer physical capacity and reputation. The next three sections sketch some relationships associated with force, with information, and with money and money surrogates.

Administration and Force: "Armed Bureaucracies"

Administrative authority requires some presence in the group from which compliance must be exacted. Therefore, some of the crucial tasks of public administration must be delegated to people who have access and standing in the subject communities. As to ethnic groups, this raises the issue of the layered composition of government service. What persons are likely to be admitted to what levels of authority?

This set of questions is most compelling when it comes to membership in a nation's military and the police, which Cynthia Enloe calls "armed bureaucracies." Political scientists must study force if they wish to understand political systems. Of course, that logic is recurrently violated, especially by American students of politics, as if they are afraid to discover some unpleasant truth they do not wish to know. Yet if force is understood as a basic resource, its use and management are not neutral unless there is consensus about its use. A plural society inherently lacks consensus; force must be the instrument by which one group controls another when conflicts cannot be resolved by bargaining or persuasion.

For "a professional group whose main concern is frequently announced as 'the problem of political power,'" writes Paul P. Van Riper, U.S. political scientists have paid astonishingly little attention to the main instrument of political power—the nation's armed forces."[33] The core question a dominant group must decide is simple. Does it dare trust members of a subordinate group with weapons? What is the composition of the civil and military forces that are permitted to carry arms?

The Problem of the Reliable Force: The Use of African Americans

There can be no more decisive administrative problem for a government than the composition of its armed forces. The question of whether African Americans could be incorporated into a reliable force was long a contentious issue among both civilian and military authorities. This point should be emphasized because at the end of the twentieth century the U.S. military may well be less segregated than any other national institution. African Americans who have reached field grades, and certainly officer rank, have generally had better scope and better opportunities than their counterparts in the corporate sector, in the world of nonprofit associations, in academia, in the entertainment industry (including commercial sports), and in organized religion.[34] The change from the historic pattern is far-reaching. As an administrative problem, the recruitment, retention, and promotion of African Americans in the military has been a controversial issue since World War II and the Korean War.

The driving force for change since the nation's earliest history has been the shortage of manpower. General George Washington, one of the colonies' largest slaveholders, encountered it when he met free blacks in the North. The question was whether they were to be admitted to the forces under his command. Washington treated it, apparently, as a problem of statecraft. He would admit blacks, unless Congress dictated differently. If he did not let them fight on the American side, the British would let them fight on theirs. But the problem was even more severe for colonists in the slave states.

The problem of forcible control, as regards public administration, is intimately associated with the history of U.S. slavery. In March 1779, when the British invaded South Carolina, the word was out that their general would give freedom to blacks who joined him. South Carolina, in a panic (reasonably so), sought help from Congress. But what was Congress to do? It had no available forces under its control. Alexander Hamilton, pragmatic as ever, urged a plan offered by a South Carolinian who proposed to raise several battalions of African slaves. Hamilton said that Congress should "give them their freedom with their muskets [which] will secure their fidelity, animate their courage, and . . . have a good influence upon those who remain, by opening a door to their emancipation."[35]

Hamilton had, of course, to confront the argument of black inferiority. He says, arguing his brief skillfully, that it is not true that blacks lack the intelligence to be soldiers. If they are stupid, he says, some military experts—including the king of Prussia—say that one cannot be too stupid to be a soldier. Besides, it is really "their want of cultivation . . . for their natural faculties are probably as good as ours." He went on, "The contempt that we have been taught to entertain for the blacks makes us fancy things that are founded neither in reason nor experience."[36] If the Laurens plan were rejected, it would come from "unwillingness to part with property of so valuable a kind [that] will furnish a thousand arguments to show the impracticability or pernicious tendency of a scheme which requires such a sacrifice."[37] Congress ultimately adopted such a plan, subject to the consent of delegates from Georgia and South Carolina—which was like making it subject to the pope's becoming a Lutheran.

The question of the corporation of blacks has been presented anew in every American war, with the exception of the Mexican War, where the only blacks involved were body servants.[38] In the War of 1812, manpower needs were severe enough that blacks were allowed to slip through the regulations—and, indeed, the statutes were briefly less restrictive—for service in the navy. But the special twist is that Andrew Jackson, never soft on the slavery question, accepted units comprised of New Orleans free blacks. Partly, his motive was like Washington's—to offset any attraction that might be offered by the British. Some 200,000 blacks served in the Union forces—army and navy—during the Civil War. By 1865, reportedly, two-thirds of the troops in the Mississippi Valley were black, and "Lincoln said that black soldiers had been decisive in bringing the Union victory."[39]

As late as World War I, members of Congress—including Congressman John Nance Garner of Texas, later vice-president under FDR—were still presenting legislation to outlaw or restrict the enlistment of blacks into the U.S. army.[40] Such legislation was never adopted. The United States entered the war officially in April 1917, and by August there was considerable pressure on the subject. The South Carolina delegation was active in opposing the training of African-American troops at Fort Jackson, S.C., fearing enforced social mixing of the races, the influence of northern black troops on local African Americans' attitudes, and the return of South Carolina's blacks from the war with new views about their social position.

Yet whites wanted blacks to be drafted; they did not want white men to be taken away in great numbers while African Americans were left behind.[41] They sought separate camps for blacks and whites, to exclude northern blacks from southern camps, and to allow only South Carolina blacks, serving under white officers, at Fort Jackson. When, in August 1917, there was a report that black troops would be sent to South Carolina, the issue became more acute. Congressman Fred H. Dominick described it as "an outrage on decency that Negro troops should be placed in the same camps with our white troops." Three days later, the South Carolina congressional delegation met with Secretary Baker and the provost marshal general, saying that they wanted treatment and justice for blacks, but "knowing . . . the social structure of the South, stabilized and bolstered by years of vigilance and trial, and the Southern white man's pride of position . . . [they hoped] that the War Department will not begin to offend these things." Congressman Manning then said they could handle black South Carolina draftees only if led by white southern officers. Congressman Asbury F. Lever later told President Wilson of the political implications of this issue and even hinted that it could mean Lever's own defeat at the polls.

The Wilson administration eventually gave in to South Carolina's claims three months later. Secretary Baker informed Manning on October 13 that in the future no blacks other than those from South Carolina would be sent to Fort Jackson. Those already there should be reduced in number as rapidly as possible by giving them an opportunity to join the stevedore and labor companies of the Quartermaster Corps.[42] Blacks from other southern states, however, were later sent to the camp.

World War II did not produce a controversy about African-American soldiers as such, but it did arouse conflict about their use in combat arms or labor battalions, about segregation both on and off posts, about their access to advanced skills such as flying, about promotion to officer rank, and about their treatment by white law officers and civilians. The controversy was essentially generated by African-American lobbyists and their white allies who applied political pressure on the president, pressure resisted by military leaders.[43] The controversy even touched Anglo-American relations because of the large number of African Americans stationed in Britain during the Normandy buildup.[44]

The Truman administration's flexibility on the subject and the personnel crisis of the Korean War led to the collapse of the old system. What did not disappear, however, was a (somewhat submerged) debate about the composition of the military and doubts about the appropriate role of blacks. The issue was very much in the public press during the Vietnam War. Edwin Newman, the distinguished newsman, noted in a book review that the author skipped over the issue of dissident blacks—the most important factor knocking the army out of shape. "The situation has reached the point . . . where only a black can write about it."[45]

The next three or four years saw more publicity on the subject of racial strife in the military. It involved apparently diverse events such as fights between black and white marines on base, the refusal of members of a crew to rejoin a naval vessel, and a sharp charge by the chief of naval operations that his senior commanders had failed in leadership and had not implemented his directives on racial relations.[46] Such issues were also necessarily entangled in the issue of whether the United States should have a military draft as a substitute for an all-volunteer force,[47] along with the overt question of whether military enlisted personnel were sufficiently well educated to perform their duties.

Of course, such matters are not much discussed today. But in 1982 a team of Brookings scholars studied the impact on national security of the racial composition of the armed services. They observed that the Soviet Union, among other nations, had similar problems. On the other hand, the social reception of U.S. blacks stationed in Germany was apparently quite bad; and similar hostility was attributed to Moshe Dayan.[48] In the 1980s, quiet discussions might have been held about the potential reliability of heavily black armed forces that might be put ashore in southern Africa under various assumed conditions.

The problem of the reliability of a military force was seen in Ulster in the early twentieth century. When the British army was called in to that impoverished province to enforce a settlement against the preferences of the Protestants, the cry went up: "Ulster will fight, and Ulster will be right!" This was no small problem for Britain, considering that Ulster had produced a significant portion of the army's officer corps.

In Asia, both the traditional (non-European) empires and European colonial empires relied on military forces that were "ethnically restrictive." In traditional polities, these forces were composed of members of a dominant group. But in colonial empires the process was often reversed, with the military force composed of some minority group that could be counted on to be reliable. With independence, other ethnic groups began to take over the military, as independence movements themselves tended to acquire an ethnic base. The newcomers to power needed to control the military forces, just as they needed the military as a source of income for group members. In due season, a new ideology arose that described the military as an instrument of national integration and development, although this ideology does not usually fit the facts. As Cynthia Enloe writes,

> In contemporary states as seemingly disparate in their political forms and levels of industrialization as China, Belgium, Canada, Syria, Iraq, the Soviet Union, South Africa, Uganda, the United States, and Guyana the capacity of state authority to enhance rather than retard national integration is jeopardized by the association of the military with one or two particular ethnic groups.[49]

Enloe may take a democratic liberal value for granted in assuming the objective of national integration. The initial objective of most ruling groups is surely stability in its own interest, and coercive measures probably suffice to maintain the level of stability they find necessary. Yet Enloe is on target in implying that, where ethnic differentiation exists, the composition of the military may easily become a point of friction or a matter requiring unusual administrative discretion. Up to the U.S. Civil War, the record shows a developing federal administrative apparatus as required by an increasingly commercial system of chattel slavery. The government's limited administrative powers were strained by the fugitive slave problem. If state and local governments in the free states refused to use their police authority to catch escaped slaves and return them to their owners, how were the slaveholders and slave traders to protect their financial value in the peculiar commerce? Could they send their own law enforcement agents in pursuit? Could owners go themselves or send private agents? Of course; but where would these agents stand when impeded and when they needed to defend their claims in the courts of the free states? In the end, this problem could only turn to the question of what federal officers would be obliged to do. What was the function of the United States marshal?[50]

The United States became, after the Civil War, a presumptively free but highly stratified society. The former Confederacy was a territory containing two populations, white and black. The white portion had greater political resources. It also had all the military resources: the police were, after all, the Confederate Army in civilian dress. And the dominant group had no intention of living on terms of formal equality with the other group.[51] If the second population, the freed blacks, were to have their condition notably improved, they required an alliance with the federal government. And if those allies were to be effective, they needed an administrative mechanism that they lacked. Even the minimal police mechanism had to be abandoned.

The reasons are not hard to find. The U.S. Congress—which is to say, the combination of forces in Congress that found political advantage in defending the freed population—vested wide discretion in the executive to achieve its purposes. But the Supreme Court systematically negated those efforts from the 1870s on. (This is almost, but not quite, a reverse mirror image of how matters played in the Congress and in the Supreme Court between the 1930s and the 1950s.) Thus, the institutions of force that became pertinent were those of state and local governments in the former Confederacy, although similar relationships could be found outside that region from time to time.

Before 1969, rural government in the American South was more or less a local government dominated by certain powerful administrators—above all, county sheriffs, who possessed all the police powers a situation required. The fact that they were elected, not appointed, and that they did not attend the FBI Academy or the International Association of Chiefs of Police in no way alters the essential administrative function they performed: discretionary use of force.

As far as I know, there has never been a systematic study of the recruitment of law enforcement officers in the United States, but one can assume that in the rural South before 1965 there were very few black deputies. One of the sheriff's crucial functions in the local systems of power was to maintain the dominance of white over black. (The matter is worth study, as I have encountered the myth that only a black deputy can arrest a black person.) The inquiry is merited when one moves from the rural South to the urban South of the same period. How was law enforcement organized and staffed in southern cities? What was the function of black police officers? What were their understood limits?

In recent decades, the relationship between the U.S. black population, especially urban blacks, and the police has also presented some of the most contentious issues. Given the operational realities of urban police work, the police force should reflect an ethnic split in the society. This is the case. A recurrent situation is one in which white police officers kill one or more young black males under circumstances viewed with anxiety and even suspicion. Confrontations between police officers and young blacks were common during the intense urban disruptions between 1966 and 1971. Black community leaders in virtually every city repeatedly demanded civilian review boards to oversee departmental judgments. If successful, such review boards would, of course, have invaded the virtually closed decision-making systems of police departments—and it is certainly reasonable to call them closed if the New York City Police Department was representative. By the same token, the organized police have vigorously, and usually successfully, resisted such proposed changes.

Police departments in most northern cities have developed a body of African-American policemen with a self-conscious interest different from that of their white colleagues. Nicholas Alex, a sociologist, analyzed some of these realities in a study based upon interviews with forty-one black police officers in New York City in the 1960s.[52] Alex's study shows only what black officers said they thought or knew about their standing or role in police work. Such reports are necessarily subject to misperception or error. But they reveal the mythologies or mental formulae by which people operate. And they are not necessarily wrong. The New York City Police Department had long resisted or discouraged applications from black candidates. Although Alex does not discuss the point directly, it is also commonly understood that the NYPD had long been an Irish-American occupational preserve. Indeed, from musical comedy to the movies, the Irish cop is a staple of popular culture.

Alex's black respondents, interviewed in the winter of 1964–1965, indicated some believable propositions. A good third of them had gone into police work because they were attracted to its capacities. They thought they could do some good. But most of them were in police work for occupational (income) reasons. It offered a good civil service opportunity, better than most would have had in the private market in New York City due to racial discrimination, among other things. Inevitably, the situation was racially stressful. Their superiors and their colleagues, as they perceived it, always saw them as *black* officers, so that their assignments and duties were race-conscious and race-specific, whether articulated or not. They also believed the general public saw them in racial terms, with many blacks expecting special favors and many whites reacting in fear and hostility. Blacks were recruited, or admitted, to the police force more because it needed blacks in situations where a white officer would be exposed to more danger or hostility.

This formation of ethnic groups within departments is not new and not limited to blacks and whites. In the decade following Alex's study, black police officers formed a national organization, reflecting their awareness of the dual position. Organized ethnic splits in police forces have been in place for a long time, and they were apparently a major factor in the troubled career of the lone Jewish officer who finally rose to the top levels of the NYPD in recent years.

The highly stratified racial structure was also reinforced by another institution of force, namely prison administration. Records show that the prison is, indeed, highly stratified. One factor is the division of the prison population into white and black groups, with internal dominion exercised by some prisoners over others.[53] Recent literature often dismisses the intervention of federal courts into various administrative routines in state and local government, including decisions by federal judges to take state prison systems directly into their own control and to mandate expenses by state legislatures. But not more than forty years ago a state prison was a place where a man surrendered full control of himself, in all respects, to prison authorities. Parchman, the prison in my native Mississippi, was noted when I was a boy as a place where a man could be whipped into such submission that he dared not turn over in his bed at night without warning the captain.

Administration and Information

When we speak of information as a social resource, we mean not only sheer facts, but also the communication of values and the use of those facts—filtered through values—as a basis for decisions. Information is both factual and symbolic. Information may be conveyed as a product to be absorbed and used as the receiver permits. Factual information may be a simple matter of the population count in the census. It is convenient, for discussion purposes, to think of three facets of the administration-information linkage in plural societies: (1) the restriction of information by one party to prevent its being available to another; (2) the use of information as a basis for decision making; and (3) the use of information as a means of inculcating values and dispensing practical instruction, that is, the educational system.

PRECLUSION OF INFORMATION

Information can be withheld under many circumstances. The most obvious is official censorship. From about 1835 until the Civil War, southern legislatures and officials, buttressed by their representatives in Congress and the concurrence of federal officials, asserted that federal control over the U.S. mails ended at the destination. The southern authorities claimed and asserted the right to seize and destroy whatever propaganda they deemed incendiary. This meant, specifically, literature of any kind that might question or attack the institution of slavery.[54] That is one kind of restriction.

We are most alert to official censorship, given the experience of the twentieth century, which has seen so much of it. But a different kind of restriction can be mobilized by the informal control mechanisms within an ethnic community. This has occurred for many years in Belgium, where the conflict is over language.[55] Belgium is divided between French-speaking areas and areas in which the predominant language is Flemish (a form of Low German similar to Dutch). Brussels, which falls within the Flemish area, was given bilingual regional status in the early 1970s.

In the mid-1840s, Brussels was about one-third French—the economic and social elite—and about two-thirds Flemish in language. By 1910 the city was 49 percent French and about 70 percent in 1947, cited as the "most recent" source in a 1973 study. In the 1920s and 1930s, Flemish speakers secured legislation to make Flanders a unilingual region. Generally, administrative and educational facilities were to be available only in Flemish; as a result, "French was no longer officially acceptable . . . [and] became a far less attractive alternative to ambitious Flemings." Consequently, "an articulate, energetic and aggressive Dutch-speaking middle class emerged for the first time and . . . gradually wrested control of Flanders from the established Francophone elite."

Flemish speakers, conceiving that bilingualism would lead to Francophone dominance in Brussels, sought further institutional changes. They sought, in effect, what we might call affirmative action to protect their language, fearing a continuing tendency toward linguistic conversion. The political problem is also indicated in that "Flemish militants [were] disturbed and dissatisfied by the [1947] census' findings. . . . They felt that the census represented a popular referendum in which respondents were asked to choose their language preferences rather than an impartial tabulation of Flemings and Francophones." Some conducted unofficial surveys that estimated that 53 percent of the population of Brussels was Flemish. However, in the 1960s the Flemish branch of the Free University of Brussels reported that over 80 percent of the population primarily spoke French. The current situation is unclear. According to the *Economist* magazine:

> There is no official count of French-speakers and Dutch-speakers because the Flemings have for years refused to allow a linguistic census that would reveal the extent of the French-speaking majority . . . The best informal count comes from the ratio of identity cards issued by the 19 communes; about 85% are in French and 15% in Dutch.[56]

The point here is that there can be severe dispute over what might otherwise be regarded as a simple matter of demographic mathematics. In the United States, substantially the same question arises when a small group is convinced that it has been undercounted. The proposition has long been advanced that African Americans, and more recently Hispanics and others, are undercounted by the census and that adjustments should be made in the published totals. The matter is controversial because it has major financial consequences and affects the apportionment of seats in Congress.[57]

There is still another sort of restriction, which violates textbook images of administrators aiding their political masters. A purposeful withholding of information occurs in many variations and at many levels. The point can be illustrated by an illustration from local government. The first concerns the effectiveness of the school board member. Whatever else may be said, board members have no impact on decisions unless they can persuade school administrators or, lacking that, can call on the authority of their position. The latter possibility exists only when a majority coalition, or at least a blocking minority, can be formed to affect decision making.

If no other member is willing to join a coalition, member X is isolated and ineffective. This is inherent in the strictest case of the plural society. As in so many other relationships I have mentioned, there are no data—not because they do not exist, but because no one has organized them and put them into the common pool. Accordingly, I resort to anecdote. In the early 1970s, I attended a session in Little Rock, Arkansas, organized by the Southern Regional Council for the benefit of black school board members from southern states. This was only a few years after the adoption of the Voting Rights Act of 1965, and tension and conflict had by no means disappeared, though physical violence against black voters was no longer practiced.

An elderly man from a rural Mississippi county (familiar to me) was present as a newly elected school board member. His problem was that other board members, and the superintendent, refused to give him the information necessary to do his job. If there were a manual from the state attorney general or state authorities, he did not know of it. If there were a friendly person in the U.S. Office of Education, he did not have that person's name or phone number, or how to get them. Nor was he given information about school budgets. I do not know how long the situation continued, but consider the ramifications. Today there are black school graduates who started first grade in this Mississippi county when this man served on the board. Can one conceive that they began in a sympathetic school environment? That their parents got reasonable support or explanations when they went to school? That they got good counseling about what courses to take and how to prepare for the next step?

INFORMATION FOR DECISION MAKING

The information nexus has an extraordinary number of twists and turns, particularly as it is reached by low-visibility decision that, once made, are almost irreversible. This is the situation of the woman whose birth certificate showed her to be "colored."[58] Few decisions can be of lower visibility than deciding what goes onto a child's birth certificate apart from specific medical information.

What can have happened with the woman who was "raised white, schooled white, [had] lived white, looked white and twice married white," yet who learned at age forty-three that her birth certificate described her as "colored"? The record indicated that "her great-great-great-great grandmother had been a black slave whose owner freed her in 1762 after she bore him four children." These facts would exempt her from being classed as Negro, according to an old statute:

> In signifying race, a person having one thirty-second or less of Negro
> blood shall not be deemed, described or designated by any public official
> in the state of Louisiana as "colored," a "mulatto," a "black," a "negro," a
> "griffe," a "quadroon," a "mestizo," a "colored person," or a "person of
> color."

However, the law had been repealed by the time of the lawsuit. The woman's parents had been issued no birth certificates, and it was concluded that "the disputed racial designations were not made by a public official but by the attending midwife or by the parents themselves." The court concluded that "individual racial designations are purely social and cultural perceptions and the evidence conclusively proves those subjective perceptions were correctly recorded at the time [the] birth certificates were issued." Here was an act of public administration with crucial consequences for a human being, an act intimately involved with ethnic group identity.

Values are a necessary part of the information nexus. When an administrator uses information to organize action or persuade others about what public policy should be, this too can be an abuse. As noted elsewhere, in the early 1970s, certain justices of the peace in Texas would refuse to marry a black-white couple who had secured a marriage license.[59]

The reality of dominant group power in many aspects of administration is too obvious to be missed. But the process is not mechanistic or unilateral. If members of a subordinate or minority group are self-conscious about group membership, they may attempt to act on the moral or psychological dictates of the group in their claim for freedom, liberation, or protection.

In the late 1960s and early 1970s, black professionals in many circumstances felt they ought to use their expertise "to help black people." Sometimes this became virtually part of the job definition. Blacks might assert such a role when a superior lacked the power to prevent them. The potentiality of such low-visibility decision making can only be stated as hypothesis. To what extent it occurs is unclear. It would be instructive to know, for instance, if black and white case workers approach the Aid to Families with Dependent Children program, and its somewhat onerous personal requirements, differently.

The reality, not appreciated by most people, is that the United States census has been persistently controversial since its inception.[60] Those who prepared the 1990 census were particularly sensitive to incipient problems. After the 1980 census, fifty-two state and local governments sued, demanding recounts. Statisticians developed a mathematically sophisticated system for recounting selected blocks and adjusting the reported figures.[61] In October 1988 the Commerce Department canceled plans to implement the recount because of allegedly unsound methodology. Critics alleged partisan motivation, as the recounts were likely to favor areas in which Republicans did not do well.[62]

We might examine what doctrines were set forth in the name of black social workers on other issues. For example, the suitability of foster parents and adequate protection of the adopted child are fundamental administrative decisions in which information plays a large role. Information on this point is a thorough mixture of ascertainable data, such as income level, and more complex research findings in disciplines such as psychology and beliefs that individuals cannot allow themselves to consider.

We might ask what behavior should be expected of social workers in the various low-visibility judgments made in the adoption process, specifically the adoption of a child of a different race from the parents. Since the 1980s this has been an emotional issue. Members of the National Association of Black Social Workers (NABSW) are very self-conscious about white racism and have produced a resolution stating that transracial adoptions have damaging psychological consequences for African-American children. Implementation of this view, of course, means policy decisions that seem to assume some inadequacy relative to race. Ironically, black-white transracial adoptions have been accomplished in Great Britain, where it has been argued that black foster parents are very successful with white children.

These interethnic relationships take other forms, of course. New York State once had strongly organized religious institutions for the care of orphans and foundlings, or children without known parents. The policy problem was how to assign children who, if they were true foundlings, could have no known religious identification. Who knows if such a child were born of Catholic, Jewish, or Protestant parents? Yet once the child was assigned, the child's religious future—insofar as religion can be shaped by childhood instruction—would be determined.

Educational administration at every level, and educational content and policy, also reflects the importance of discretion regarding information. The action may be purposeful or accidental. But it is not trivial. One anecdote concerns the public schools of a very upper-middle-class neighborhood, in a midwestern city, with a world-famous university. The kindergarten class contained two black children, one boy and one girl. By chance the mother of the boy learned that these children were asked to dance for the amusement of their peers. The practice was stopped when the parents intervened with the principal. But countless such low-visibility incidents must occur that are never detected.

Perhaps the most decisive aspect of the administration-information linkage that concerns cultural plurality is the problem of testing students for intelligence, aptitude, or academic competence. The matter is saturated with ambiguity. On the one hand, it is apparent that some individuals have greater intellectual capacity than others. But it is increasingly unclear how far those capacities are inborn and to what extent they are learned. But there is lingering credence given to the concept, rooted in nineteenth-century science, that there are important "natural" moral and intellectual differences between the races and that the Caucasian race is inherently at the top.

The administrative process, at least in the United States, emerges from a long history in which intelligence has been a criterion for decisions about opportunities, specifically education and employment, and testing became the specific means of making the criterion operational. As it evolved, school testing became the means by which psychology became *the* public and private policy science.

Testing has served at least two social functions, neither overtly declared, but both real. The first is to structure the pattern of power and prestige. It follows as a matter of policy that inferior people should be weeded out, placed as a matter of social difference in their "natural" categories. Nor has the argument been absent from the policy scene in recent times. In the early 1970s, Sir Keith Joseph voiced the argument that taxpayers in the United Kingdom was sustaining, under the welfare state, the less competent and intelligent parts of the population.

The U.S. white population has never accepted predetermined stratification by race. But the function of sustaining existing patterns of power and prestige through testing is sharply perceptible on the racial scene in the United States. The function is exclusionary: to discover criteria that white people can meet and that black people cannot meet to the same degree, and to make those criteria grounds for decision making about burdens and opportunities.

The concept of white superiority, of course, antedates the scientific era.[63] It was present among the Founders, as the opinions of Jefferson show; but these opinions can be matched by those of Jay and Hamilton. White superiority is present in the slavery-era debates regarding whether or not African slaves had souls. Claims of white superiority on biblical grounds were met with biblical rebuttals. Nineteenth-century science upheld those claims. Even today, as African Americans overcome one allegation of deficiency after another, a new one is discovered and new research is called for to investigate "innate" racial differences.

That search continues, as reflected in debates about the views of various candidates for appointment during the Reagan administration. Given the cultural assumption of white superiority, to be intellectually or politically persuasive, anyone opposed to that bias must show definitively that a purportedly superior individual is not superior. This is impossible, as new tests will inevitably be produced to prolong the debate. The matter is not purely theoretical. James E. Jones points out, for instance, that testing for industrial employment began to be implemented in the 1960s.[64] It may be a coincidence, but it is curious that this was the first time the elimination of open racial discrimination in hiring became a serious possibility.

If one function of testing is exclusionary, another function is to ration a valuable commodity in limited supply. Testing as a rationing mechanism allows "progressive" elites to protect themselves without adopting the troglodytic discrimination against other groups practiced by their predecessors. By the same token, to the extent that testing is accepted as legitimate, it allows opportunity to be rationed in an "objective" way without creating antagonism toward the rationers. Finally, it is simply a means of easing the task for recruiters, although it may sometimes be a good indicator of job performance.

It was precisely in response to litigation, in behalf of African American claimants, that the United States Department of Labor development a "score adjustment" process for a test used for referrals to private employers of persons seeking certain categories of blue-collar jobs. The "score adjustments" gave additional points to African-American and Hispanic persons, whereas relying on raw scores would have always led to referral lists overwhelmingly composed of white persons. This testing procedure was defended by its advocates, on the basis that the raw scores did not better predict on the job performance, and therefore should not be treated as reliable.[65] Suffice it to say, however, the adjustment procedure was bitterly opposed by the people generally unfavorable to affirmative action,[66] and even the people favorable found it politically impossible to sustain. Therefore, Congress forbade the process. It is, in part, in the atmosphere of debate about ethnic plurality in the United States that other attempts have been made to develop a broader concept of testing. Bernard Gifford, an educator-social scientist, and executive of Apple Computer, has been a strong advocate of the view that educational and employment testing must be restructured in order to use effectively "a shrinking, entry-level work force increasingly composed of linguistic, racial, and ethnic minorities, whose talents are often underdeveloped and underutilized."[67]

INFORMATION, VALUES, AND EDUCATIONAL ADMINISTRATION

Education as a system of symbolic information is designed, among other things, to shape children's identities and aspirations and to dispose them to submit to authority. In this context, administrative decision making about education may be one of the most highly controverted areas. In the Belgian case, to which I have referred, schooling is said to be an important means for the assimilation of Flemish children into French-speaking society. Many Flemish parents apparently sent their children to French schools because of the social and professional advantages it gave them. But they also did so because Brussels had an inadequate supply of Flemish schools. The situation has been altered in recent years. Evidently, Flemings now constitute a national majority in Belgium, and bilingualism works in their favor. They demand strict respect for the bilingual law and achieve the best jobs, both in the civil service and the public sector. French-speaking parents, the journalists now report, are "starting to send their children to Dutch-speaking schools to improve their prospects of finding a good job."[68]

The powerful effect of schooling, and recognition of this power, is precisely the reason the United States has had Catholic primary and secondary schools since the nineteenth century. Catholics believed that the common schools routinely taught Protestant values at a time when overt hostility between Catholic and Protestant was much more noticeable than it is today.

Administration and Money or Money Surrogates

The connection between public administration and money or money surrogates is hard to overemphasize. However, the underlying approach here is discretion in human activity, not merely about contemporary governance; thus we illustrate the importance of ethnic differentiation and economic matters in a situation far removed from the present concept of the public.

If there is a substantial difference between one group and another in access to jobs and decent sources of income, group conflict will appear. Given the importance of administrative decisions relevant to employment, public adminstration will be the scene of such conflict.

The principle is illustrated by accounts from ancient periods long before secular government as we know it existed, and surely long before the concept of a *public* that includes all persons. Richard Hooker, the Anglican theologian, noted the presence of ethnic identification and discrimination in the early Christian communities. When "it was the ancient custom of the Church to yield the poor much relief, especially widows . . . there were [those who] grudged that others had too much and they too little, the Grecian widows shorter commons [daily food allotments] than the Hebrews."[69] Hooker, being aligned with authority, showed little regard for the poor "who are always querulous and apt to think of themselves as less respected than they should be." The biblical account in the book of Acts (chapters 6 and 15) explains how the apostles set up an organized food distribution system so that the ethnic dispute would not divert so much time and psychic energy from the main purpose.

Similar experiences might be found in relief efforts in various parts of the world. In 1927, a great Mississippi flood displaced people into temporary camps. A complaint reached the Coolidge administration that African-American families were kept in the camps longer, given less adequate food, clothing, and medicine, that black men were forced to work on the levees more than other men, that blacks (unlike whites) could not leave or enter without passes, and so on. Secretary of Commerce Hoover arranged for a study, coordinated with the Red Cross, to study the situation and make recommendations. Researchers found the most satisfactory conditions "where the local colored people have had an opportunity to assist in the administration of affairs."[70]

Such relationships must have presented themselves in the New Deal years, both in the programs of direct relief by the Federal Government and in the Federal-state programs. There is some fragmentary evidence concerning Georgia in the early New Deal. The state had received loans from the Reconstruction Finance Corporation to allow it engage in job programs. Most white workers under this program "never received more than 90 cents a day for RFC work, and blacks often got only 40 cents a day, the average wage being about 50 cents a day for 10 hours work. Michael Holmes, the author cited here, when the relief programs were reorganized, the purely federal agencies being removed, and authority being shifted to the state, "blacks, rural residents, and women . . . were the first to be removed from lists" of employees.[71]

Administrative decisions also affect the private economy. While economic theory emphasizes the efficiency and superiority of market decisions unfettered by "political" influence, the political scientist is aware of certain qualifications. Markets do not exist in nature; markets are defined by rules, and rules are defined and enforced according to prior social judgments— which is to say political judgments—that determine what transactions are mandatory, permissible, and impermissible.

The rules relating to property and its use are within our consideration. An administrative decision about the use of property is involved whenever there is a question about what the public official having authority will enforce.

Ray Bromley, an anthropologist, illustrates how this works from field research in highland Ecuador.[72] Rural producers bring their goods to marketplaces in market centers, where the administrative rules are made and applied by the municipal councils. How these rules are made and executed is a textbook example of the dominant groups' advantage over the lower ones through collusive regulation. In these Ecuadorean towns, local officials engage in various forms of petty authority, using the rules as instruments with which to tyrannize over other people in face-to-face situations. Bromley indicates two specific kinds of such actions. Indian (and evidently black) traders are sometimes forced to sell at prices that they deem too low. This seems less like price control than a shakedown. One peasant reported, "Sometimes [white buyers] call the police and make us sell by force. They lie and say: 'This *indio* offered to sell at this price, but now that I give him the money, he won't sell.' As the policeman is a relative or friend of the buyer, he forces us to sell."

Bromley further indicates that officials allow white traders to set different prices for Indian buyers. Municipal authorities "may even formally accept the unequal treatment of Indians in the marketplace," permitting cloth vendors, for example, to use special measures when selling fabric to the Indians: selling several centimeters short of a specified length. Such abuse recalls the U.S. South before the civil rights movement. In the highlands of Ecuador, "it is mutually acceptable that the 'white' may insult, or even strike, an Indian, but never vice versa."

Milton J. Esman observed a situation of Malaysia that was both similar to and different from the situation in Ecuador or the pre–civil rights South. Esman's report contains no hint that either the Malay or Chinese believed that they could rule the other. Economic power and skills tended to be concentrated in the Chinese community, while political power, including the civil service, tended to be concentrated in the Malay community. In that respect, Malaysia was different; the point of similarity is economic conflict. But conflict arose from the fact that the Malays were economically far behind the Chinese.[73]

Administrative decision making about economic benefits has had differential effects in still other areas, notably in matters of contracting and related public expenditure, and in matters where government gives loans or guarantees loans in the private market. The decision about whom government will have as supplier, or whose customer government will be, has historically been one of the most crucial points of decision. The struggle over personnel, to which we turn below, is primarily a struggle over income. But the struggle over contracts is a struggle over the opportunity to accrue capital, and has been of vast importance at many times and in many parts of the world.

Finally, we turn to administrative decision-making and the problem of jobs, both private sector and public sector. In general, we forecast that decision makers will make decisions where they can contain compliance costs for themselves as much as possible. The resistance of some constituency outside the agency is a compliance cost, but it is a less burdensome cost, under most circumstances, than a compliance cost that immediately raises resistance from those who are within the decision maker's authority. This should be understood in the long perspective on the development of policy regarding racial discrimination in the private job market in the United States and the later development of policy regarding racial discrimination in the public sector in the United States.

The concept of an *active* policy against private-sector discrimination is specifically traceable to President Franklin Roosevelt's Executive Order 8802 (1941).[74] However, such a policy, generated by the White House itself, did not become a reality until the Kennedy administration, and may be even more accurately identified with Lyndon Johnson.[75] One might even argue that the serious pursuit of an affirmative action policy did not occur until the first years of the Nixon administration.

President Roosevelt's executive order introduced the language of "fair employment practice," which later became "equal employment opportunity." The executive order signaled that the individual decisions about money (via access to employment) would now be made by federal officials.

The modern concept of affirmative action dates from a plan put forth by the Department of Labor, when George Schultz was secretary, about five months into the Nixon administration. At that time, the Commission on Civil Rights was a high-prestige body, though without enforcement power. When the new administration came to office, the commission had criticized the executive branch's enforcement of various orders that had taken legal effect. During the Kennedy and Johnson administrations, notably the latter, the president had taken the position that companies should not simply wait for complaints, but should act affirmatively to hire people they had previously turned away.

Public employment provides a straightforward example of the challenge of the plural society. Its purpose is to provide a means for getting the public's work done. But control of the public payroll has other, latent functions as well. The merit principle has come to be that no one should be on the payroll who does not deserve the position; furthermore, merit should more or less reflect neutral competence, measured by some objective standard. Absent this criterion, public employment might be used—as it was in nineteenth-century England—to provide income for the less competent sons of the aristocracy and gentry.[76] Or, as in the United States, it might still be used as patronage rewards for those who had labored to support the winning party or candidate. Instead, *merit* is ostensibly the criterion.

However, public employment is also measured by those from whom it is withheld as well as those on whom it is conferred. Recruitment, retention, training, promotion, and pay are basic personnel decisions.

The composition of the ranks of U.S. professional administrators, relative to the population as a whole, reflects how far dominant groups have retained the economic benefits of controlling the government, namely the opportunity to secure income and perquisites.

The classified civil service, when established in 1883, included about 14,000 employees, of whom 620 were blacks employed in Washington.[77] This suggests something slightly in excess of 4 percent of the classified service in that city. In 1892 the Civil Service Commission listed 2,393 Negro employees in Washington. Statistics of this period are of questionable validity; but the impression remains that the Negro civil service saw sustained, vigorous, and definite growth, at least until the Wilson administration. Early in this century, when government was relatively small, racial discrimination within the federal work force was common but not firmly consolidated.

The same Woodrow Wilson who advocated a civil service based on competence disappointed those who hoped he would give a lead in improving the status of African Americans. A century ago, the largest government employers were the Treasury Department and the Post Office. These two agencies were especially notable for African Americans, since they offered the largest number of jobs for well-educated blacks. In the Wilson administration, the heads of these departments were permitted to alter the previous policy, to the extent of reducing employment possibilities for African Americans and introducing a measure of formal segregation in the workplace.

Republican administrations, from Harding through Hoover, may have avoided large national policy issues that interested the overt black leadership. But civil service and personnel policy shifted so that individual blacks could be hired onto the federal payroll. Krislov—relying heavily upon Laurence W. J. Hayes—reports that black employment, which had gone down to slightly under 5 percent in the Wilson years, rose to almost 10 percent by the end of the Hoover administration. Formal antidiscrimination in civil service law began to appear in the early 1930s, though discrimination was still practiced in government agencies. The same trends that produced change in the federal service also began marginally to affect state and local government.

In 1962 Louis Friedland, briefly acting director of Michigan's antidiscrimination agency, provided a useful capsule review of the history up to that time.[78] At that time, "fair employment practices legislation" was still high on the agenda of civil rights groups. Would an active program to eliminate discrimination in the public sector be followed? If so, would it be done within the civil service agencies or by some external agency? Friedland concluded that his state's agency had demonstrated its expertise and did not unnecessarily challenge the prerogatives of the Civil Service Commission.

Electoral victory has been a major factor in easing discriminatory practices. Peter Eisinger found in a study of cities where blacks held high office, that once blacks achieved political control, the proportion of black public administrators rose dramatically:

> Black professionals in Norfolk grew to nearly perfect proportionality from a baseline of next to nothing. Black workers achieved a nearly perfect fair-share in New Orleans, increasing their numbers by two-thirds. In Little Rock, there was a dramatic gain in the number of black administrators, and there was a similar gain in Oakland. But nothing equals the change that occurred in Oklahoma City, where the black administrator fair-share score went from a mere 2 in 1973 to 129 in 1980.[79]

The federal government has also brought its weight to bear, to some extent, in trying to get local governments to adopt affirmative action plans. In 1973, Frank Thompson presented an analysis of Oakland, California, that shows something of the process in local government where officials are *relatively* friendly and interested in affirmative action.[80] Oakland had the usual features of a large black population (approximately 50 percent) and economic decay. Oakland operated with a council-manager government and a civil service staff (under a personnel director) that constructed and administered tests, advised on education and experience requirements, participated in an oral examination board, and generally offered advice on recruitment. When Oakland's government came under sustained pressure from the black community, with the assistance of some federal informational inquiries and a good deal of publicity, the city government offered a sort of contained response. City officials sought to retain control over the personnel process, but at the same time tried to make what response they could. Thompson's case material refers to a relatively adaptive city government. Eisinger, as mentioned, refers to the adaptation that comes when there is a dramatic increase in the perceptible political power of blacks in large cities.

Where control did not shift, administrative resistance was likely. But the other side of the personnel picture is sustained resistance to changing the old pattern, especially affirmative action requirements. In the 1970s, Mitchell Rice and William E. Verner, Jr., circulated an inquiry to seventy-one municipalities in Texas asking for copies of their affirmative action programs.[81] Only 45 percent, or thirty-two municipalities, actually replied. Those who did not respond probably either had not initiated affirmative action or, even more likely, did not want to make themselves vulnerable to external public relations criticism or legal action.

The most dramatic evidence of a protracted resistance to compliance was in the Alabama State Police case, *United States v. Paradise* (1987). In a closely divided decision representing fifteen years of litigation, the U.S. Supreme Court upheld an order that had originated in the Federal District Court in Alabama.[82] In 1972 the court found that the Alabama Department of Public Safety (which administers the state police) had discriminated against African Americans for many years. In thirty-seven years there had never been a black trooper of any rank. The court issued an order setting hiring quotas. Seven years later, by 1979, no blacks had reached the upper ranks. As of November 1, 1978, there were 232 corporals, but not one of them was black. The court issued a Partial Consent Decree. The department was to develop a plan to promote corporals, the next rank above patrolman, with no adverse impact on blacks and with certain other guidelines.

In 1981, two years after the partial consent decree and a year after the deadline for compliance, the court issued a further decree providing for administering a test, reviewing the test results, and other measures. After a further series of complicated technical steps, the court concluded that insufficient progress was being made. It therefore ordered, "for a period of time only," that the state police would promote officers on a one-for-one basis (one black, one white) if qualified blacks were available. After the department promoted eight blacks and eight whites, the district court suspended the 50 percent requirement. The U.S. Department of Justice appealed the court order on the legal theory that race-conscious remedies are unconstitutional and the only people entitled to benefit from affirmative action decisions are specific individuals who could prove in court that they were personally disadvantaged by some past discriminatory practice.

From Practice to Theory:
Notes for Conceptual Development and Empirical Inquiry

The intellectual problem here is to work toward a political theory of administration that provides a better understanding of the simultaneity of continuity and disruption—administrative turbulence. We are searching for the terms by which working hypotheses may be framed to guide further study.

Practice should not necessarily be held up as a norm. This is an important point, given the strong moral tradition underlying much of political science and public administration theory. What theory most adequately describes and explains what occurs? What research would best determine if theory has produced the best forecasts?

Three Basic Resources and Agency Performance

How can we develop hypotheses about the relation between three basic resources—force, information, and money or money surrogates—and administrative decision making in the plural society?

ADAPTING TO THE USE OF FORCE

The fact of intense cleavage between group A and group B will cause an emphasis to be placed on the instrumentalities of force. This should lead us to expect that the reliability of the military institution will be a key consideration, and that decision making will be predicated upon the supposition that its reliability must not be compromised. We cannot emphasize too strongly that the illustrative material about the United States and the role of African Americans in the military is not our main argument, though that is where the illustrative material originates for the most part. This cannot be unique in human experience, nor in the contemporary world, unless there is not now and has not been in the past any other society with a similar structure.

In the plural society, the shortage of necessary personnel will be a driving force, leading to the accommodation in the military of persons who otherwise would not be equally acceptable. The American experience, from which this rough inference is derived, is that this pressure from the shortage of otherwise suitable personnel was experienced from the time of the Revolutionary War until the time of the Korean War. General George Washington, a slaveowner, made the pragmatic decision to accept free Africans into forces under his command in the North. If they were not permitted to fight on his side, he reasoned, they would be permitted to fight on the British side. He was not forced to deal with the question in the South, though Hamilton—his ambitious young aide, let us recall—offered a similar concept for the South. Andrew Jackson, whose personal career and attitudes were even more entangled with slavery, made a similar pragmatic decision about accepting support of free persons of color in New Orleans. The administrative decision is to convert these outside people into marginal resources, to be utilized at the margin. In successive situations, the American political-military authorities found themselves forced by necessity to open the services to less and less restricted roles until we reach something like the situation of the 1990s. A second version of the plural military situation is represented by the case of various colonial empires in which the dominant group is able to make choices among possible recruits from several ethnic groups and to use members of one group to exercise control over the others.

The plural society also experiences the problem of how to compose its instrumentalities of force in the civilian sector. (1) To a very large degree, the instumentalities of force, as they developed prior to the Civil War, were related to the problem of slave control in the South and of slave capture in the North. There were, of course, other significant elements, but these were the elements that imposed a pressure for arbitrariness into the system. (2) The slave capture issue disappeared with the disappearance of slavery, but the mechanisms for control over African Americans may have become more intense because control officially was supposed to have expired, but socially was demanded by one part of the population.

In the urban North, the police system would appear to have become essentially a set of ethnic preserves, the consequences of which are still being lived out and adjusted in the 1990s. The same point can be made with regard to the prison system, as the other important part of the system of overt coercion.

WHERE ETHNICITY AND INFORMATION INTERSECT

The situations we have discussed prove that information is not necessarily neutral, but is closely connected to the exercise of power. This entails whether information will be sought or procluded from being developed, to whom it is presented, and how it will be used to structure choices.

The low-visibility decision to write the word "colored" on the birth certificate of a female born in Louisiana in 1934 created *information* that had great consequences for the child and others connected with her. The administrative decision to conduct a census in Belgium and the decision not to adjust certain figures in the 1990 United States census represent other choices about expected benefits and values. A new census in Belgium was expected to show numbers unfavorable to the Flemish-speaking population; although making adjustments to the 1990 U.S. census was expected to yield advantages to many, it did not favor the interests of the Bush administration.

The discussion above also suggests other elements in which values and preferences, amounting virtually to dogma, enter the administrative process. An illustration is the position of the National Association of Black Social Workers on the subject of transracial adoptions. The discussion also refers to pragmatic adaptations in which information is more or less created by an arbitrary administrative procedure in order to satisfy some other social need, as the random assignment of religious identification to foundlings to satisfy the needs of the religious groups providing their care. Finally, in discussing information as an element in the administrative process that has political consequences, I have discussed the crucial question of academic testing as a means of rationing social benefits.

ETHNICITY AND MONEY AND MONEY SURROGATES

The third set of illustrations make the point that ethnicity affects administrators as they allocate resources to fulfill human needs. Accounts from biblical times and from the writings of Richard Hooker testify to the power of administrators who allocate food. Public contracts are a modern example of the same kind of power. If a government purchases goods and services, access to markets and control of the purchasing process are of major importance. When ethnic groups control the administrative units that purchase goods, they have the power to benefit the networks of which they are a part. Further, because government can intervene in employment decisions, administrators can influence who has access to jobs, both public and private.

Agency Techniques, Missions, and Strategies

The problem of maintaining power is fundamental to the administrative agency. Cooperation of others, inside and outside the agency, is essential for the exercise of power. An agency must have the support not of the clientele it serves, but of the constituency or interest group that has the capacity to support or refuse to support the agency.

An agency's prime mission—how it performs those services essential to the agency's clientele—emerges from various influences: the agency decision maker's core values and beliefs; organizational demands imposed by an agency's doctrines, preferences, and established practices; and external forces. The strategies an agency will follow in the face of ethnic differentiation in a plural society is shaped by all these influences.

If social groups are clearly separate and unequal in power, agencies will tend to define their prime missions around those with power so as to allow them to ignore the power minority. The higher the prestige and importance attached to the agency's function, the more likely it is to claim that ethnicity is irrelevant to its function. The U.S. State Department and other agencies concerned with foreign affairs are apt, in the national interest, to disclaim any concern with minority groups. Similarly, the Treasury Department, the Council of Economic Advisers, the Federal Reserve Board, and the Office of Management and Budget approach national economic decisions with virtually no regard for the unemployment statistics of any specific minority group. As social groups alter their status in the power scheme, agencies change their responses to those groups.

An agency can change its prime mission so as not to offend a vital constituency. The story of the Bureau of Agricultural Economics provides an example in its Coahoma County study that "allegedly" raised the race issue—in gross violation of the prime mission of an agricultural agency. The agency staffers who initiated the study neglected to notice that the agency's prime mission was to serve the interests of large planters who depended on the cheap labor of submissive African-American agricultural workers.

The Labor Department redefined itself just before World War I. By statute, its job referral service was designed for European immigrants. But that clientele, who could not vote and had little social power, was not a constituency. Labor defined itself to extend its constituency to encompass all working people at a time when the power of the labor movement was growing.

Ethnic differentiation can be incorporated as a part of an agency's mission of custodial assistance. Agencies may pay some attention to the concerns of subordinate groups if they do not challenge fundamental power. This explains how the Office of Education (originally the Bureau of Education) could take an active interest in African-American education, even when it was an explosive issue in the agricultural South. This is how an agency official such as Ambrose Caliver could carry out a vigorous program of research; there were no active interests in the education coalition able to stop it.

Finally, agencies can adopt a control strategy dictated by a dominant group, or a group that fears a challenge. The Mormons in Utah in 1857, Japanese Americans in World War II, and Native Americans and African Americans at various stages of our nation's history provide examples. Control strategies reveal a deep ambiguity in the Department of Justice between its law enforcement responsibilities, which has sometimes included a commitment to reducing racial stratification, and its investigative side, committed to the control of sedition and other threats.

Group Resources and the Structure of the Group Situation

Agency strategies should also be considered in relation to group resources and the overall situation of these groups—their power resources relative to each other. For instance, Milton Esman shows that in Malasia the Malay population dominated electoral politics and the civil service, while the Chinese dominated business. Administrative behavior would have to recognize the fact that neither group dominated the other, that both groups had leaders that could make commitments for their members.

Agencies also have internal ethnic strains. Pay, power, and prestige within an agency are affected by the larger society. In the United States as late as the 1960s, the "first blacks" were appointed to ordinary, middle-level or senior administrative posts. Thus much ethnic conflict arises from the professional and personal ambitions of persons of various ethnic groups within the agencies themselves.

The possibility of members of minority groups entering an administrative agency is affected by its prime mission, especially when they are needed to serve others of the same group. It was easier to hire African-American case workers when their clientele would be African-American; however, not until the past two decades could one assume that a white client, even a poor one, would be assigned to an African-American case worker.

Administrators' conceptions of their jobs are also affected by their group membership. Lenneal Henderson discovered that few administrators undertook "advocacy" activities: defined as joining certain organizations, changing a job conception as a result of their convictions, donated to civic or professional organizations, or participated in demonstrations on their behalf. Exceptions were African-American administrators, who were more likely to have engaged in such activities; however, curiously, Henderson found no important differences between the behavior of white and African-American administrators.

Conclusion

This volume has called for a political theory of administration—specifically, to explain "turbulence in the environment of operating administration." Ethnic conflict within a larger society is a powerful exogenous influence on the behavior of agency administrators, which in turn becomes a means of further defining the depth and extent of such conflict.

In the search for empirical studies that will help us define our concepts, social scientists must define *plurality* and *integration*. If, on the basis of the knowledge of ethnic relationships, one could not predict how administrators will relate to those over whom they have authority, one might conclude that a society is integrated. If—conversely—one can virtually always predict these relationships on the basis of difference, this would constitute the perfect case of the plural society.

Social scientists should also inquire into the dynamics of group relationships outside the administrative system—depending on how far ethnic differentiation is regarded as morally legitimate and legally sanctioned. The moral legitimacy of ethnic differentiation depends on how it is treated under law.

The plural society and ethnic differentiation are sources of great turbulence in public administration. Indeed, when human beings are unable to resolve conflicts without coercion, administrative government assumes the critical responsibility of protecting the political system from collapse. Northern Ireland, since 1922, has been an example of a plural society held together by economic need and coercion imposed by the British government. In 1947, India—a pure administrative government under British rule—was partitioned into the Republic of India and Pakistan. The transition exhibited not merely turbulence, but the absolute triumph of disruption over continuity, the collapse of the civil service administration under the pressures of a plural society. This, too, is a result that students of public administration might well ponder.

These chapters are designed, let us recall, to advance the hypothesis that public administration is central to politics. With that as my point of departure, my subject is turbulence: the interplay between continuity and disruption. The administrator's task is to maintain continuity and avoid disruption. Whether they study public or private organizations, analysts must repeatedly either discover their own form of politics or promulgate analyses of management so far removed from reality as to be worthless. This is often interpreted as divorcing public administration from politics. As a rule, people dislike politics. Politics deals *necessarily* with conflict, with aspects of human experience and behavior that can be exhilarating and ennobling, yet can also be quite ugly—so people wish not to acknowledge them. Whether the dislike of politics is universal or only a Western phenomenon, it is manifest in American culture; it is particularly evident in the pejorative language used to describe politicians and in popular habits of thought about public administration.

As a result, many people wish to address questions about management and organization theory in a way they think is rigorous and free of the "opinions," "uncertainties," or "irrationalities" associated with politics. This requires a form of analysis from which "politics" is removed. This, however, is mere escapism. Politics is both a necessary and rational means of reconciling multiple objectives. Solipsism, psychosis, and ultimate quietism are all escapes from politics, if only by surrendering all power to others.

All people must depend on group decisions made on the basis of many criteria; the idea that decisions can follow a single criterion of rationality is absurd. Illustrations of conflicts caused by multiple criteria flood into the mind. University hospitals are frequently confronted by the promotion and tenure claims of an emergency room physician who is known to give good service to patients but who will never publish in the *New England Journal of Medicine*. The rector and vestry of a small parish have the problem of how to cope with a fellow parishioner who holds the same ultimate beliefs that they do but who may be disruptive in the life of the parish. Similar illustrations could be taken from the activities of a university economics department or could be introduced into Herbert Simon's discussion of the organization of a business school. From these small examples of micropolitics, we can move to higher and higher levels of interorganizational decision making—interagency, interdepartmental, intercorporation, interstate, international.

It is not that there are no objective or single-value decisional criteria. But conflict is so pervasive that any organizational effort to ignore politics will be nullified by results. Results will mandate adjustments that are political whether they are called by that name or not.

The study of public administration becomes, in part, a study of how to sustain continuity and quell disruption. The administrator does not always favor surface continuity, and creating disturbance may be a way of wielding sufficient power to reestablish firmer control. Of course, disruption may ironically be induced or provoked by an administrator to achieve the quiescence needed to assure further continuity. There are reports, for instance, of Asian societies in which administrators have sometimes encouraged massacres to forestall what they consider worse disorder. The very concept of the *agent provocateur* is that of one who induces a group to do something that, in turn, precipitates retaliation by the authorities. Such ideas illustrate why our conceptions can only be provisional hypotheses. American thinking, in the twentieth century, can conceive of literal massacres as administrative strategies. It is even more true that administrative theorists (and some administrators) do not necessarily favor surface continuity. Some theories of administration— such as the New Public Administration—are predicated on the value of non-violent disruption.

The intellectual problem, accordingly, is to trace the conceptual and empirical consequences of any particular approach to our hypothesis about public administration. In this vein, even given a concept of public administration as most conventionally understood, the present literature in the field is impoverished by its separation from earlier twentieth-century predecessors. In due course, we may create both a more orderly set of theory and a more orderly aggregation of data if we search for continuity, not disruption, and decide whether any given source of disruption is intellectually functional or a useless diversion.

Today we face both an opportunity and the necessity for a new departure.

The study of public administration must leave its self-assigned intellectual ghetto, and political science must learn that without a firm grounding in the realities of administering the law, it will always miss the realities of power. This epilogue thus proposes three themes as a basis for new research from which new theory may be derived.

Hence the first major theme, stated in the first two chapters, is that political science may profit from drawing more confidently on the work of our intellectual predecessors. There is an unrealized potential for a political theory of administration. Technology has changed enormously, and the language in which administrative concepts are expressed has changed also. Our research objectives should be to discover what problems are worthy of inquiry, to consolidate the concepts set forth already, to reframe them into hypotheses to guide inquiry, and to reevaluate what is intellectually credible to assert in light of this renewed investigation. A fresh approach is needed. Despite much criticism and attempted refinement of these ideas, public administration continues to be analyzed as though it can be separated from politics. As reflected in Peter Self, Fred W. Riggs, and others, theorists still insist on this distinction to make it possible to study administration independently of politics. The intellectual purpose of this approach is to sustain an administrative process in a democratic polity.

From the literature on the politics of administration (Herring and others), it was a short logical step to the bureaucratic politics literature (of the William T. R. Fox variety) in which policy was conceived as the product of competitive adjustments among agencies and agency interests. The scope of public administration was increasingly limited to issues of detail—often of great practical importance, but which did not command broad intellectual interest. The consequence was that the major intellectual issues that could have been associated with the field were displaced to other disciplines.

Political scientists after World War II gradually lost confidence in their own work and began to seek guidance and sanction from intellectual work in other fields. This loss of confidence affected the whole field. Political scientists interested in public administration could not achieve their ends by merely pursuing their own intellectual interests, but by redefining them using the nomenclature of other lines of inquiry. For some political scientists (though very few), the issues became questions of management. For still others, the potentialities of organization theory seemed appealing. Others found liberation in the idea of systematic inquiry into the nature of bureaucracy, under the influence of Max Weber.

New nomenclature often entailed the pursuit of different ideas, interesting in themselves, but often increasingly removed from the core problems of political science. These several currents of administrative thought continue to mingle and separate. They sometimes amount to statements about the same phenomena in different languages, and there is a necessary confusion in discussions of policy, politics, and *politique*. But the meanings are often the same. Moreover, the major landmarks in the study of administration have different meanings to different scholars. Organization theory focuses primarily on interpersonal factors, and to some extent on the interaction of individuals holding individual positions. While many theories account for the impact of environment on how the law is administered, the question of when and how the environment affects administrative decision making or how administrators themselves control the world outside their entity, exceeds the scope of organization theory. However, we must repeatedly return to these crucial elements of politics if the organization of control is our main subject of inquiry.

The quest for a political theory of administration also implies taking a serious approach to the work outside the academy, confronting the realities of the social world. The distinction between theory and application, between public and private, has often proved intellectually harmful when treated as ritual. The reason there is a management science, for instance, is that there are great problems of execution of which political scientists are generally unaware. In principle, the problems are not beyond our ken, but completely within the scope of our normal concepts. For example, the concept of "stakeholders" is a means of recognizing that the corporate decision maker must take account of various relationships that are political in character, regardless of whether any public authority is involved. The truth of this statement is also clear to anyone who participates in the affairs of the church. Similarly, despite the doctrine that a firm's chief executive officer is in complete control, relations among executives, boards of directors, and subordinate employees in a firm exhibit the same characteristics as those in government as studied by political scientists.

Those seeking a theory of administration will be subjected to pressures that divert attention from central *scholarly* questions. Such pressures, after all, are inherent in human experience. On the other hand, they also generate scholarly interests. For example, the small organization is susceptible to profound divisions and tensions. What do scholars know and say about enhancing cooperative relationships? I suggest, in an academic world that is rapidly changing, that scholars might study why there is such a propensity to factions, schisms, and distasteful behavior in university departments.

The second major theme (stated in chapters 3–5) is the need for new inquiry into the roles, uses, and limits of dogma as a means for crossing from theory and research into practice. The analytical principles undergirding administration theory are not restricted to public government and organizations as they make demands on public government. This fact also raises a problem in thinking: does reduction of turbulence in the intellectual environment mean a parsimonious neglect of disturbing facts? As I point out in chapter 3, one must necessarily make choices before undertaking action or research, whether these choices are purposeful or reflect inherited beliefs. Objective scrutiny will reveal that certain administrative theories were designed to facilitate an established administrative practice. Practice itself is made necessary by political dogma, which guides choice. We all hold political beliefs and preferences—dogma—that we are prepared not to examine. It is thus necessary to construct a theory of administration to fit the dogma. We may persist in adopting such a compatible theory even though experience makes it so thoroughly hard to accept that one escapes the burden of dissonance reduction only by an act of faith. The dogma of executive leadership as justifying a strong presidency was articulated in the Brownlow Report and given new life in the 1980s by judges committed to a Hamiltonian theory of the separation of powers. The preclusion of research may also be the result, of course, of conflict about dogma within a discipline.

At the same time, we are faced with the pathological consequences of dogma. The dogmatist may persistently advocate a given position in the face of compelling new facts. It is easy to say that this is wrong, but such condemnation does not resolve a problem for the decision maker. Yet when dogma precludes new thought or the interpretation of new data from experience old and new, it frustrates the best efforts of empirical theory.

Whether this kind of blockage has occurred with regard to the nature of executive leadership and the efficacy of central executive direction, is a natural question. Following the assumptions of bureaucratic theory, to attribute such political responsibility to public officials is wishful thinking. Under bureaucratic theory, the administrative process stands on its own, being self-contained and beyond external control. One may ask whether judicio-political theory, extending the dogma of executive leadership advanced as common sense by the Brownlow propositions, may not create further turbulence in U.S. public administration.

Management science, in its various forms, is attractive not so much because it is demonstrably superior, but because it provides an effective reinforcement for the dogma of management prerogative. Management science provides what bureaucratic theory cannot provide—namely, a positive program and method that purports to be decision making without politics. The human relations movement is an adaption that still serves the prerogative concept, but manages to induce more loyalty, provide for more voice, and diminish unwanted exits by employees—all without the weapon of fear.

This volume also examines the problem of dogma and the uses of administrative law in the United States. Both lawyers and political scientists run the risk of failing to recognize certain important realities of the U.S. experience in public administration. Challenges and political combat lead to results that must be articulated in "rational" terms, and concepts thus invented are ultimately reified: they take on lives of their own. By taking a lesson from cultural anthropology and looking at systems and values of a different order, we get a different perspective on administrative law. It is a means of appealing decisions made by administrators and enables central authorities to supervise those at lower levels, thus helping to maintain the alignment of policy, program, and operational detail. In centralized, highly complex regimes lacking legitimate political opposition, administrative law may be a way for rulers to oversee the actions of their agents. A challenge to the legality of an official's action speaks only to the presumed errors or departures of that official, not the legitimacy of the ruler or the ruler's policies.

The third major theme of this book (chapters 6–8) is that there are major exogenous sources of disruption in administration that need further examination. Here one focuses on two phenomena that are likely to produce disruptions: physical technology and ethnic differences in the society. The impact of technology on public administration should be given more attention. A basic concept expounded in political science literature is that political conflicts found elsewhere in society will also affect decisions about scientific and technical issues. Somewhat in conflict with this proposition is a secondary implication: that political decision makers are incapable of making wise choices about matters of science, especially as the science-based choices now are so pervasive, far-reaching and irreversible in their consequences. Finally, there is the ever present thrust, grounded in Marxist theory, that posits the exploitative character of capitalist decision making regarding issues of science and technology. On the other side, literature in the tradition of Frank H. Knight and Friedrich von Hayek and their followers asserts that government regulation is basically inefficient or has adverse consequences.

These issues are worthy of discussion. But chapters 6–7 present a different conception of intellectually strategic choices. The history of public administration and its relation to technology reveals underlying political processes because technology *necessarily has political consequences.* History abounds with examples of major changes in administrative practice caused by technological change. If they essentially reflect the same patterns of action as occur in the wider contemporary world, then we are closer to making fundamental observations about human action. If they are qualitatively different, we have helped to establish boundaries for studying something unique to administrative practice, and thus give a qualitative distinction to the term *modern.*

Changes in physical technology have had three important consequences for administration of the law. (Alternatively, one could say that physical technology is the independent variable with regard to three important dependent variables.) Technology affects the structure and organization of work, which become qualitatively different; technology affects the communications structure and the possibilities of central control; and technology affects government officials' decisions both as to capital investment and regulation.

It would be useful to inquire into the relationship between technology and the enforcement of legislation. If those with administrative responsibility are willing to enforce legislation, when does enforcement require a technology of force? When does it require a technology of information that is merely cognitive? When must the information be more than cognitive? How is one to administer a declared public policy ("execution of the state will") that is designed to serve some party's advantage? What about legislation that vests an entrepreneurial function in a government unit?

We must identify the unfolding technological changes that are likely to influence administration. Such changes have important social consequences. The importance of physical technology today is demonstrated in public action, or public controversy, on a variety of fronts: (1) communications technology, and the degree to which its regulation leads to regulation of the content of information transmissions—a genuine First Amendment problem with important political and economic implications; (2) the massive technological enterprises that produce hazardous wastes; (3) the technologies of contemporary financial transactions, particularly with the emergence of twenty-four-hour global trading; (4) genetic screening and genetic engineering; and (5) computerized weapons systems, including the Strategic Defense Initiative, or the computer capacity for launch-on-warning, in which human command can be dispensed with upon receipt of a warning that enemy missiles have been launched.

The parallel exogenous factor treated here concerns public administration in the plural society (chapter 8). The plural society has a compelling and turbulent impact on administration. If administration is the exercise of discretion regarding the public use of force, money, and information, then one must ask by whom? against whom? for whom? how? to what purpose? These questions accentuate a neglected problem: the fact of ethnic plurality and its impact on administration of the law.

Intense cleavages between group A and group B in a society will force an emphasis on the instrumentalities of force and on ensuring a reliable military and a dependable civilian police. Yet subordinated groups must be included in those forces. How is this to be achieved?

Ethnic differences have sometimes meant the preclusion of information, information given to some persons and withheld from others, the use of information to structure choices that have a lifelong impact on individual lives. The low-visibility decision to classify persons by race on birth certificates is an administrative decision, as is the decision whether or not to conduct a language-use census in Belgium. Controversy in which information plays a large role is evident in decisions affecting child welfare and adoption and academic testing as a means of rationing social benefits—even as a means of excluding certain social groups.

Ethnic differences also affect the administration of the law in the distribution of goods and services. Decisions regarding the allocation of food and shelter, public contracts whereby the government is a purchaser of goods or of services, regulations that govern access to the market and protection of property, and decision making about both private and public employment procedures are all examples.

How force, information, and money (or money surrogates) are handled in plural society is also related to other issues. The problem of achieving, maintaining and exercising power, a fundamental matter to the administrative agency, are all affected by an agency's constituency and its prime mission.

Agency strategies have to cope with the relative power of ethnic groups. Are these groups merely informal organizations, but with leaders who can articulate aspirations and make binding commitments for the group?

The anecdotes, cases, and stories recounted in chapter 8 accentuate other issues as well. The internal management of an agency will be affected by plurality in the polity, since pay, power and prestige within the agency—even the possibility of joining the agency, depends on an individual's ethnic identity.

The aim of this book is to contribute to a political theory of administration that will offer greater clarity on five intellectual and practical problems in human action. Problem 1: explaining and foretelling the growth, stabilization, or decline of institutions that constrain the use of force, money, and information by formal administrative structures. Problem 2: explaining the different capacities of administrative institutions to acquire and to exercise discretion about the use of force, money, and information. Problem 3: understanding the structural features of the administrative system, including bargaining-and-command relationships between superiors and subordinates; the requirements of "field administration"; and decision making about the extent of central control, devolution, and negotiated power sharing. Problem 4: administrative initiative in policy making. Problem 5: the extent to which our knowledge permits us to understand administrative and organizational design as predicting, as forecasting or merely as prophecy.

Finally, there is no empirical distinction between political power and bureaucratic power. There are only different manifestations of political power, and different modes of rising to power. The higher civil servant is quite as much a practitioner of power as the elected officeholder. The political reality lies in the relationship to the action, not the form of office that initiates action. "The life blood of administration is power" is a proposition with which we concur. The point can be extended. The life blood of power is administration.

NOTES

Introduction

1. *Jerusalem Post*, "Spotlight," April 14, 1990, 8B.

2. Cited in Matthew Holden, Jr., " 'Imperialism' in Bureaucracy," *American Political Science Review* 60 (1966): 943.

3. Matthew Holden, Jr., *The Centrality of Administration to Politics*, Working Papers in Public Administration no. 1 (Charlottesville: Institute of Government, University of Virginia, 1984).

4. Morris Janowitz, William Delany, and Deil S. Wright, *Public Administration and the Public* (Ann Arbor: Bureau of Government, Institute of Public Administration, 1953).

5. Henry J. Friendly, "Some Kind of Hearing," 123 University of Pennsylvania Law Review (1967), 2167, in *The Legal Foundations of Public Administration*, ed. Donald D. Barry and Howard Whitcomb (St. Paul: West, 1981), 4, n. 10.

6. Bryan Jones, *Governing Buildings and Building Government: A New Perspective on the Old Party* (University: University of Alabama Press, 1985).

7. Austin Ranney, letter to the author, March 25, 1969.

8. E. N. Gladden, *A History of Public Administration*, 2 vols. (London: Frank Cass, 1972).

9. A. Leo Oppenheim, *Mesopotamia* (Chicago: University of Chicago Press, 1977), 95–109, 235–49.

10. D. Mackenzie Brown, *The White Umbrella: Indian Political Thought from Manu to Gandhi* (Berkeley and Los Angeles: University of California Press, 1958), 53–58; Carolyn Webber and Aaron Wildavsky, *A History of Taxation and Expenditure in the Western World* (New York: Simon and Schuster, 1986), 78–90.

11. H. H. Scullard, *From the Gracchi to Nero* (London: Methuen, 1963), 110.

12. George Steindorff and Keith R. Seele, *When Egypt Ruled the East* (Chicago: University of Chicago Press, 1968), chap. 9.

13. A. N. Sherwin-White, *Roman Foreign Policy in the East: 168 B.C. to A.D. 1* (London: Duckworth, 1984), 267–28.

14. David Braund, ed., *The Administration of the Roman Empire, 241B.C.–A.D.193*, Exeter Studies in History no. 18 (Exeter: Department of History and Archaeology, 1988).

15. J. D. Fage, *An Introduction to the History of West Africa* (Cambridge: Cambridge University Press, 1962), 18–39, provides a brief overview of the major African political units.

16. H. H. Gerth and C. Wright Mills, eds., *From Max Weber: Essays in Sociology* (New York: Oxford University Press, 1946), 209.

17. For a somewhat idealized treatment, see Cheik Anta Diop, *Pre-colonial Black Africa from Antiquity to the Formation of the Modern States* (Westport, Conn.: Lawrence Hill, 1987), 43–129.

18. Christopher Bellavita, ed., *How Public Organizations Work: Learning from Experience* (New York: Praeger, 1990).

19. Hannah Pitkin, *Fortune Is a Woman* (Berkeley and Los Angeles: University of California Press, 1984.

20. My reference is based on conversations with my colleague Henry J. Abraham, who was the prime minister's undergraduate contemporary.

21. I am obliged to B. Guy Peters for comments on this point.

Chapter 1. The "Accumulated Wealth of Concepts, Questions, and Generalizations"

1. Having observed motivation and work habits among government executives, corporate executives, professors, and lawyers, I have concluded that scholars inflict more painful demands upon themselves, against more subjective and elusive criteria, with a higher probability of failure and more modest rewards for success, than any of the others.

2. Charles E. Lindblom, "In Praise of Political Science," Review Essay, *World Politics* 9 (January 1957): 240–53.

3. For this figure of speech, applied to scholarship, I am indebted to Brantly Womack.

4. See Leonard Schapiro, Foreword to *Government and Opposition* 1:1 (November 1965).

5. Cf. Dante Germino, *Machiavelli to Marx* (Chicago: University of Chicago Press, 1972); and S. I. Benn and R. S. Peters, *The Principles of Political Thought* (New York: Free Press, 1965). Outside the European tradition, see E.I.J. Rosenthal, *Political Thought in Medieval Islam* (Cambridge: Cambridge University Press, 1962), which reflects a clearer awareness of administration.

6. While some distinction between *executive* and *administrative* came into political science via William F. Willoughby, it was not a prominent idea even in the 1920s. Charles E. Merriam, *American Political Ideas: Studies in the Development of Political Thought, 1865–1917* (New York: Macmillan, 1926), illustrates this by treating *administration* by cross-reference to *executive*.

7. See Charles S. Hyneman, *The First American Neutrality* (Urbana: University of Illinois Press, 1934); *Bureaucracy in a Democracy* (New York: Harper, 1954); *Popular Government in America* (New York: Atherton, 1968); *American Political Writing in the Founding Era* (Indianapolis: Liberty Press, 1983); *The Supreme Court on Trial* (New York: Atherton Press, 1963); and *The Study of Politics* (Urbana: University of Illinois Press, 1959). Hyneman was department chair at Northwestern University at a crucial period when that institution begin its profound shift toward becoming a virtual center of

behavioral political science. That shift was intensified under his successor, Richard C. Snyder (see *Approaches to the Study of Politics*, ed. Roland A. Young [Evanston: Northwestern University Press, 1958]).

8. Sir Henry Taylor, *Autobiography of Henry Taylor*, 2 vols. (New York: Harper, 1885); see also *Dictionary of National Biography* 9:410–12.

9. Sir Henry Taylor, *Notes from Life* and *The Statesman* (London: Kegan Paul, Trech, [1836] 1883), 211.

10. Plato, *The Laws*, trans. Trevor J. Saunders (Baltimore: Penguin, 1970), 221–22.

11. Ibid., 230–31.

12. The following discussion is based on Dom Hubert Van Zeller, *The Holy Rule: Notes on St. Benedict's Legislation for Monks* (New York: Sheed and Ward, 1958), 33, 36, 420.

13. This paragraph is based on Niccolò Machiavelli, *The Prince and the Discourses* (New York: Modern Library, 1950), 85–86, 192–93, 242.

14. Jean Bodin, *Six Books of the Commonwealth*, abr. and trans. M. J. Tooley (Oxford: Basil Blackwell, 1955), esp. 84–96.

15. Thomas Hobbes, *Leviathan*, ed. Michael Oakeshott (Oxford: Basil Blackwell, 1960), chap. 23.

16. Jean-Jacques Rousseau, *The Social Contract*, trans. Charles Frankel (New York: Hafner, 1947). 51–52.

17. Woodrow Wilson, "The Study of Administration," *Political Science Quarterly* 2 (1887): 197–222.

18. Robert J. Morgan, who has studied James Madison's political philosophy, emphasized the Framers' concept that Europe was bankrupt and provided no lessons for the new nation to copy.

19. Dwight Waldo, *The Administrative State: A Study of the Political Theory of American Public Administration* (New York: Ronald Press Company, 1948), esp. 1–21.

20. See Austin Ranney, *The Doctrine of Responsible Party Government* (Urbana: University of Illinois Press, 1962), chaps. 3, 6.

21. *The Papers of Woodrow Wilson*, ed. Arthur S. Link (Princeton: Princeton University Press, 1969), vol. 7, *passim*.

22. Frank J. Goodnow, *Comparative Administrative Law* (New York: Putnam, 1893); *Municipal Home Rule: A Study in Administration* (New York: Macmillan, 1895, 1897); *Municipal Problems* (1897, 1911); *City Government in the United States* (1904, 1906); and *Municipal Government* (New York: Century, 1909, 1919).

23. Charles Grove Haines and Marshall E. Dimock, eds., *Essays on the Law and Practice of Governmental Administration* (Baltimore: Johns Hopkins Press, 1935).

24. Ranney, *The Doctrine of Responsible Party Government*, 109.

25. Dwight Waldo, *The Administrative State* (New York: Ronald Press, 1948), 79; John A. Fairlie, "Public Administration and Administrative Law," in *Essays on the Law and Practice of Governmental Administration*, ed. Haines and Dimock, 3–43.

26. Alice B. Stone and Donald C. Stone, "Early Development of Education in Public Administration," in *American Public Administration: Past, Present, Future*, ed. Frederick C. Mosher (University: University of Alabama Press, 1975), 27.

27. *The Papers of Woodrow Wilson*, 32:502–03.

28. Ibid.

29. The following two paragraphs are based on *The Papers of Woodrow Wilson*, 5:49–54.

30. "The Study of Administration," *The Papers of Woodrow Wilson*, 5:357–80.

31. This paragraph is based on "The Study of Administration," *The Papers of Woodrow Wilson*, 5:538, 386–87. Seligman was later the first editor of the *Encyclopedia of the Social Sciences* and in 1910 became chair of what is now the National Urban League (Nancy J. Weiss, *The National Urban League, 1910–1940* [New York: Oxford University Press, 1974], 41).

32. Woodrow Wilson, "The Study of Administration," in *Classics of Public Administration*, 2d ed., ed. Jay M. Schafritz and Albert C. Hyde (Chicago: Dorsey, 1987), 1.

33. Vincent Ostrom, *The Intellectual Crisis in American Public Administration* (University: University of Alabama Press, 1973), 28–29.

34. Paul P. Van Riper, "The Administrative State: Wilson and the Founders," in *A Centennial History of the American Administrative State*, ed. Ralph K. Chandler (New York: Free Press, 1987), 9. Also see Waldo, *The Administrative State*, 26, n. 12.

35. Leonard D. White, *Introduction to the Study of Public Administration* (New York: Macmillan, 1926), 9.

36. *The Papers of Woodrow Wilson*, 7:112–58.

37. Ostrom, *The Intellectual Crisis in American Public Administration*, 28–29.

38. William F. Willoughby, *The Government of Modern States* (New York: Appleton-Century, 1936).

39. Wilson, "The Study of Administration," in *Classics of Public Administration*, ed. Schafritz and Hyde, 21–22.

40. Ibid., 18.

41. Ibid., 24.

42. See Harold F. Gosnell, *Boss Platt and His New York State Machine* (Chicago: University of Chicago Press, 1924).

43. Wilson, "The Study of Administration," in *Classics of Public Administration*, ed. Schafritz and Hyde, 18.

44. Ibid.

45. Ibid., 23.

46. Ibid., 24.

47. Ibid., 19.

48. Ibid.

49. V. O. Key, "Politics and Administration," in *The Future of Government in the United States*, ed. Leonard D. White (Chicago: University of Chicago Press, 1942), 146.

50. Frank J. Goodnow, *Politics and Administration: A Study in Government* (New York: Macmillan, 1900), v.

51. There was a vast literature on functionalism. See Stephen L. Wasby, *Political Science: The Discipline and Its Dimensions* (New York: Scribner, 1970), 98–108.

52. Gabriel Almond and G. Bingham Powell, *Comparative Politics* (Boston: Little, Brown, 1966).

53. Goodnow, *Politics and Administration*, 15–19, and chaps. 1, 2, 4, *passim*.

54. Ibid., 79.

55. Ibid., chap. 1.

56. Ibid.

57. Ibid.

58. Ibid.

59. Wilson, "The Study of Administration," in *Classics of Public Administration*, ed. Schafritz and Hyde, 23.

60. James Stever, "Mary Parker Follett and the Quest for Pragmatic Administration," *Administration and Society*, August 1986, 162.

61. Frank J. Goodnow, *Municipal Government*, 2d ed. (New York: Century, 1919).

62. Dwight Waldo, "Public Administration and Culture," in *Public Administration and Democracy: Essays in Honor of Paul Appleby*, ed. Roscoe C. Martin (Syracuse: Syracuse University Press, 1965), 39–61, is one of the attempts to define contemporary American society as "an administrative culture" and to define the administrative subculture within the United States.

63. Wilson, "The Study of Administration," in *Classics of Public Administration*, ed. Schafritz and Hyde, 16–17, 20, 22.

64. Goodnow, *Politics and Administration*, 9.

65. William F. Willoughby, *The Principles of Public Administration* (Washington, D.C.: Brookings, 1927); and "The Science of Public Administration," in *Essays in Political Science, In Honor of Westel Woodbury Willoughby*, ed. John Mabry Mathews and James Hart (Baltimore: Johns Hopkins Press, 1937), 39–63.

66. Leonard D. White, *Introduction to the Study of Public Administration* (New York: Macmillan, 1939), first came out in 1926 and dominated the field until the 1950s. Herbert A. Simon, Don Smithburg, and Victor A. Thompson, *Public Administration* (New York: Knopf, 1950), was the important challenger to the White textbook.

67. White, *Introduction to the Study of Public Administration*, 3.

68. Ibid., 460.

69. Marshall E. Dimock, "The Meaning and Scope of Public Administration," in *Frontiers of Public Administration*, ed. John M. Gaus, Leonard D. White, and Marshall E. Dimock (Chicago: University of Chicago Press, 1937), 7.

70. Willoughby, "The Science of Public Administration," in *Essays in Political Science*, ed. Mathews and Hart.

71. This paragraph is based on Dimock, "The Meaning and Scope of Public Administration," 7.

72. The following paragraph is based on Hindy Lauer Schachter, *Frederick W. Taylor and the Public Administration Community: A Reevaluation* (Albany: State University of New York Press, 1989), 19–20.

73. Ibid.

74. Ibid. 72–73.

75. James Clay Thompson and Richard F. Vidmer, *Administrative Science and Politics in the USSR and the United States* (New York: Praeger, 1983); and Thomas F. Remington, *Building Socialism in Bolshevik Russia: Ideology and Industrial Organization, 1917–1921* (Pittsburgh: University of Pittsburgh Press, 1984).

76. U.S. House of Representatives, Labor Committee, *Peonage in Western Pennsylvania, Hearings on H. R. 90 Authorizing Committee to Investigate the Taylor System and Other Systems of Shop Management*, August 1, 1911 (Washington, D.C.: Superintendent of Documents, 1911); and House Special Committee to Investigate Taylor and Others Systems of Shop Management Under Authority of H.R. 90.

Chapter 2. Why and How Political Science Surrendered Public Administration

1. Charles E. Lindblom, "In Praise of Political Science," Review Essay, *World Politics* 9 (January 1957): 240–53. The phrase, "Knowledge gets lost," from my colleague Herman Schwartz, powerfully captures the whole idea.

2. Jonathan Bendor, "Review Article: Formal Models of Bureaucracy," *British Journal of Political Science* 18 (1988): 362–70.

3. E. Pendleton Herring, *Public Administration and the Public Interest* (New York: McGraw-Hill, 1936), vii.

4. Ibid.

5. Herring's analysis of the Internal Revenue Service shows how far ahead of the intellectual curve he was. Despite the importance of money and taxation, few scholars have undertaken an empirical analysis of the revenue service of any country.

6. Samuel P. Huntington, "The Marasmus of the ICC," *Yale Law Journal*, 1952.

7. Herring, *Public Administration*, 213.

8. Jeffrey Pressman and Aaron Wildavsky, *Implementation*; Laurence J. O'Toole, "Goal Multiplicity in the Implementation Setting: Subtle Impacts and the Case of Wastewater Treatment Privatization," *Policy Studies Journal* 18 (Fall 1989): 18, n. 3; and Laurence J. O'Toole and Robert S. Mountjoy, "Interorganizational Policy: A Theoretical Perspective," *Public Administration Review* 44 (1984), 491–503.

9. James W. Fesler, *Area and Administration* (University, Ala.: University of Alabama Press, 1949; and "Approaches to the Understanding of Decentralization," *Journal of Politics* 27 (1965): 536–66.

10. Schuyler C. Wallace, *Federal Departmentalization* (New York: Columbia University Press, 1941); David B. Truman, *Administrative Decentralization: The Chicago Field Offices of the United States Department of Agriculture* (Chicago: University of Chicago Press, 1940); Earl Latham, with William D. Carey, Arthur Svenson, Milton Mandell, and Wallace Sayre, *The Federal Field Service: An Analysis With Suggestion for Research* (Chicago: Public Administration Service, 1947).

11. Alice B. Stone and Donald C. Stone, "Early Development of Education in Public Administration," in *American Public Administration: Past, Present, and Future*, ed. Frederick C. Mosher (University, Ala.: University of Alabama Press, 1975), 19.

12. Lent D. Upson, *Letters on Public Administration, from a Dean to His Graduates* (Detroit: Citizens Research Council of Michigan, 1954).

13. Robert K. Merton, *Social Theory and Social Structure* (New York: Free Press, 1952).

14. Rowland Egger, "The Period of Crisis: 1933 to 1945," in *American Public Administration: Past, Present, and Future*, ed. Frederick C. Mosher (University, Ala.: University of Alabama Press, 1975), 63.

15. Ibid., 66.

16. Ibid., 66–67.

17. David Easton, *The Political System: An Inquiry into the State of Political Science* (New York: Alfred A. Knopf, 1953), 3.

18. Ibid., 22.

19. Kenneth Culp Davis, "Some Reflections of a Law Professor about Instruction and Research in Public Administration," *American Political Science Review* 47 (1953): 739.

20. Joseph P. Harris ("Kenneth Culp Davis, 'Reflections of a Law Professor on In-

struction and Research in Public Administration': An Exchange," *American Political Science Review* 48 [1954]: 174–86) offered elements of a reply, but these were cast in terms that are not immediately comprehensible to the intellectual newcomer and would not encourage a provost's faculty research committee faced by a grant application from a political science faculty member who wanted to study the relevant problems.

21. Oskar Morgenstern, *The Question of National Defense* (New York: Random House, 1959), 263–64.

22. Ibid., 264.

23. Lindblom, "In Praise of Political Science."

24. Easton, *The Political System*, 22. The explanatory footnote refers to "H. Simon, *Administrative Behavior* . . . which develops a theory in the field of administration."

25. Thomas Hammond, "In Defense of Luther Gulick's 'Notes on the Theory of Organization,'" *Public Administration* 68 (Summer 1990): 143–73.

26. Mary Parker Follett, *The Speaker of the House of Representatives* (New York: Longmans, 1902). See also Terence Harwick, "Integrative Administration: The Contribution of Mary Parker Follett," Ph.D. diss., University of Southern California, 1985.

27. I am obliged for the comment of Joseph D. Cooper on this point.

28. Henry C. Metcalf and L. Urwick, *Dynamic Administration* (New York: Harper and Brothers, 1940), 13.

29. Peter Drucker, *Adventures of a Bystander* (New York: Harper and Row, 1979), 262–63.

30. *DAB*, IX, Supplement One, ed. Harris E. Starr (New York: Scribner, 1944), 308. Also see the obituary for Mary Parker Follett, *New York Times*, December 21, 1933, 21.

31. *Black's Law Dictionary*, 5th ed. (St. Paul: West, 1979).

32. Mary Parker Follett, "The Process of Control," in *Papers on the Science of Administration*, ed. Luther H. Gulick and L. S. Urwick (New York: Institute of Public Administration, 1937), 167.

33. The following discussion is based on Mary Parker Follett, *Creative Experience* (New York: Longmans, Green, 1930), xi.

34. Harold D. Lasswell, *The Future of Political Science* (New York: Atherton Press, 1963), 95–122.

35. These observations are derived from conversation with each of the colleagues mentioned.

36. John M. Gaus, "A Theory of Organization for Public Administration," in Leonard D. White, John M. Gaus, and Marshall E. Dimock, eds., *Frontiers of Public Administration* (Chicago: University of Chicago Press, 1937), 66–91.

37. John M. Gaus, in *Reflections on Public Administration* (University, Ala.: University of Alabama Press, 1947).

38. The following discussion is based on Luther H. Gulick, "Notes on a Theory of Organization," in *Papers on the Science of Administration*, ed. L. H. Gulick and L. S. Urwick (New York: Institute of Public Administration, 1937), 7, 9–11, 13, 37.

39. The following discussion is based on Herbert A. Simon, *Administrative Behavior: A Study of Decision-Making Processes in Administrative Organization*, 3d ed. (New York: Free Press, 1976), 20–44. Chapter 2 much of what is found in various readers under the title, "Proverbs of Administration." See also ibid., 249, n. 1, citing Gulick's essay, "Science, Values, and Public Administration," in *Papers on the Science of Administration*,

ed. Gulick and Urwick, 191–93. See esp. chaps. 10 and 11 on organizational loyalties and identification. See 198–247 for the anatomy of organization. Something of the sort is also present in the final chapter entitled, "The Business School: A Problem in Organizational Design." Throughout this book, his notes and asides reflect an extremely broad knowledge of legal, historical, and conventional political science studies of the time.

40. John Viscount Morley, *Politics and History* (New York: Macmillan, 1923), 6–7.

41. Thomas Hammond, "In Defense of Luther Gulick's 'Notes on the Theory of Organization,'" *Public Administration* 68 (1990): 143–73, 3.

42. Larry B. Hill, "Taking Bureaucracy Seriously," presented at the annual meeting of the American Political Science Association, 1986.

43. Charles Goodsell, *The Case for Bureaucracy: A Public Administration Polemic* (Chatham, N.J.: Chatham House Publishers, 1983).

44. Norton E. Long, *The Polity*, ed. and intro. Charles Press (Chicago: Rand McNally, 1962).

45. Woodrow Wilson, "The Study of Administration," in *Classics of Public Administration*, ed. Schafritz and Hyde, 22.

46. J. Donald Kingsley, *Representative Bureaucracy: An Interpretation of the British Civil Service* (Yellow Springs, Ohio: Antioch Press, 1944), 5.

47. Harold J. Laski, "Bureaucracy," in *Encyclopedia of the Social Sciences*, ed. Edwin R. A. Seligman (New York: Macmillan, 1930), 3:70.

48. Ibid.

49. Max Weber, *Theory of Social and Economic Organization*, ed. and trans. Talcott Parsons and A. M. Henderson (New York: Free Press and Falcon's Wing Press, 1947); see also *Max Weber: A Selection of Texts*, ed. Stanislav Andreski (London: Allen and Unwin, 1983), chaps. 3, 4.

50. Gordon A. Craig, "The Kaiser and the Kritik," *New York Review of Books* 35 (February 18, 1988); J. P. Mayer, *Max Weber and German Politics* (Salem, N.H.: Ayer, 1956); Wolfgang J. Mommsen, *Max Weber and German Politics*, trans. Michael S. Steinberg (Chicago: University of Chicago Press, 1984).

51. Mommsen, *Max Weber and German Politics*, viii, 415–47.

52. The following discussion of Weber's lecture is based on *From Max Weber*, ed. Gerth and Mills, 127–28.

53. Friedrich von Hayek et al., *Capitalism and the Historians* (Chicago: University of Chicago Press, 1963); *The Road to Serfdom* (Chicago: University of Chicago Press, 1944).

54. Herman Finer, *The Road to Reaction* (Boston: Little, Brown, 1945).

55. Joseph A. Schumpeter, *Capitalism, Socialism, and Democracy* (New York: Harper, 1962).

56. The following paragraphs are based on *From Max Weber*, ed. Gerth and Mills, 77–127.

57. Andreski, ed., *Max Weber: A Selection of Texts*; and Michel Crozier, *The Bureaucratic Phenomenon* (Chicago: University of Chicago Press, 1967).

58. Robert A. Dahl and Charles E. Lindblom, *Politics, Economics, and Welfare* (New York: Harper, 1963), 234, n. 6.

59. The following paragraphs are based on *From Max Weber*, ed. Gerth and Mills, 196–244.

60. Edward C. Page, *Political Power and Bureaucratic Authority* (Brighton: Wheatsheaf, 1985).

61. Gerth and Mills, eds., *From Max Weber*, 232.

62. Ibid., 233.

63. See, for example, James M. Beck, *Our Wonderland of Bureaucracy: A Study of the Growth of Bureaucracy in the Federal Government and Its Destructive Effect upon the Constitution* (New York: Macmillan, 1932).

64. Crozier, *The Bureaucratic Phenomenon*.

65. Ibid.

66. Ibid.

67. Hannah Arendt, *The Origins of Totalitarianism* (New York: Meridian, 1960), 213–15.

68. Ibid.

69. Unless otherwise indicated, I have drawn material from Florence N. Trefethen, "A History of Operations Research," in Joseph F. McCloskey and Florence N. Trefethen *Operations Research for Management*, ed. Joseph F. McCloskey and Florence N. Trefethen (Baltimore: Johns Hopkins Press, 1954), 3–35.

70. See Edward S. Quade, ed., *Analysis for Military Decisions* (Chicago: Rand McNally, 1964); and Charles J. Hitch, *Decision-Making for Defense* (Berkeley and Los Angeles: University of California Press, 1965).

71. Michael J. White, "The Impact of Management Science on Political Decision-Making," Northwestern University, Cooperative International Program on Studies of Operations Research and Management Sciences, Program Publication no. 2–71, March 1971; Gerald E. Thompson, *Management Science: An Introduction to Quantitative Analysis and Decision-Making* (New York: McGraw-Hill, 1976).

72. On CPM, see John D. Glaser, "The Critical Path Method," in *The Encyclopedia of Management*, ed. Carl Heyel (New York: Van Nostrand Reinhold, 1982), 188–91; and "Integrated Project Management," ibid., 485–86; on PERT, see Robert W. Miller, "PERT (Program Evaluations and Review Technique)," ibid., 868–74; on PPBS, see Susan G. Hadden, ed., "Symposium on Expert Systems," *Journal of Policy Analysis and Management* 8 (1989): 183–208.

73. Gary Chapman, "A New Generation of High-Technology Weapons," in *Computers in Battle: Will They Work?*, ed. David Bellin and G. Chapman (Boston: Harcourt Brace Jovanovich, 1987), 88–89.

74. Dorothy Leonard-Barton and John J. Sviolka, "Putting Expert Systems to Work," *Harvard Business Review* (March-April 1988), 93. Also, cf. Marvin Minsky, "Introduction," *Robotics*, ed. Minsky (Garden City, N.Y.: Anchor, 1985), 12–13.

75. On applications to industry, see William B. Ashe, Charles H. Foster, and William H. Stanback, "An Expert System for Analysis of U.S. Regulatory Laws Concerning Electric Power Generation, Final Report," for SYS 777, Knowledge Based Systems, Department of Systems Engineering, School of Engineering and Applied Science, University of Virginia, Charlottesville, May 2, 1986; on defense applications, see Kamal N. Karna, ed., *Expert Systems In Government Symposium*, Washington, D.C., October 24–25, 1985; Expert Systems in Government Symposium, October 22–24, 1986; IEEE Computer Society Press, 1986; and *Approximate Reasoning in Expert Systems*, ed. Madan M. Gupta et al. (Amsterdam: Elsevier, 1985).

76. Gaus, *Reflections*.

77. F. L. Harrison, *Project Management* (New York: John Wiley, 1981), chap. 11.

78. See Michael Syrett, "Project Chiefs Learn to Widen Their View," *Sunday Times*, May 17, 1987, 89, describing an Ashridge Management College Course entitled "Leading Projects Effectively."

79. R. Edward Freeman, *Strategic Management: A Stakeholder Approach* (Boston: Pitman, 1984), 31.

80. Arthur F. Bentley, *The Process of Government* (Chicago: University of Chicago Press, 1908); Charles B. Hagan, "The Group as a Concept in Political Science," in *Approaches to the Study of Politics*, ed. Roland A. Young (Evanston: Northwestern University Press, 1958); Pendleton Herring, *Group Representation Before Congress* (New York: Russell and Russell, 1928); Grant McConnell, *Private Power and American Democracy* (New York: Knopf, 1966); and David B. Truman, *The Governmental Process* (New York: Alfred A. Knopf, 1953).

81. Gaus, *Reflections*.

82. Long, *The Polity*.

83. Richard E. Neustadt, *Presidential Power: The Politics of Leadership* (New York: John Wiley, 1960).

84. James Clay Thompson and Richard F. Vidmer, *Administrative Science and Politics in the USSR and the United States* (New York: Praeger, 1983), 27.

85. Philip Converse, "Generalization and the Social Psychology of 'Other Worlds,' " in *Metatheory in Social Science: Pluralisms and Subjectivities*, ed. Donald W. Fiske and Richard A. Schweder (Chicago: University of Chicago Press, 1983), 55.

86. In this respect, economics offers some useful history on techniques for confronting internal contradictions. See C. Addison Hickman, *J. M. Clark* (Cambridge: Cambridge University Press, 1975).

Chapter 3. The Dogma and Theory of Executive Leadership

1. Leonard D. White, *The Federalists: A Study in Administrative History* (New York: Macmillan, 1961); *The Jeffersonians: A Study in Administrative History* (New York: Free Press, 1951); *The Jacksonians: A Study in Administrative History, 1829–1861* (New York: Macmillan, 1954); and *The Republican Era* (New York: Macmillan, 1958).

2. See White, *The Jacksonians*, 46–49.

3. Woodrow Wilson, *Congressional Government* (Boston: Houghton Mifflin, 1887), 253–54.

4. Edward S. Corwin, *The President: Office and Powers, 1787–1957* (New York: New York University Press, 1957).

5. Louis Brownlow, in *A Passion for Politics*, describes his career in journalism and politics, including his relationship to Woodrow Wilson and his tenure as a commissioner of the district government. The book ends with a reference to his coming career as a professional leader in public administration.

6. Paul P. Van Riper, "Luther H. Gulick, Public Administration and Classical Management: A Self-Portrait With Comments," presented at the annual meeting of the American Society for Public Administration, 1980.

7. Leonard D. White, "Preface," and Charles E. Merriam, "The Education of

Charles E. Merriam," in *The Future of Government in the United States*, ed. White (Chicago: University of Chicago Press, 1942), v–vii, 1–24.

8. U.S. President's Committee on Administrative Management, *Report of the Committee with Studies of Administrative Management in the Federal Government, Submitted to the President and Congress in Accordance with Public Law No. 379, 74th Cong., 2d sess.* [the Brownlow Report] (Washington, D.C.: GPO, 1937).

9. Matthew Holden, Jr., *President, Congress, and Racial Stratification*, Ernest T. Patterson Memorial Lecture, Political Science Department, University of Colorado, 1984; and "Race and Constitutional Change in the Twentieth Century," in *African Americans and the Living Constitution*, ed. John Hope Franklin and G. R. McNeil (Washington, D.C.: Smithsonian Institution Press, 1995), 117–43.

10. Paul S. Reinsch, ed., *Readings on American Federal Government* (Boston: Ginn and Co., 1909), 47. Reinsch was a professor of political science at the University of Wisconsin, and later U.S. minister to China.

11. Jesse Macy, *Party Organization and Machinery* (New York: Century, 1904).

12. U.S. President's Committee on Administrative Management, *Report of the Committee*, 49; the entire discussion takes up two pages of the report.

13. For speculations on this distaste for the congressional process, see Matthew Holden, Jr., "Congress on the Defensive," *National Political Science Review* 1 (1988).

14. James MacGregor Burns, *Congress on Trial* (New York: Harper, 1949).

15. E. E. Schattschneider, Review of James MacGregor Burns, *Congress on Trial*, in *Political Science Quarterly* 65 (1950): 141.

16. The Committee on the Constitutional System is a group of private citizens in which the leadership has come principally from C. Douglas Dillon, Lloyd Cutler, and Senator Nancy L. Kassebaum. See Donald L. Robinson, *Government for the Third American Century* (Boulder: Westview, 1989); and *Reforming American Government: The Bicentennial Papers of the Committee on the Constitutional System* (Boulder: Westview, 1985); James L. Sundquist, *Congressional Reform and Effective Government* (Washington, D.C.: Brookings, 1992). I have been one of the more skeptical participants in the committee's discussions, for reasons partly reflected in Robinson, *Government for the Third American Century*, 55, and Robert C. Wood, *Whatever Possessed the President?* (Amherst: University of Massachusetts Press, 1994).

17. Charles O. Jones, "Presidential Negotiation With Congress," in *Both Ends of the Avenue: The Presidency, the Executive Branch, and Congress in the 1980's*, ed. Anthony King (Washington, D.C.: American Enterprise Institute, 1983), 96–130, esp. 123–27.

18. Matthew Holden, Jr., " 'Imperialism' in Bureaucracy," *American Political Science Review* 60 (1966): 943–51.

19. Richard E. Neustadt, *Presidential Power: The Politics of Leadership* (New York: John Wiley, 1960).

20. Barbara Kellerman, *The Political Presidency: The Practice of Leadership* (New York: Oxford University Press, 1984).

21. Bert A. Rockman, *The Leadership Question: The Presidency and the American Political System* (New York: Praeger, 1984).

22. U.S. President's Committee on Administrative Management, *Report*, 2.

23. See the title of Goodnow's *Politics and Administration*, and the discussion in chap. 1.

24. *Bowsher v. Synar*, 478 U.S. 714 (1986); *Synar v. United States*, 626 F. Supp 1374 (1986).

25. *Synar v. United States*, 626 F. Supp 1398, emphasis added.

26. *Northern Securities Co. v. U.S.*, 193 U.S. 197 (1904).

27. *Myers v. U.S.*, 272 U.S. 52 (1926).

28. President's Committee on Administrative Management, *Report of the Committee with Studies on Administrative Management in the Federal Government* (Washington, D.C.: GPO, 1937), 39–40.

29. Rexford G. Tugwell was an important person in the New Deal. A former professor at Columbia, he had gone to Washington with Roosevelt, had been assistant secretary of agriculture, was governor of Puerto Rico in its transition to commonwealth status. For more than two decades after World War II he was a vigorous interpreter of the New Deal, exponent of public planning, and advocate of constitutional reform. He was long a fellow of the Center for the Study of Democratic Institutions.

30. *Synar v. United States*, 626 F. Supp 1374.

31. William E. Leuchtenburg, "The Case of the Contentious Commissioner," in *Freedom and Reform: Essays in Honor of Henry Steele Commager*, ed. Harold M. Hyman and Leonard W. Levy (New York: Harper and Row, 1967), 276–312.

32. *Moultrie v. Martin*, 690 F2d 1078 (1982).

33. *Synar v. United States*, 626 F. Supp 1374.

34. Ibid., emphasis added.

35. There is a neglected historical thesis in that personnel is an "executive" function constitutionally available only to the President. Henry Adams, "Civil Service Reform," in *The Great Secession Winter and Other Essays*, ed. George Hochfeld (New York: Sagamore Press, 1958).

36. *In Re Sealed Case*, 838 F2d 476 (USCA, DC, 1988).

37. Frank W. Miller, Robert O. Dawson, George E. Dix, and Raymond I. Parnas, *Prosecution and Adjudication* (Westbury, N.Y.: Foundation, 1991), 695–712.

38. See Chief Judge Silberman, *In Re Sealed Case* on the arrangement of criminal jurisdiction in the Constitution.

39. Ibid.

40. The following discussion is based on White, *The Jacksonians*, esp. 507–08.

41. The issue is also confused by the fact that federal district judges have authority to fill U.S. attorney positions on a temporary basis, as a result of which there was a noticeable political controversy in Massachusetts in 1987 (*Boston Globe*, August 19, 1987, 4B). If the issue were so clear-cut in principle, the system could not tolerate any variation.

42. Silberman, *In Re Sealed Case*.

43. Quoted in Richard Loss, ed., *Corwin on the Constitution* (Ithaca: Cornell University Press, 1981).

44. John P. Roche, "The Founding Fathers: A Reform Caucus in Action," *American Political Science Review* 55 (1961): 807.

45. William L. Anderson, "Intention of the Framers," *American Political Science Review* 49 (1955): 345.

46. James Madison, letter to Thomas Ritchie, September 15, 1821, in Albert Furtwangler, *The Anthority of Publius: A Reading of the Federalist Papers* (Ithaca, N.Y.: Cornell University Press, 1984), 36.

47. Richard A. Posner, *The Federal Courts: Crisis and Reform* (Cambridge, Mass.: Harvard University Press, 1985), 336–39.

48. James A. Dorn and Henry G. Manne, eds., *Economic Liberties and the Constitution* (Fairfax, Va.: George Mason University Press and Cato Institute, 1987); Bernard H. Siegan, *Economic Liberties and the Constitution* (Chicago: University of Chicago Press, 1980).

49. Alexander Hamilton, *The Letters of Pacificus and Helvidius* (1845; rpt. Delmar, N.Y.: Scholars' Facsimiles and Reprints, 1976).

50. Ralph Huitt, address presented to the Wisconsin Political Science Association, October 1970; Luther H. Gulick, "Notes on a Theory of Organization," in *Papers on the Science of Administration*, ed. Gulick and L. S. Urwick (New York: Institute of Public Administration, 1937).

51. Daniel J. Meador, ed., *The President, the Attorney General, and the Department of Justice* (Charlottesville: White Burkitt Miller Center of Public Affairs, University of Virginia, 1980).

52. John G. Heinberg, "Centralization in Federal Prosecutions," *University of Missouri Law Review* 15 (June 1950): 244–58.

53. James Eisenstein, "Counsel for the United States: An Empirical Analysis of the Office of United States Attorney," Ph.D. diss., Yale University, 1968, chap. 4.

54. Ibid.

55. Carl Bernstein and Bob Woodward, *All the President's Men* (New York: Simon and Schuster, 1974).

56. Adam Yarmolinsky, "Ideas Into Programs," in *The Presidential Advisory System*, ed. Thomas E. Cronin and Sanford D. Greenberg (New York: Harper, 1969).

57. Leon Festinger, *Conflict, Decision, and Dissonance* (Stanford: Stanford University Press, 1964). There is a similarity to the problem of military doctrine. Cf. Barry R. Posen, *The Sources of Military Doctrine* (Ithaca: Cornell University Press, 1984).

Chapter 4. Dogma, Interests, and Administrative Law as Politics, I

1. Kenneth Culp Davis, "Reflections of a Law Professor on Instruction and Research in Public Administration," *American Political Science Review* 47:3 (September 1953), 728.

2. Donald D. Barry and Howard R. Whitcomb, *The Legal Foundations of Public Administration* (St. Paul: West Publishing, 1981), 1–2.

3. *Black's Law Dictionary*, 6th ed. abr. (St. Paul: West Publishing, 1991), 29; also see J. Myron Jacobstein and Roy M. Mersky, *Fundamentals of Legal Research* (Westbury, Conn.: Foundation, 1990), 9.

4. Jacobstein and Mersky, *Fundamentals of Legal Research*, 9.

5. David B. Truman, *The Governmental Process: Political Interests and Public Opinion* (New York: Knopf, 1951), 33.

6. Ibid.

7. Many forms of political theory are associated with particular professions or methods of learning. See Alan Keith-Lucas, "The Political Theory Implicit in Social Casework Theory," *American Political Science Review* 47:4 (December 1953): 1076–91, as an example of a study of the political theory of a profession.

8. Richard B. Stewart, "The Reformation of American Administrative Law," in *The*

Federal Agencies Essays of Politics and Power, ed. Howard Ball (Englewood Cliffs, N.J.: Prentice-Hall, 1984).

9. Jerry L. Mashaw, *Bureaucratic Justice: Managing Social Security Disability Claims* (New Haven: Yale University Press, 1985), 3.

10. Frank J. Goodnow, *Social Reform and the Constitution* (New York: Macmillan, 1911).

11. See John A. Fairlie, "Public Administration and Administrative Law," in *Essays on the Law and Practice of Governmental Administration: A Volume in Honor of Frank Johnson Goodnow*, ed. Charles G. Haines and Marshall E. Dimock (Baltimore: Johns Hopkins University Press, 1935), 3–43.

12. Richard J. Pierce, Jr., Sidney A. Shapiro, and Paul R. Verkuil, *Administrative Law and Process* (Westbury, Conn.: Foundation, 1992), 5, n. 12; and Kenneth E. Warren, *Administrative Law in the Political System* (St. Paul: West Publishing, 1988), 418.

13. Martin Shapiro, *The Supreme Court and Administrative Agencies* (New York: Free Press, 1968) is an exception, as is Shapiro's broad interest. Since about 1980, there have been textbooks by Lief Carter, Phillip Cooper, Barbara Hinkson Craig, David Rosenbloom, Kenneth Warren, and William West.

14. Davis, "Reflections of a Law Professor."

15. Ibid., 730–39.

16. Ibid., 739.

17. Ibid., 750.

18. Dwight Waldo, *The Administrative State* (New York: Ronald Press, 1948), 79.

19. This interpretation was offered by Frank Untermyer, professor emeritus of political science, Roosevelt University, who was himself a student in this period.

20. Marver H. Bernstein, *Regulating Business by Independent Commission* (Princeton: Princeton University Press, 1955).

21. "Appendix I: Detailed Statistical Tables: Annual Reports of the Director, Administrative Office of the United States Courts, Twelve Month Period Ended September 30, 1993," *United States Courts: Selected Reports*, AI-3–AI-6, 1993.

22. See David L. Bazelon, *Questioning Authority: Justice and Criminal Law* (New York: New York University Press, 1989), esp. the introduction by Justice William J. Brennan.

23. See *Calvert Cliffs Coordinating Committee* v. *United States Atomic Energy Commission*, 449 F. 2d 1109 (1971).

24. See Al Kammen, "U.S. Court's Liberal Era Ending," *Washington Post*, January 27, 1985.

25. *Synar v. United States*, 629 F. Supp. 1374 (1986).

26. C. A. Miller, quoted in Vincent M. Barnett, Jr., "Judicialization of the Administrative Process," *Public Administration Review* 8 (1948): 132.

27. Telephone information, Ms. Karen Rudman, Administrative Office of the United States Courts, December 31, 1992.

28. James W. Doig and Erwin C. Hargrove, *Leadership and Innovation: A Biographical Perspective on Entrepreneurs in Government* (Baltimore: Johns Hopkins University Press, 1987).

29. Conversation with the author when he and Clapp were commissioners of the Public Service Commission of Wisconsin.

30. William L. Cary, *Politics and the Regulatory Agencies* (New York: McGraw Hill,

1967); Doris Kearns Goodwin, *No Ordinary Time: Franklin and Eleanor Roosevelt* (New York: Simon and Schuster, 1994).

31. *Black's Law Dictionary*, 819.

32. Ibid., 936.

33. Ibid., 937.

34. Ibid.

35. *Oesterich v. Selective Service System Local Board No. 11*, 393 U.S. 233 (1968).

36. *Citizens to Preserve Overton Park v. Volpe*, 401 U.S. 402.

37. *Nader v. Allegheny Airlines*, 426 U.S. 290 (1976).

38. Pierce, Shapiro, and Verkuil, *Administrative Law and Process*, 190.

39. *ICC v. Chicago, R.I., & Pac. Railway*, 218 U.S. 88, 110 (1910), cited in Richard M. Travis, "Primary Jurisdiction: A General Theory and Its Application to the Securities Exchange Act," *California Law Review* 63 (1975).

40. *Texas and Pacific Railway v. Abilene Cotton Co*, 204 U.S. 426, 448 (1907), cited in ibid.

41. Travis, "Primary Jurisdiction," 927–28.

42. *Nader v. Allegheny Airlines*.

43. *Wall Street Journal*, June 6, 1985, 46.

44. *Decatur v. Paulding*, 14 Pet 497 (1840).

45. W. Patrick Strauss, "James Kirke Paulding," in *American Secretaries of the Navy*, ed. Paolo E. Colletta (Annapolis: Naval Institute Press, 1980), 1:165–66.

46. *Decatur v. Paulding*.

47. Donald A. Axelrod, *A Budget quarter: Critical Policy and Management Decisions* (New York: St. Martin's, 1989), 45–84.

48. William A. Robson, *Justice and Administrative Law: A Study of the British Constitution* (London: Macmillan, 1928), 37.

49. Davis, "Some Reflections of a Law Professor."

50. Richard A. Posner, *The Federal Courts: Crisis and Reform* (Cambridge, Mass.: Harvard University Press, 1985), 83.

51. *American School of Magnetic Healing v. McAnulty*, 187 U.S., 103.

52. Ibid., 108.

53. Roscoe Pound, *The Future of the Common Law* (Cambridge, Mass.: Harvard University Press, 1937); Richard Rose, *Lesson Drawing in Public Policy* (Chatham, N.J.: Chatham House, 1994).

54. Lord Hewart, *The New Despotism* (New York: Cosmopolitan Book Corp., 1929), 42–43.

55. Carlton J. H. Hayes, *British Social Politics* (Boston and New York: Ginn and Co., 1913).

56. James M. Beck, *Our Wonderland of Bureaucracy: A Study of the Growth of Bureaucracy in the Federal Government and Its Destructive Effect upon the Constitution* (New York: Macmillan, 1932), esp. 85.

57. Ibid., 177.

58. Kenneth F. Warren, *Administrative Law in the Political System* (St. Paul: West Publishing, 1988), 395, n. 162.

59. Paul Verkuil, "The Emerging Concept of Administrative Procedure," *Columbia Law Review* 78 (1978): 9.

60. D. B. Hardeman and Donald C. Bacon, *Rayburn: A Biography* (Austin: Monthly Press, 1987).

61. Thomas C. McCraw, *Prophets of Regulation* (Cambridge: Belknap Press, 1984), 153–209.

62. Ingo Walter, ed., *Deregulating Wall Street: Commercial Bank Penetration of the Corporate Securities Market* (New York: Wiley, 1985).

63. Second Acceptance Speech, Democratic National Convention, June 27, 1936, in *F.D.R. Speaks: Authorized Edition of Speeches, 1933–1945*, ed. Henry S. Commager (New York: Crown Publishers, 1960).

64. See James T. Patterson, *The Conservative Coalition in Congress* (Lexington: University of Kentucky Press, 1967).

65. Richard B. Morris, *Government and Labor in Early America* (New York: Columbia University Press, 1946); Karen Orren, *Belated Feudalism: Labor, the Law, and Liberal Development in the United States* (Cambridge: Cambridge University Press, 1991); Christopher L. Tomlins, *The State and the Unions* (Cambridge, Mass.: Harvard University Press, 1960).

66. Earl Latham, "The Body Politic of the Corporation," in *The Corporation in Modern Society*, ed. Edward S. Mason (Cambridge, Mass.: Harvard University Press, 1960).

67. Tomlins, *The State and the Unions*.

68. See U.S. House of Representatives, House Reports, 76th Cong., 3d sess. (Jan. 3, 1940–Jan. 3, 1941), vol. 7 (Washington, D.C.: GPO, 1941); H. Rpt. 1902, *Report on Investigation of National Labor Relations Board, Intermediate Report of Special Committee to Appoint Pursuant to H. Res. 258)*; see also H. Rpt. 3109, final report.

69. Hardeman and Bacon, *Rayburn*.

70. Barnett, "Judicialization of the Administrative Process," 131.

71. Davis ("Some Reflections of a Law Professor," 750) provided a selection of the sample questions that he deemed worthwhile: (1) "What are the effects upon administrative policies of conducting general investigations of the broad problems that lie behind masses of small adjudications, as compared with the prevalent system of treating each problem in each adjudication?" (2) "What are the effects upon administrative policies of granting or withholding from private parties the right to compel prosecutions?" (3) "What are the effects upon administrative policies of greater autonomy in professional staffs, increased subdelegation, more decentralization, heavier reliance on methods of informal supervision as compared with methods of formal adjudication and formal rulemaking?" and (4) "What in fact are the mechanics of lobbying before particular regulatory agencies, what are the successes and failures of the lobbying forces, what are the losses of the groups that are under-represented in these processes . . . ?"

Chapter 5. Dogma, Interests, and Administrative Law as Politics, II

1. Richard B. Stewart, "The Reformation of American Administrative Law," in *Federal Administrative Agencies: Essays on Power and Politics*, ed. Howard Ball (Englewood Cliffs, N.J.: Prentice-Hall, 1984), 31.

2. C. A. Miller, quoted in Vincent M. Barnett, Jr., "Judicialization of the Administrative Process," *Public Administration Review* 8 (1948): 132.

3. James M. Beck, *Our Wonderland of Bureaucracy: A Study of the Growth of Bureaucracy in the Federal Government and Its Destructive Effect upon the Constitution* (New York: Macmillan, 1932).

4. *Universal Camera Corp. v. NLRB*, 340 U.S. 474 (1951), esp. 478–79, 490.

5. *Black's Law Dictionary*, 6th ed. abr. (St. Paul: West Publishing, 1991), 819.

6. Ibid., 936.

7. Joseph P. Harris, *The Advice and Consent of the Senate* (Berkeley and Los Angeles: University of California Press, 1953), 178–93.

8. David B. Truman, *The Governmental Process* (New York: Knopf, 1953), chap. 14.

9. Based on a conversation with Robert W. Perdue, sometime deputy general counsel of the Federal Power Commission.

10. Truman, *The Governmental Process*, chaps. 4–5.

11. Daniel Fiorino, "The Federal Courts and the Regulatory Process: The Cases of Natural Gas and Broadcasting," Ph.D. diss., Johns Hopkins University, 1977, 162.

12. Richard J. Pierce, Jr., Sidney A. Shapiro, and Paul R. Verkuil, *Administrative Law and Process* (Mineola, N.Y.: Foundation, 1985), 177–78.

13. Marver H. Bernstein, *Regulating Business by Independent Commission* (Princeton: Princeton University Press, 1955).

14. The Final Rule, issued May 25, 1984 [Docket RM83–71: Order no. 380], was designated *Elimination of Variable Costs from Certain Natural Gas Pipeline Minimum Commodity Bill Provisions*.

15. Order no. 436, *Regulation of Natural Gas Pipelines After Partial Wellhead Decontrol*, 17. This was a final rule and statement of policy, issued slightly less than a year and a half after no. 380 (October 9, 1985 [RM85–1-000], pts. A-D).

16. Docket RM 91–11–000: *In Re: Pipeline Service Obligations and Revisions to Regulations Governing Self-Implementing Transportation Under Part 294 of the Commission's Regulations*.

17. *Association of National Advertisers, Inc. v. Federal Trade Commission*, Civil Action No. 78–1421 (U.S. District Court, District of Columbia), 406 F. supp. 996.

18. As Douglas writes, "I took Gerhard Gesell, just out of law school, and pitted him against Dean Acheson in the New York Stock Exchange investigation—which started with Whitney defalcation and reached into the mechanisms that made such acts easy." William O. Douglas, *Go East, Young Man: The Early Years* (New York: Random House, 1974), 267.

19. *Association of National Advertisers, Inc. v. Federal Trade Commission* (No. 79–1117), U.S. Court of Appeals, District of Columbia Circuit (627 F. 2d 1151); 5 Media L. Rep. 2233; 19801 Trade Cas (CCH) (Certiorari Denied June 16, 1980. See 100 S. Ct. 3011).

20. Michael Pertschuk, *Revolt Against Regulation: The Rise and Pause of the Consumer Movement* (Berkeley and Los Angeles: University of California Press, 1982), 109–10, 113.

21. Kenneth Culp Davis, "Reflections of a Law Professor on Instruction and Research in Public Administration," *American Political Science Review* 47:3 (September 1953), 749–52.

22. Richard A. Posner, *The Federal Courts: Crisis and Reform* (Cambridge, Mass.: Harvard University Press, 1985), 336–39.

23. Paul Korman, an attorney in private business, pointed this out to me in the late 1970s when he was a staff member at FERC. What little we know about rule making is

suspended between a recitation of the mechanical steps under the Administrative Procedure Act and the routine cynicism of media reporting.

24. *Calvert Cliffs Coordinating Committee, Inc. v. United States Atomic Energy Commission*, 449 F. 2d 1109 (1971) and *Duke Power Co. v. Carolina Environmental Study Group*, 438 U.S. 59 (1978).

25. *Vermont Yankee Nuclear Power Corp. v. Natural Resources Defense Council, Inc., et al.*, 435 U.S. 519 (1978).

26. Ibid., 557–58.

27. *Johnson v. Robison*, 415 U.S. 361 (1974).

28. Stewart, "The Reformation of American Administrative Law," 34.

29. Ibid., 35.

30. Daniel J. Fiorino, "Judicial Administrative Interaction in Regulatory Policy-Making," *Administrative Law Review* 28 (winter 1976), 41–88.

31. Robert C. Wood, *Remedial Law; When Courts Become Administrators* (Amherst: University of Massachusetts Press, 1995).

32. *Environmental Defense Fund v. Hardin*, 428 F. 2d 1093 (District of Columbia Circuit, 1970); and *Environmental Defense Fund Inc., v. Ruckershan*, 439 F. 2d (District of Columbia Circuit, 1971).

33. Pierce, Shapiro, and Verkuil, *Administrative Law and Process*, 187.

34. *Jaffree v. Wallace*, 837 F. 2d 1461 (1988); and *Jaffree v. Wallace*, No. 82–554-H.

35. Stewart, "The Reformation of American Administrative Law," 34.

36. This paragraph and the next are based on U.S. House of Representatives, Subcommittee on Oversight and Investigations, "Moss Criticizes Court, Justice Department for Interference with a Valid Congressional Inquiry," Press Release no. 19, Aug. 6, 1975, 1.

37. Cf. *FTC v. Pillsbury*, 355 F. 2d 952 (USCA, DC, 1966).

38. Matthew Holden, Jr., "Bargaining and command by Heads of U.S. Government Departments," *Social Science Journal* 25 (1988), 255–76.

39. Erwin G. Krasnow, Lawrence D. Longley, and Herbert A. Terry, *The Politics of Broadcast Regulation* (New York: St. Martin's Press, 1982), 67.

40. Matthew Holden, Jr., "The Presidency and the Regulatory Process: Energy," in *Governance VI, New Insights on Governance: Theory and Practice*, ed. K. W. Thompson (Lanham, Md.: University Press of America, 1990), 174–90.

41. William F. Fox, Jr., *Understanding Administrative Law* (New York: Matthew Bender, 1994), 47, n. 1.

42. Krasnow, Longley, and Terry, *The Politics of Broadcast Regulation*, 67.

43. Douglas, *Go East, Young Man*, 309.

44. Ibid.

45. Edward Howrey, *Washington Lawyer* (Ames: University of Iowa College of Law, 1983), 225–64.

46. William L. Cary, *Politics and the Regulatory Agencies* (New York: McGraw Hill, 1967), 7.

47. David M. Welborn, *Regulation in the White House: The Johnson Presidency* (Austin: University of Texas Press, 1993), 105.

48. James L. Baughman, *Television's Guardians; The FCC and the Politics of Programming, 1958–1967* (Knoxville: University of Tennessee Press, 1985).

49. James C. Miller III, *The Economist as Reformer: Revamping the FTC, 1981–1985* (Washington, D.C.: American Enterprise Institute for Public Policy Research, 1989).

50. As witness to the scene, this is how I would characterize the behavior of Charles B. Curtis, FERC chairman between 1977 and 1980.

51. Miller, *The Economist as Reformer*, 44, 49.

52. Richard A. Posner, *The Federal Courts: Crisis and Reform* (Cambridge, Mass.: Harvard University Press, 1985); Jerry L. Mashaw, *Bureaucratic Justice: Managing Social Security Disability Claims* (New Haven: Yale University Press, 1985), 18–19.

53. Don Phillips, "FAA Won't Require Child Safety Seats," *Washington Post*, Sept. 15, 1992, A1.

54. *Synar v. United States*, 629 F. Supp. 1374 (1986).

55. Pierce, Shapiro, and Verkuil, *Administrative Law and Process*, 104–05.

56. Ibid., 106.

57. David L. Bazelon, *Questioning Authority: Justice and Criminal Law* (New York: New York University Press, 1989).

58. Al Kammen, "U.S. Court's Liberal Era Ending," *Washington Post*, January 27, 1985.

59. *Vermont Yankee Nuclear Power Corp. v. Natural Resources Defense Council, Inc., et al.*, 435 U.S. 519 (1978). I wish to acknowledge the helpfulness of a short paper on the relevance of organizational theory to *Vermont Yankee* by Birte Iversen, a Danish student in my seminar on administrative law and public policy in fall 1992.

60. Bradley C. Canon, "Organizational Contumacy in the Transmission of Judicial Policies: The *Mapp, Escobedo, Miranda,* and *Gault* Cases," 20 *Villanova Law Review* 1 (November 1974), 50–79.

61. Stewart. "The Reformation of American Administrative Law," 31.

62. Ibid., 34.

63. Cary, *Politics and the Regulatory Agencies*, preface.

64. Ibid., 64.

Chapter 6. Politics, Technology and Administrative History, I

1. Schapiro, Foreword to *Government and Opposition*.

2. Leonard D. White, *Introduction to the Study of Public Administration* (New York: Macmillan, 1926), 4.

3. Leonard D. White, *Introduction to the Study of Public Administration*, rev. ed. (New York: Macmillan, 1939), 16.

4. See Richard C. Cortner, *A "Scottsboro" Case in Mississippi: The Supreme Court and Brown v. Mississippi* (Jackson: University Press of Mississippi, 1986).

5. See Kamal N. Karna, ed., *Expert Systems in Government Symposium* (Washington, D.C.: IEEE Computer Society Press, 1986); Madan M. Gupta et al., eds., *Approximate Reasoning in Expert Systems* (Amsterdam: Elsevier, 1985); and Susan G. Hadden, ed., "Symposium on Expert Systems," *Journal of Policy Analysis and Management* 8 (1989), 183–208.

6. Victor Ehrenberg, *The Greek State* (New York: Norton, 1960), 70.

7. Leonard D. White, *The Jacksonians: A Study in Administrative History, 1829–1861* (New York: Macmillan, 1954), esp. chap. 23.

8. Carlo M. Cipolla, *Clocks and Culture* (New York: Norton, 1978).

9. E. N. Gladden, *A History of Public Administration* (London: Frank Cass, 1972), 1:19–20.

10. Harold Innis, *The Bias of Communication* (Toronto: University of Toronto Press, 1971), 3–4.

11. Margery Davies, *The Woman's Place Is at the Typewriter: Office Work and Office Workers, 1870–1930* (Philadelphia: Temple University Press, 1982).

12. Carolyn C. Cooper, "Sylvio A. Bedini, *Thomas Jefferson and His Copying Machines*," *American Historical Review* 91 (1986): 461; see also Sidney Hart, "Peale and the Mechanical Arts," in *New Perspectives on Charles Willson Peale*, ed. Lillian B. Miller and David C. Ward (Pittsburgh: University of Pittsburgh Press, 1991), 250.

13. Janet Hermann, *The Pursuit of a Dream* (New York: Vintage Books, 1983), 20.

14. Leonard D. White, *The Republican Era* (New York: Macmillan, 1958), 102.

15. This paragraph is based on Lent D. Upson, *Letters on Public Administration—from a Dean to His Graduates* (Detroit: Citizens Research Council of Michigan, 1954), 87, 101–02.

16. Davies, *The Woman's Place*.

17. White, *The Republican Era*, 390–92.

18. Herbert Kaufman, *The Limits of Organizational Change* (University, Ala.: University of Alabama Press, 1971), 31–38.

19. See L. S. Urwick, "Organization as a Technical Problem," in *Papers on the Science of Administration*, ed. Luther H. Gulick and L. S. Urwick (New York: Institute of Public Administration, 1937).

20. See Leah Grubbs, "Chief Executive Officer Communication in the American Corporate Environment," Ph.D. diss., University of Texas, 1984; JoAnne Yates, *Control Through Communication: The Rise of System in American Management* (Baltimore: Johns Hopkins University Press, 1989), esp. chap. 2.

21. Judith Merkle, *Command and Control: The Social Implication of Nuclear Defense* (New York: General Learning Press, 1971), 2, n. 4.

22. Edward Gibbon, *Decline and Fall of the Roman Empire* (New York: Modern Library, 1930), vol. 1.

23. Samuel Eliot Morison, *Admiral of the Ocean Sea* (Boston: Little, Brown, 1942), 89.

24. Albert B. Donworth, *Why Columbus Sailed* (New York: Exposition Press, 1953), 82–104. See also Jean Merrien, *Christopher Columbus: The Mariner and the Man* (London: Odhams Press, 1958); and Felipe Fernandez-Arnesto, *Columbus and the Conquest of the Impossible* (New York: Saturday Review Press, 1974), both stimulating but non-scholarly sources.

25. The following discussion is based on Benjamin Franklin, *A Biography in His Own Words*, ed. Thomas Fleming (New York: Newsweek, 1972), esp. 177, 187.

26. The following discussion is based on White, *The Federalists*, chap. 38, 486–87.

27. Harold Nicolson, *The Congress of Vienna* (New York: Harcourt, Brace, 1946), 2.

28. Ibid., 64–65.

29. See the reference to *Decatur v. Paulding* in chap. 4 of this volume as it deals with the nineteenth-century courts' unwillingness to review administrative actions.

30. The following discussion is based on White, *The Jacksonians*, 486–87.

31. Much of this is reflected in T. Harry Williams, *Lincoln and His Generals* (New York: Knopf, 1952).

32. William H. Seale, *The President's House* (Washington D.C.: White House Historical Association, 1986), 1:374.

33. The following discussion is based on Lowell M. Limpus, *History of the New York Fire Department* (New York: Dutton, 1948).

34. Elias Colbert and Everett Chamberlin, *Chicago and the Great Conflagration* (Cincinnati: Vent, 1982).

35. Seale, *The President's House*, 1:494.

36. See Francis L. Loewenheim, Harold D. Langley, and Manfred Jonas, eds., *Roosevelt and Churchill: Their Secret Wartime Correspondence* (New York: Saturday Review Press–Dutton, 1975).

37. White, *The Jacksonians*, 487.

38. See Robert F. Kennedy, *Thirteen Days* (New York: Norton, 1969).

Chapter 7. Politics, Technology and Administrative History, II

1. John M. Gaus, *Reflections on Public Administration* (University, Ala.: University of Alabama Press, 1947), 9.

2. W. Henry Lambright, *Governing Science and Technology* (New York: Oxford University Press, 1976), chaps. 2 and 3.

3. Ibid., 56.

4. James L. McCamy, *Science and Public Administration* (University, Ala.: University of Alabama Press, 1960), 52–60.

5. Daniel C. Roper, *The United States Post Office* (New York: Funk & Wagnalls Company, 1917), 48–64, generally contains the information on the Post Office's relationships with the steamship companies and with the railroad companies.

6. Geoffrey D. Austrian, *Herman Hollerith: Forgotton Giant of Information Processing* (New York: Columbia University Press, 1982).

7. Abbott Payson Usher, *A History of Mechanical Invention* (Boston: Beacon Press, 1959), 235–36.

8. E. N. Gladden, *A History of Public Administration* (London: Frank Cass, 1972).

9. Report to the Chairman, Committee on Government Operations, House of Representatives, By the Comptroller General of the United States, *Social Security Administration's Computer Systems Modernization Effort May Not Achieve Planned Objectives* (Washington, D.C.: General Accounting Office (GAO/IMTEC-85-16, September 30, 1985), 1–2.

10. Ibid., 4.

11. General Accounting Office, Letter to Hon. Lowell Weicker, Jr. and others, "Social Security Administration's Progress in Modernizing its Computer Operations (IMTEC-85-15)," August 30, 1985.

12. Ibid.

13. *Washington Post*, September 6, 1989, C1.

14. Harold Sackman, *Computers, System Science and Evolving Society* (New York: John Wiley, 1961).

15. John M. Gaus, "A Theory of Organization for Public Administration," in *Frontiers*

of Public Administration, ed. John M. Gaus, Leonard D. White, and Marshall E. Dimock (Chicago: University of Chicago Press, 1936).

16. John U. Nef, *War and Human Progress* (Cambridge: Harvard University Press, 1950); cf. William H. McNeill, *The Pursuit of Power: Technology, Armed Force, and Society Since A.D. 1000* (Chicago: University of Chicago Press, 1982).

17. John Ise, *United States Oil Policy* (New Haven: Yale University Press, 1926).

18. Robert Sobel, *RCA* (New York: Stein and Day, 1986), chap. 1.

19. Lord Snow, *Science and Government* (New York: New American Library, 1962); and Ronald Clark, *Tizard* (London: Methuen, 1965), 105–65.

20. John Erickson, "The Air Defence Problem, 1939–40: British and Soviet Roads to Radar Compared," in *W.J.M.M.: Political Questions, Essays in Honor of W.J.M. Mackenzie*, ed. Brian Chapman and Allen Potter (Manchester: University of Manchester Press, 1974), 81–99.

21. I. B. Holley, Jr., "A Detroit Dream of Mass-produced Fighter Aircraft: The XP-75 Fiasco," *Technology and Culture* 28:3 (July 1987), esp. 588–91, is my source on the difficulties.

22. Ibid., 587.

23. Ibid., 589.

24. Donald F. Kettl, *Government by Proxy* (Washington: CQ Press, 1988), 22.

25. Gaus, *Reflections*, 14.

26. Leonard D. White, *Introduction to the Study of Public Administration*, rev. ed. (New York: Macmillan, 1939), 15.

27. McCamy, *Science and Administration*.

28. John Ellis, *The Social History of the Machine Gun* (New York: Pantheon Books, 1975), 155.

29. Harry Trebing, "The Chicago School Versus Public Utility Regulation," *Journal of Economic Issues* 10:1 (March 1976): 97–121.

30. Julian Levi, *Introduction to Legal Reasoning* (Chicago: University of Chicago Press, 1947).

31. Leonard D. White, *The Jacksonians: A Study in Administrative History, 1829–1861* (New York: Macmillan, 1954), 443–48.

32. President of the United States, *Decision and Report to Congress on the Alaska Natural Gas Transportation System* (Washington, D.C.: Executive Office of the President, Energy Policy and Planning, September 1977).

Chapter 8. Public Administration and the Plural Society

1. Robert B. Gordon and David J. Killick, "Adaptation of Technology to Culture and Environment," *Technology and Culture* 34 (April 1993), 243.

2. Textbooks tend to describe affirmative action as applied to personnel policy. See Rayburn Barton and William L. Chappell, Jr., *Public Administration: The Work of Government* (Glenview, Ill.: Scott, Foresman, 1985); George E. Berkley, *The Craft of Public Administration* (Boston: Allyn and Bacon, 1984); Robert B. Denhardt, *Public Administration: An Action Orientation* (Belmont, Calif.: Wadsworth, 1995); George J. Gordon, *Public Administration in America* (New York: St. Martin's, 1985); Nicholas Henry, *Public Administration and Public Affairs* (Englewood Cliffs, N.J.: Prentice-Hall, 1992); Allan W.

Lerner and John Wanat, *Public Administration: A Realistic Reintegration of Contemporary Public Management* (Englewood Cliffs: Prentice-Hall, 1992); Felix A. Nigro and Lloyd G. Nigro, *Modern Public Administration* (New York: Harper & Row, 1985); Dennis Palumbo and Steven Maynard-Moody, *Contemporary Public Administration* (New York: Longman, 1992); and Grover Starling, *Managing the Public Sector* (Belmont, Calif.: Wadsworth, 1993).

3. *Federalist* no. 10 (New York: Modern Library, 1952); David B. Truman, *The Governmental Process* (New York: Knopf, 1952); Henry W. Ehrman, ed., *Interest Groups on Four Continents* (1958).

4. H. Gordon Skilling, *Interest Groups in Soviet Politics* (Princeton: Princeton University Press, 1971), was criticized for advocating an interest group interpretation of Soviet politics well before Gorbachev appeared on the world scene.

5. James Yoho, a faculty member at Wilkes University, adapted this concept to John Cabot's mode of soliciting royal support for explorations of North America.

6. Truman, *The Governmental Process*, chap. 14.

7. Some scholars distinguish racial from ethnic groups, arguing that the experience of white immigrants in the United States is qualitatively different from that of African-descended persons. See Dianne M. Pinderhughes, *Race and Ethnicity in Chicago Politics: A Reexamination of Pluralist Theory* (Urbana: University of Illinois Press, 1987); and Andrew Greely, *Ethnicity in the United States* (New York: John Wiley, 1974).

8. John Merriman Gaus, *Reflections on Public Administration* (University, Ala.: University of Alabama Press, 1947).

9. James G. March and Herbert A. Simon, *Organizations* (New York: John Wiley, 1958).

10. *Max Weber: The Theory of Social and Economic Organization*, trans. A. M. Henderson and Talcott Parsons (Glencoe: Free Press and Falcon's Wing Press, 1947)

11. *Jane Doe v. State of Louisiana*. Through the Department of Health and Human Resources, Office of Vital Statistics and Registrar of Statistics, no. CA-1120, Court of Appeal of Louisiana, Fourth Circuit, 479 So. 2d 369 (October 18, 1985), 372.

12. John S. Furnivall, *Colonial Policy and Practice* (Cambridge: Cambridge University Press, 1948).

13. Woodrow Wilson, "The Study of Administration," in *Classics in Public Administration*, ed. Jay M. Shafritz and Albert C. Hyde (Chicago: Dorsey Press, 1987), 17.

14. Gordon A. Craig, "The Kaiser and the Kritik," *New York Review of Books* 35 (February 18, 1988): 18.

15. Wolf R. Bohning, "Foreign Workers in Post-War Germany," *New Atlantis* 2:1 (1970): 12–38.

16. Hannah Arendt, *The Origins of Totalitarianism*, 2d ed. (New York: Meridian Books, 1958), 185.

17. See Matthew Holden, Jr., "Bargaining and Command by Heads of U.S. Government Departments," *Social Science Journal* 25 (1988): 255–76.

18. See Matthew Holden, Jr., " 'Imperialism in Bureaucracy," *American Political Science Review* 4 (1966): 943–51.

19. Leonard J. Arrington, *Brigham Young: American Moses* (New York: Knopf, 1985); Roy F. Nichols, *The Stakes of Power, 1847–1877* (New York: Hill and Wang, 1970), 70.

20. Alexander Leighton, *The Governing of Men: General Principles and Recommenda-*

tions Based on Experience at a Japanese Relocation Camp (Princeton: Princeton University Press, 1945).

21. Michael D. Green, *The Politics of Indian Removal: Creek Government and Society in Crisis* (Lincoln: University of Nebraska Press, 1982), xv.

22. Burke Marshall, *Federalism and Civil Rights* (New York: Columbia University Press, 1962); Matthew Holden, Jr., "Race and Constitutional Change in the 20th Century," in *African Americans and the Living Constitution*, ed. John Hope Franklin and Genna Rae McNeil (Washington, D.C.: Smithsonian Press, 1995), 117.

23. U.S. Attorney General, *Activities in the Department of Justice*, U.S. Senate 66th Cong., 1st sess., docket no. 153, 1919.

24. Francis E. Rourke, "The Politics of Administrative Organization," *Journal of Politics* 19:3 (August 1957), 463–64.

25. Ibid., 464.

26. Charles M. Hardin, *Freedom in Agricultural Education* (Chicago: University of Chicago Press, 1955), 155.

27. Ibid., chap. 13.

28. Ibid., 166.

29. Ibid., 167.

30. Harry Kursh, *The United States Office of Education: A Century of Service* (Philadelphia: Chilton Books, 1965), 61.

31. Ibid., 15.

32. See Ambrose Caliver, *Rural Elementary Education Among Negroes under Jeans Supervising Teachers* (Washington, D.C.: GPO, 1933), *Background Study of Negro College Students* (Washington, D.C.: GPO, 1933), *Education of Negro Leaders: Influences Affecting Graduate and Professional Studies*, U.S. Office of Education Bulletin no. 3 (Washington, D.C.: GPO, 1948).

33. Paul P. Van Riper, "A Survey of Materials for the Study of Military Management," *American Political Science Review* 49:3 (September 1955), 828.

34. Past may not be prologue if the consequence of military downsizing is to remove from military service the cadres from which replacements would come.

35. Alexander Hamilton, letter of March 14, 1779, to John Jay, quoted in *The Negro in American History* (Chicago: Encyclopedia Brittanica), vol. 3: *Slaves and Masters, 1567–1854*, 414.

36. Ibid.

37. Hamilton, letter of March 14, 1779, to John Jay.

38. Jack D. Foner, *Blacks and the Military in American History* (New York: Praeger, 1974), 12–13.

39. Patricia L. Faust, ed., *Historical Times Illustrated Encyclopedia of the Civil War* (New York: Harper and Row, 1896), 63.

40. The Matthew Holden, Jr., Archives, *Tabulation of Bills and Proposed Resolutions Relative to Afro-Americans, the 57th Through the 80th Congresses* (Charlottesville, Va., 1987).

41. Robert Milton Burts, *Richard Irvine Manning and the Progressive Movement in South Carolina* (Columbia: University of South Carolina Press, 1974), 161, citing a letter from Manning to Secretary of War Newton D. Baker, December 7, 1917.

42. Ibid.

43. Richard M. Dalfiume, *Desegregation of the U.S. Armed Forces: Fighting on Two Fronts, 1938–1953* (Columbia: University of Missouri Press, 1975), esp. 42, 84; Holden, "Race and Constitutional Change in the Twentieth Century," 134–35.

44. Graham Smith, *When Jim Crow Met John Bull: Black American Soldiers in World War II Britain* (London: Tauris, 1987).

45. Edwin Newman, review of Ward Just, *Military Men, New York Times Book Review*, December 20, 1970, 3.

46. See remarks by Congressman Augustus F. Hawkins, D-Calif., *Congressional Record* (House), September 10, 1960. E7333; House Armed Services Committee, Special Subcommittee to Probe Disturbances on Military Bases, *Inquiry Into the Disturbances at Marine Corps Base, Camp Lejeune, N.C., on July 20, 1969*, HASC 91–32, December 15, 1969; and the same subcommittee's report on disturbances at Camp Pendleton, Calif., February 15, 1970, HASC 91–43; and Orr Kelly, "Discipline Breakdown Plagues Marines," *Washington Star*, August 13, 1969, A1. See also Everett R. Holles, "130 of Crew Defy Order to Join Aircraft Carrier," *New York Times*, November 10, 1972, 1; and Wallace Terry, *Bloods: An Oral History of the Vietnam War by Black Veterans* (New York: Random House, 1984), 191–205. Norman, now a group vice president at Amtrak, was a naval officer during the Vietnam War who served for a time as an aide to Admiral Elmo Zumwalt.

47. Major General L. Gordon Hill, Jr., Chief of Public Information, Department of the Army, letter to the *New York Times*, March 11, 1979.

48. Martin Binkin and Mark J. Eitelberg, with Alvin Schneider and Marvin M. Smith, *Blacks and the Military* (Washington, D.C.: Brookings, 1982), 84–119. On the specific German matter and on the views attributed to Dayan, whose reported comments about the intelligence and education of American black soldiers were along the lines of those more recently attributed to Prime Minister Nakasone, the study stopped (119, nn. 96–97) with little more than brief quotations from the newspapers. In view of the experience of the team, and of the access of Brookings researchers to the Pentagon, the Armed Services Committees, and to foreign political and defense analysts, it would be fruitful to have a fuller exploration of the matter.

49. Cynthia H. Enloe, "Ethnicity in the Evolution of Asia's Armed Bureaucracies," in *Ethnicity and the Military in Asia*, ed. DeWitt C. Ellinwood and C. H. Enloe (New Brunswick, N.J.: Transaction Books, 1981), 1–14.

50. R. Kent Newmyer, *Supreme Court Justice Joseph Story* (Chapel Hill: University of North Carolina Press, 1958) describes the travail this placed upon Justice Story, a renowned constitutional commentator who upheld the federal obligation to return fugitive slaves. He was, ironically, the mentor of Charles Sumner, who came to hold opposite views. See Sumner, *The Crime Against Kansas* (New York: Arno Press, 1969), speeches given in the Senate on May 19–20, 1856, that precipitated Sumner's beating by Congressman Preston Brooks of South Carolina.

51. William A. Dunning, *Essays on the Civil War and Reconstruction* (New York: Harper Torchbooks, 1965).

52. Nicholas Alex, *Black in Blue: A Study of the Negro Policeman* (New York: Meredith Corporation, 1969).

53. James B. Jacobs, *Stateville: The Penitentiary in Mass Society* (Chicago: University of Chicago Press, 1977), 138–211.

54. Frederic A. Bancroft, "The Early Anti-Slavery Movement and African Colonization," in *Frederic Bancroft: Historian*, ed. Jacob E. Cooke (Norman: University of Oklahoma Press, 1957), 147; and Russell B. Nye, *Fettered Freedom: Civil Liberties and the Slave Controversy, 1830–1860* (Urbana: University of Illinois Press, 1972), 41–85.

55. The following discussion is based on Jeffrey Obler, "The Regulation of Linguistic Conflict in Brussels," presented at the annual meeting of the American Political Science Association, 1973, esp. 3, 7; Leo Tindemans, "Regionalised Belgium—Transition from the Nation-State to the Multinational State," *Memo from Belgium*, no. 151–52 (Brussels: Ministry of Foreign Affairs, External Trade and Cooperation in Development, 1972).

56. *Economist*, April 18, 1987, 47.

57. Spencer Rich, "Political Power and Money at Stake in Census Undercount Fight," *Washington Post*, January 12, 1988, A19.

58. This discussion is based on *Jane Doe v. State of Louisiana*.

59. Matthew Holden, Jr., *The Centrality of Administration to Politics*, Working Papers in Public Administration, no. 1 (Charlottesville: Institute of Government, University of Virginia, 1984).

60. William Alonso and Paul Starr, eds., *The Politics of Numbers* (New York: Russell Sage, 1987).

61. Barbara Bailar, "The Miscounting of America," *Washington Post*, March 6, 1988, C3.

62. Marjorie Sun, "Plan to Assess Census Undercounting Dropped," *Science* 239 (January 19, 1988): 456–57.

63. Winthrop Jordan, *White over Black: Amerian Attitudes Toward the Negro, 1550–1812* (Baltimore: Penguin, 1969).

64. James E. Jones, "The Genesis and Present Status of Affirmative Action in Employment: Economic, Legal and Political Realities," *Iowa Law Review* 70 (1985), 900.

65. Alexandra K. Wigdor, "Fairness in Employment Testing," *Issues in Science and Technology*, Spring 1990), 54–58.

66. Robert G. Holland, "Big Brother's Test Scores," *National Review*, September 5, 1990, 35–36.

67. *From Gatekeeper to Gateway: Transforming Testing in America* (Chestnut Hill, Mass.: National Commission on Testing and Public Policy, Boston College, 1990), ix.

68. Obler, "The Regulation of Linguistic Conflict in Brussels."

69. Richard Hooker, *Of the Laws of Ecclesiastical Polity* (London: J. M. Dent Sons, 1954), 2:436.

70. American National Red Cross, *The Final Report of the Colored Advisory Commission Appointed to Cooperate with the American National Red Cross and the President's Committee on Relief Work in the Mississippi Valley Flood Disaster of 1927* (Washington, D.C.: American National Red Cross, 1919), 17–27.

71. Michael Holmes, *The New Deal in Georgia: An Administrative History* (Westport, Conn.: Greenwood, 1975), 21.

72. Ray Bromley, "Market Center and Market Place in Highland Ecuador: A Study of Organization, Regulation, and Ethnic Discrimination," in *Cultural Transformations and Ethnicity in Modern Ecuador*, ed. Norman E. Whitten, Jr. (Urbana: University of Illinois Press, 1981).

73. This paragraph is based on Milton J. Esman, *Administration and Development in Malaysia* (Ithaca: Cornell University Press, 1972), esp. 266, 282.

74. Malcolm Ross, *All Manner of Men* (New York: Reynal & Hitchcock, 1948); and Louis Kesselman, *The Social Politics of FEPC* (Chapel Hill: University of North Carolina Press, 1948.

75. Jones, "The Genesis and Present Status of Affirmative Action in Employment."

76. Hans-Eberhard Mueller, *Bureaucracy, Education, and Monopoly: Civil Service Reforms in Prussia and England* (Berkeley and Los Angeles: University of California Press, 1984), 96–100.

77. Samuel C. Krislov, *The Negro in Federal Employment: The Quest for Equal Opportunity* (Minneapolis: University of Minnesota Press, 1967, 19.

78. Louis L. Friedland, "Fair Employment Practices in the Public Service," *Public Personnel Review* (April 1962), 109–13.

79. Peter K. Eisinger, *Black Employment in City Government, 1973–1980* (Washington, D.C.: Joint Center for Political Studies, 1983), 48.

80. Frank Thompson, "Bureaucratic Response to Minority Challenge: The Case of Recruitment," presented at the annual meeting of the American Political Science Association, 1973.

81. Mitchell Rice and William E. Verner, Jr., "Affirmative Action in Texas Municipalities: Compliance With EEOC Standards," Decision Sciences in the Public and Private Sectors: Theory and Applications, SWAIDS Conference, Eleventh Annual Conference, March 19–22, 1980, n. 1.

82. *United States v. Paradise*, 55 Law Week 4211 (nos. 85–999).

Epilogue

1. Al Carthill, *The Lost Dominion* (London: G. P. Putnam, 1924), 93–94.

2. Ithiel deSola Pool, *Technologies of Freedom* (Cambridge: MIT Press, 1983).

INDEX